Praise for Creative Careers

"*Creative Careers* is a practical tool that will help you begin to see how to turn your creative inkling into a career—not just something you wish you could have some day."

—*Andrea Kay, syndicated columnist and author of* Life's a Bitch and Then You Change Careers *and* Work's a Bitch and Then You Make It Work

---

"*Creative Careers* is an outstanding resource for up-and-coming young artists and their families. As we move into a new, creative economy the information on these pages thoroughly debunks the old stereotype of the 'starving artist.' Opportunities abound like never before and employers are in hot pursuit of the best and brightest creative talent.

The profiles of real artists on the job included in this book are particularly interesting and add an important real world component to the information. This is a 'must-have' for any library, career resource center or prospective art student."

—*Sue Hinkin, Dean of Career Services, Savannah College of Art and Design*

"This book is a unique resource for artists in all disciplines, as it provides valuable insight into creative careers via real-life professional profiles."

—*Elisa Seeberman, Director of Career Services, The University of the Arts*

"This book is a valuable resource for those aspiring to a career in Arts and Letters. It's chock full of real-world advice from people who have been there and done that. Not only would it make a perfect graduation gift, it's the quintessential remedy for those stuck in jobs that pay the bills but make it a chore to get out of bed every Monday morning."

—*Scott Hoffman, Managing Member, Folio Literary Management, LLC*

Creative
CAREERS

Paths for Aspiring Actors, Artists, Dancers, Musicians and Writers

ELAINA LOVELAND
Author of *Creative Colleges*

Creative Careers: Paths for Aspiring Actors, Artists, Dancers, Musicians and Writers
(2nd Edition)
By Elaina Loveland

Published by SuperCollege, LLC
3286 Oak Court
Belmont, CA 94002
www.supercollege.com

Credits: Cover: TLC Graphics, www.TLCGraphics.com. Design: Monica Thomas
Layout: The Roberts Group, www.editorialservice.com

Trademarks: All brand names, product names and services used in this book are trademarks, registered trademarks or trade names of their respective holders. SuperCollege is not associated with any college, university, product or vendor.

Disclaimers: The author and publisher have used their best efforts in preparing this book. It is intended to provide helpful and informative material on the subject matter. Some narratives and names have been modified for illustrative purposes. SuperCollege and the author make no representations or warranties with respect to the accuracy or completeness of the contents of the book and specifically disclaim any implied warranties or merchantability or fitness for a particular purpose. There are no warranties which extend beyond the descriptions contained in this paragraph. The accuracy and completeness of the information provided herein and the opinions stated herein are not guaranteed or warranted to produce any particular results. SuperCollege and the author specifically disclaim any responsibility for any liability, loss or risk, personal or otherwise, which is incurred as a consequence, directly or indirectly, of the use and application of any of the contents of this book.

ISBN: 9781932662344
Manufactured in the United States of America
10 9 8 7 6 5 4 3 2 1

Cataloging-in-Publication Data
Elaina Loveland
Creative Careers: Paths for Aspiring Actors, Artists, Dancers, Musicians, and Writers
        2nd Edition
        p.   cm.
        Includes appendices
        ISBN   9781932662344
        1. Careers
        2. Reference
                                        I. Title
                                        3. Education

ACKNOWLEDGEMENTS

WRITING A BOOK OFTEN TAKES ON A LIFE OF ITS OWN, and this book would not have been possible without the assistance and support of the many people whom I would like to thank here.

Thank you to all the people who so graciously took the time to share their experiences about their careers. Your words of wisdom will hopefully make a difference in a young person's life as they examine what their path will be. Your contributions for this book are its gems. Undoubtedly, your story will make a difference to someone, somewhere, which was my purpose in embarking on this book project in the first place. Your personal touch makes me proud that I could bring careers "to life" through showing your experience.

Sharon Ritchey, thank you for leading me to Kristen Ball, who assisted me with research for this project.

Kristen Ball, I can't thank you enough for being there for me whenever I needed assistance throughout the stages of creating this book. You are an incredible professional.

Julie Bogart, my friend and fellow writer, thank you for your help finding real people who were willing to talk with me. I wouldn't have found such fascinating subjects without you.

Nancy Rasmussen, at the University of the Arts, and Linda Tierney and Seth Michalak at Savannah College of Art and Design: thank you all for reaching out to your alumni to inform them of this project so I could contact the most successful alumni to be interviewed for this book. Your institutions should be proud to have such successful people working in creative fields that can guide younger generations toward a rewarding future.

Last, but not least, thank you to my family: my mother, father, and brother, whose continual support never wavers. And to Robert Liddy, who has known me since childhood and has always listened with a thoughtful ear about my writing. Thanks for your support as well—you are also family to me.

HOW TO USE THIS BOOK

THIS BOOK COMBINES STATISTICAL INFORMATION ON VARIOUS CAREERS as well as advice from real people in creative jobs. Because facts alone do not fully show what a career is actually like, real people shared their experience and advice through interviews about their career path. Hopefully, the combination of the reference material about careers and the real-world perspective will provide readers with a more complete picture of what creative jobs are actually like. This, in turn, should enable other individuals to make well-informed career choices that will lead them on a more fulfilling path in life.

Unless noted otherwise, career data and/or descriptions were obtained or adapted from The Bureau of Labor Statistics, U.S. Department of Labor, *Occupational Outlook Handbook*, 2008-09 Edition on the Internet at http://www.bls.gov/oco (as of September 2008).

TABLE OF CONTENTS

INTRODUCTION

Envisioning a Creative Career

DETERMINING ONE'S LIFELONG OCCUPATION IS one of the most important decisions an individual will ever make. People choose career paths for a myriad of reasons: prestige, earning potential, a distinct career path, having summers off, etc. Usually a person will gravitate toward activities and careers that incorporate skills at which he or she excels. For example, it would seem natural for a person who is excellent in math to pursue a career in accounting, while someone who stands out in the field of science might make medical school a goal.

An interest in the arts usually starts sometime during childhood or young adulthood. Often people who are inclined toward music, theater, dance, writing, art, design and fashion envision themselves in art-related vocations. For this group of people, however, a career path may not be as solid or dependable in some people's minds as those occupations sometimes termed the more "practical" jobs.

There are those individuals who strive to make their careers their life's work. Many of these people are creative; in fact, they usually have a passion for one or more of the arts. But sometimes, artists who want to use their creativity as the primary work of their careers can become discouraged by those who fear that a creative person will become a "starving artist."

For some creative careers, particularly in performance, work can be part-time or even limited to a certain part of the year. Because of this and other similar factors, artists can indeed experience fluctuations in their ability to "earn a living." However, at the top of these performing career paths, particularly with acting and music, attaining a high income is not unrealistic. Some starving artists do become well-known musicians, painters, authors, and fashion trend-setters, perhaps even "stars" of stage and screen—and everyone knows that stars make more money than even the highest paid professionals in the fields of law and medicine. And these stars started somewhere, probably at the very first rung of the ladder. They took a risk, and luckily, they got the reward. But usually, only the most talented, the most ambitious, and the most fortunate will become stars.

Where does that leave the rest of us who want to use our creative energy every day and earn money for it? Fortunately, for creative people, there is no better time to choose a career on a creative path. The term "successful artist" is no longer relegated to those who hold the "star" positions of performer, published author, or famous artist. Choosing a career in the arts doesn't have to mean feast or famine, success or starvation, make it or break it, or any other expressions such as these. In the twenty-first century, there are numerous art careers and job opportunities that require a passion for an artistic field and that hold the possibility for success on many levels.

Take a moment and look around you: nearly everything you see was the fruit of an artist's imagination. The chair you are sitting on was created by a furniture designer. That last movie you saw was written by a screenwriter. The cover of the book you are reading was designed by a graphic artist. The music in that ad you heard on the radio this morning was composed by a musician. The Web site you visit most frequently is customized and perhaps maintained by a Web designer. A talent manager represents your favorite actor. The dance moves you love in a favorite commercial, movie, musical or dance concert were created by a choreographer. And the list goes on. We live in a world that is fashioned by creative people. Our natural environment is enhanced by artists' work, and not all of them are entertaining us—most of them are not entertainers—most of them add their unique talent to create something useful for everyday people or to promote the arts. They all have real jobs with benefits. They are not starving. In fact, the arts is big business. Approximately 1.9 million Americans consider their primary occupation as artist, and their aggregate income is estimated at $70 billion annually, according to *Artists in the Workforce*, a June 2008 report published by the National Endowment for the Arts. Obviously, the artists themselves are earning salaries, as well as the thousands of people who work in jobs to support their efforts.

In recent years, the availability of creative jobs has exploded due to the advent of the Internet. Web sites all require artists to make them visually appealing and writers to produce quality content. People have come to rely on the Internet as part of their daily lives, which means that there is a continual need for people to use their creative skills to insure a quality Web experience that will keep us informed and entertained.

Additionally, this new thrust in the arts has not replaced jobs that are in the earlier, more traditional print world. There are more books and magazines and written material being created than ever before. Just look at all of the mail you receive. Consider the sheer magnitude of magazines on your local bookstore newsstand and the shelves and shelves of books in two- and three-story bookstores in most suburban and urban areas. All these books and magazines were produced by writers and artists, and those jobs are growing while even more new jobs are created by the increasing use of Web technology. This means more opportunity in creative fields—not less as some people might think.

If you are an aspiring actor, artist, dancer, musician, or writer, by all means, do whatever it takes to achieve your dream. But keep in mind that your ultimate goals may change, and fortunately, there are many paths you can take that still use your background in the arts and provide you with a satisfying career. You can have it all. You can find valuable, worthwhile work using your artistic skills and have a good quality of life from your earnings. You may decide that, in fact, your dream job is not what you initially thought it was—it may be here, described in these pages. There may be a creative career waiting for you to discover that is not in the shape you thought it would be—and maybe, your future is even better than you imagined.

Chapter 1

Careers for Actors

Beyond acting on stage or in front of a camera, one can find an abundance of careers in the business of entertainment. It takes a great many people who work behind the scenes to bring a theatrical production together or to produce a television show or film. Although acting is the job that comes to mind to most people who are drawn to the field of entertainment, other skilled careers may be of interest as well. An actor is only one part of the picture: everything that is seen or heard onstage or in a television show or movie must be designed by someone. The creation of a simulated real-life environment requires specialists in a variety of vocations to make a believable reality come to life for the public to view.

Actor

Job Description: Actors perform in stage, radio, television, video, or motion picture productions. They also work in nightclubs, theme parks, commercials, and "industrial" films produced for training and educational purposes. Some actors do voice-over and narration work for advertisements, animated features, books on tape, and other electronic media, including computer games.

Training and Educational Qualifications: Most aspiring actors participate in high school and college plays, work in college radio stations, or perform with local community theater groups. Formal dramatic training, either through an acting conservatory or a university program, is generally necessary. Some continue their academic training and receive a Master of Fine Arts (MFA) degree.

Job Outlook: Employment of actors is expected to grow about as fast as the average for all occupations through 2016. Competition for jobs will be stiff for many reasons, mostly because the large number of highly trained and talented actors generally exceeds the number of available parts.

Salary: Median hourly earnings of actors are $11.61. The middle 50 percent earn between $8.47 and $22.51. The lowest 10 percent earn less than $7.31, and the highest 10 percent earn more than $51.02 an hour. Median annual earnings are $16.82 an hour in performing arts companies and $10.69 in motion picture and video industries. Annual earnings data for actors is not available because of a wide deviation in the number of hours worked by actors. Additionally, there is a variance in earnings due to the short-term nature of many jobs, many of which may last for 1 day or 1 week. Actors who are members of the Screen Actors Guild (SAG) earn a minimum daily rate of $759 or $2,634 for a 5-day week.

Significant Facts:

- Acting assignments typically are short term—ranging from 1 day to a few months—which means that actors frequently experience long periods of unemployment between jobs. Often, actors, producers, and directors must hold other jobs in order to sustain a living.

- Employment in motion pictures and in films for television is centered in New York and Hollywood. However, small studios are located throughout the country.

- Many professional actors rely on agents or managers to find work, negotiate contracts, and plan their careers. Agents generally earn a percentage of the pay specified in an actor's contract.

INDUSTRY RESOURCES:

Actors Equity Association
165 West 46th Street
New York, NY 10036
Phone: (212) 869-8530
Internet: www.actorsequity.org

Screen Actors Guild
5757 Wilshire Boulevard
Los Angeles, CA 90036-3600
Phone: (323) 954-1600
Internet: www.sag.org

American Federation of Television and Radio Artists (AFTRA)
260 Madison Avenue
New York NY 10016-2401
Phone: (212) 532-0800
Internet: www.aftra.com

Profile: Actor

Name: Joyce
Age: 57
Title: Actor

Education: BFA Drama
Years in Industry: 33

CAREER LADDER:

Film:

A Price above Rubies
Roommates
Lorenzo's Oil

The Rescue
Life in the Food Chain
Just Like in the Movies

Television:

Rear Window (with Christopher Reeve)
Cosby
Law & Order (6 various seasons and roles)
Molly Dodd
Kate & Allie
The Equalizer
Mr. Merlin
Fifth of July (PBS) with Cynthia Nixon as my
    daughter, Richard Thomas as my brother
Gregory K

The Gentleman Bandit
Ethel Is an Elephant
The Single Life
Wrong for Each Other
Another World
Ryan's Hope
All My Children
One Life to Live

Broadway and Off Broadway:

The Water Children	Playwrights Horizon
One the Bum	Playwrights Horizon
Prelude to a Kiss	Circle Rep and Broadway
Fifth of July	Circle Rep, Mark Taper Forum, Broadway
Extremities	Westside Arts Theater
Reckless	Circle Rep
The Miss Firecracker Contest with Holly Hunter	Manhattan Theater Club and Westside Arts
The Hands of Its Enemy	Manhattan Theater Club
Hot L Baltimore	Circle In the Square
Talley and Son	Circle Rep, Mark Taper Forum
Back in the Race	Circle Rep
The Runner Stumbles	Circle Rep with Bill Hurt
Who Killed Richard Cory	Circle Rep
Love and/or Death	Circle Rep

Regional Theater:

Bluish	Alliance, Atlanta
'Night Mother with Eileen Heckart	Alliance, Atlanta
The Traveling Squirrel	Long Warf, New Haven
Hot L Baltimore	Seattle ACT

Q&A

Where are the best cities to live to find jobs like yours?
Atlanta, Chicago, Los Angeles, New York.

What is your typical day like?
My typical day now is not reflective of my career, because in the last two years, work has dropped off alarmingly. This is not unusual for women in my industry. Now, I average an audition every other day or so. The norm throughout my career was 3–7 a day, mostly for commercials. However, the "shelf life" for that kind of work is far shorter than theater and even TV.

For most of the years in my career, I caught a train around 8:04 a.m. into New York City and then ran around the city to whatever location the audition or booking was scheduled to take place. The time spent would be determined by the efficiency of the casting people and the importance of the audition; for example, auditions for plays took more time than those for radio spots. I went from place to place until all the work/auditions were done and then I caught a train back to Connecticut.

When I acted in a play in New York City, I arrived at the theater by 6:30 p.m. to rest and get ready for the night's performance (rehearsals took the entire day from 9:00 a.m. to 6:00 p.m.). I would perform the show and catch the 10:30 or 11:30 p.m. train. If I didn't have auditions, I drove in late in the afternoon, which left plenty of time for a light meal and rest at the theater before the show. I have always been an actor who likes to be in the theater at least 1.5 hours ahead of the show.

What is your favorite part of your job?
The joy of acting.

What do you dislike about your job?
I dislike not working enough and the sheer grind of auditioning as opposed to performing.

Have you had any turning-point or "light bulb" moments in your career that have helped you get to where you are today?
I would have to say that having the perseverance to get a reading for *Hot L Baltimore* some 30 years ago was my "moment." I was hired to replace another actress. This event began an association with Lanford Wilson and the director Marshall Mason that led me to become a member of the Circle Repertory Company, a business relationship that lasted for over 20 years. It opened a world of working with new, live, exciting playwrights and other beginning actors; we did not know at the time that we were making history in New York City theater—but we did.

Q&A

How did you know you wanted to pursue this career?

For some unknown reason, it is simply the only thing I ever wanted to do—I was called to it.

How did you get into this industry?

I got into the industry by banging on doors to get an agent, and by trying over and over and over to be seen for off-Broadway shows that did not want to read me. My turning point happened when I joined the Circle Repertory Company as I described.

What do you consider your greatest professional accomplishment?

I was a member of the prestigious Circle Repertory Company in NYC for over 20 years. We were a small group of actors, directors and writers who worked as a company. The writers wrote for us, and even though actors would float in and out on other jobs, there was a core that worked frequently together. Amongst the company were Bill Hurt, Jeff Daniels, Lisa Emory, Helen Stenborg, Barnard Hughes, Amy Wright, MaryLouise Parker, Robin Bartlett, Bobo Lewis and many more. We originated the works of Lanford Wilson, Milan Stitt, Craig Lucas, Julie Bavasso, Corrine Jacker and a number of other American playwrights.

To what professional associations do you belong?

I am a member in Screen Actors Guild, Actors Equity and American Federation of Television and Radio Artists. I served on the National Board of Directors of AFTRA for over 15 years. I am presently also a Trustee on the AFTRA Health and Retirement Funds.

What advice do you have for others who would like to pursue this career?

Get really good training and focus on becoming a substantial stage actor. The craft of being truthful and solid in eight performances a week can translate to other media well. Do not set out to be a celebrity or a "star." Most of us aren't stars, and even those who become one rely on tremendous technique to support their talent. Dedication and discipline is the key.

Camera Operator

Job Description: Camera operators use television, video, or motion picture cameras to shoot a wide range of material, including television series, studio programs, news and sporting events, music videos, motion pictures, documentaries, and training sessions.

Training and Educational Qualifications: Employers usually seek applicants with a good eye, imagination, and creativity, as well as a good technical understanding of how the camera operates. Television, video, and motion picture camera operators and editors usually acquire their skills through on-the-job training or formal postsecondary training at vocational schools, colleges, universities, or photographic institutes.

Job Outlook: Employment of camera operators and editors is expected to grow about as fast as the average for all occupations in the next years through 2016. Rapid expansion of the entertainment market, especially motion picture production and distribution, will spur growth for the camera operator vocation. In addition, computer and Internet services will provide new outlets for interactive productions. Growth will be tempered, however, by the increased off-shore production of motion pictures.

Salary: Median annual earnings are $40,060 for television, video, and motion picture camera operators. The middle 50 percent earn between $26,930 and $59,440. The lowest 10 percent earn less than $18,810, and the highest 10 percent earn more than $76,100. The median annual earnings reported for a camera operator in the motion picture and video industries is $44,010 and $32,200 in radio and television broadcasting.

Significant Facts:

- Workers acquire their skills through on-the-job or formal postsecondary training.

- Technical expertise, a good eye, imagination, and creativity are essential.

- Keen competition for job openings is expected because many talented people are attracted to the field.

INDUSTRY RESOURCES:

International Cinematographer's Guild
80 Eighth Avenue, 14th Floor
New York, NY 10011
Phone: (212) 647-7300
Internet: www.cameraguild.com

National Association of Broadcast Employees and Technicians
501 Third Street, NW, 6th floor
Washington, DC 20001
Phone: (800) 882-9174
Internet: www.nabetcwa.org

Profile: Cinematographer

Name: Christopher

Age: 43

Title: Cinematographer

Employer: Self-employed

Education: BA History, MFA Motion Picture Production

Years in Industry: 21

CAREER LADDER:

Production Assistant, Driver, Grip, Electrician, Gaffer, 2nd Unit DP, Cinematographer

Did you have an internship in this field prior to starting your job?

After completing graduate school, I was offered an opportunity to observe Owen Roizman, ASC, shoot *The Addams Family*. This was not an official internship, but it was a marvelous experience from which I learned a great deal.

Where are the best cities to live to find jobs like yours?

While every country has a filmmaking community, and many cities abroad and in the United States have a production industry of some sort or another, the filmmaking capital of the United States is Los Angeles. New York is probably second. Although many films are shot on locations around the world, the key creative people on the set often come from one of the filmmaking capitals.

What is your typical day like?

There are two types of typical days for a cinematographer. One involves production; the other involves looking for work. Working as a freelance craftsperson, there is little job security and certainly no guarantee of future employment. On a typical production day, I arrive to the designated set (either on location or on stage) early. I like to have a few minutes of quiet to myself before I begin. I walk through the day's scheduled work with the director and assistant director and other department heads. Then I have some breakfast prepared by the caterer and step onto the set ready to work, prior to the official call time. The director then stages the action, and together we block the camera and set marks for the actors. After this, the actors are released to wardrobe and makeup while we light the set, often using "stand ins" of similar height, build and complexion, who are wearing similar clothes to what the actors will wear. When we are ready, the actors return; we roll cameras and we shoot. Each scene is broken down into the many shots required to present it properly and we reconfigure, re-block, re-light and re-shoot from each required angle until the scene is completed. Then we move on to the next scene.

After we have been at work for six hours, we break for lunch. We then return to work for another six hours until "wrap" is called. If we are to work more than that, a second meal (dinner) will be provided. At wrap, I usually walk through the next day's work with the director and AD before going to the production office or to a trailer to watch the

Profile: Cinematographer

Q&A

footage from the previous day's shoot with the director. These "dailies" let us know how we are doing. We might also watch some cut scenes provided by the editor who is editing the film as we shoot, often just a day or two behind the production.

At the end of such a day, I return home, or if working on location, return to my hotel, where I shower, eat and often then meet again with the director to discuss tomorrow's work. After that I sleep to get ready to do it all again. Some films can take 30, 40, 60, or 120 days. Sometimes they involve travel and extended time away from home and family. Other films are shot closer to home and on shorter schedules. They each have their own challenges and opportunities.

On days when I am not shooting, I am often reading scripts, meeting with producers and directors or networking with my friends and associates in order to find the next job.

What are your job responsibilities?

As a cinematographer, I am responsible for photographing the action that comprises the shots—the building blocks of a film. Before filming begins, I select the necessary camera and lighting equipment needed, and I choose the best medium on which to shoot, whether film or video, 35mm or HD. I often work with the director to determine the preferred aspect ratio for the film and then shoot tests to establish a common language and dialogue with the director and production designer so that all our efforts will work in concert with one another. Once filming begins I team with the director to stage the action, place the camera, and select the lens. It is my responsibility to design and supervise the lighting on every shot. I determine the correct exposure each time that we shoot, and I interact with the lab to ensure that the proper processes are used to achieve the results I want. I also must work with the director and script supervisor to ensure that the shots we deliver to the editor will cut seamlessly together, and I must make sure that the lighting, the focal lengths, camera distance, height and subject size are all appropriate for the film we are making.

I lead the camera crew, which consists of an operator, first assistant (focus puller), second assistant, and loader. On many shows, there are multiple cameras, and a crew is needed for each, though one loader can often load for multiple cameras. I also instruct the gaffer (chief lighting technician) regarding what I want in terms of lighting, direction, quality, quantity and color, directions which sometimes must be as specific as which lighting unit to use. I also instruct the key grip regarding what we need from his crew in terms of rigging, camera support and light control. These department heads, in turn, lead their respective crews in executing the needs for each shot.

As a trusted and valued creative collaborator, I will often watch versions of the film with the director and editor, and I offer comments as requested. I will assist in color grading the elements for any special effects,

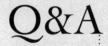

Q&A

and I will supervise the final color grading of the release prints, and the telecine transfer of the film to tape for its video or DVD release.

What is your favorite part of your job?

I like it all—the creativity, the collaboration, the close associations with other creative people, the excitement that comes from an uncertain future, the quiet time at home between jobs, the time away on location, sometimes traveling to distant locations (some more exotic than others), the feeling I get when an audience responds well to the film we have worked so hard to make. I also like the diversity—every job is different, and I am fortunate to work on feature films, television commercials, documentaries, television programs—it's always changing with many opportunities to learn, to grow and to meet new people. When not shooting, I teach both undergraduate and graduate students at The USC School of Cinematic Arts, and I enjoy being able to share my experiences with them. I like feeling their excitement and enthusiasm.

What do you dislike about your job?

Time away from my family, excessively long hours, sometimes bad catering, and sometimes less-than-ideal living accommodations.

Have you had any turning-point or "light bulb" moments in your career that have helped you get to where you are today?

There have been many. Every film provides countless opportunities to learn and to grow if one is open and receptive, and I am. While mastery of one's craft is essential to the job, ultimately it is our relationships with others that do the most for us. Despite the time and budget pressures, it is essential to treat everyone encountered with respect and dignity. Today's production assistant is very likely tomorrow's producer, so treat her well, and she may offer you an opportunity.

How did you know you wanted to pursue this career?

I've been interested in photography and in films since I was 8 years old. Frequent visits to the Edison Museum in East Orange New Jersey to watch the early films (*The Great Train Robbery*) sparked my interest and held it firm.

How did you get into this industry?

Nepotism. My father was a television director in New York, and he was in California directing a cable show when I first came out on vacation, shortly after graduating from college. I visited him on the set and decided to stick around for a few days. I began helping out where I could, working for free. Soon I found myself working 18 hours a day without pay, and I loved every minute of it. I quickly gravitated toward the grips and electricians and started working with them. After a few weeks, I left California and returned to Maine until my phone rang, and I was asked to return to California by the production manager of the same show. This time, they would pay me,

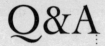
Profile: Cinematographer

Q&A

and provide a hotel room for me. Without hesitation, I moved to California, though at the time I had no idea how long I would stay.

Most of my jobs come through word of mouth, through recommendations. Some are initiated by a director or producer stumbling onto my Web site, and some come through the efforts of my agent. I have also worked with fellow USC professors and have been hired by former students. I have worked with friends and associates with whom I attended UCLA, and with total strangers. I have met people at parties who have hired me, and I have been overlooked by closer friends and associates. Much of what happens in this business is a matter of timing, and of being in the right place, being present, and having a willingness to roll with the punches (of which there are many).

What do you consider your greatest professional accomplishment?

To date, my greatest professional accomplishment is my commitment, ability and success at maintaining both an exciting, challenging and often unpredictable career while being part of a wonderful and loving family. In my work, I always push myself to try new ideas, and to push the boundaries of where I feel safe so that I can explore new less safe, uncharted waters. I select projects that interest me, challenge me, and offer me opportunities to stretch and to grow creatively.

If you weren't doing this job, what similar careers might you consider?

I think I would become a naval architect, designing boats with classic lines and proportions, but constructed using modern techniques and materials; boats that are both aesthetically pleasing as well as a joy to sail.

To what professional associations do you belong and what publications and Web sites do you read?

I am a member of The International Alliance of Theatrical and Stage Employees and Motion Picture Machine Operators, Local 600. Local 600 is also known as the Cinematographer's Guild or the ICG (International Cinematographer's Guild). I read *American Cinematographer* and *ICG* magazine every month. I read *Variety* and *The Hollywood Reporter* less regularly. Some sites I visit are www.cameraguild.com, www.theasc.com, and www.cinematography.net.

What advice do you have for others who would like to pursue this career?

My best advice is to pursue what you love to do, because you will spend a lot of time doing it, and you will likely spend as much or more time chasing it. As you are doing it, find something you love more than film. Have a life outside of filmmaking. Be nice to others. Be tenacious in your pursuits, and never stop learning.

Costume Designer

Job Description: Costume designers design the wardrobe for performers in stage, television, theater, dance and opera productions. Before completing costume sketches, they study the production and its characters by reading the script, meeting with the director, and researching the time period, location and mood of the piece. They then prepare renderings with fabric swatches. Some costume designers will also supervise costume production.

Training and Educational Qualifications: While there is no set path to a career in costume design, aspiring designers should consider a college degree in fashion design, fine arts, theater technology, art history or theatrical design and spend as much time as possible gaining experience in costuming with a school or community theater group. Designers need a wide variety of specialized skills such as drawing, sewing, tailoring, and pattern making, so one pursuing such a path would want to get training in those areas. Some costume designers may elect to pursue a master's degree in fine arts.

Job Outlook: Costume design is frequently considered a specialty of fashion design. Competition is expected to be keen, while relatively few job openings will arise because of low job turnover and a small number of new openings created annually.

Salary: Median annual earnings for fashion designers are $62,610. The middle 50 percent earn between $42,140 and $87,510. The lowest 10 percent earn less than $30,000, and the highest 10 percent earn more than $117,120.

Significant Facts:

- More than 1 out of 4 fashion designers are self-employed.

- Fashion designers, including costume designers, usually have a 2-year or 4-year degree.

INDUSTRY RESOURCES:

Costume Designers Guild Local #892
4730 Woodman Avenue, Suite 430
Sherman Oaks, CA 91423
Phone: (818) 905-1557
E-mail: cdgia@earthlink.net
Internet: www.costumedesignersguild.com

Costume Society of America
203 Towne Centre Drive
Hillsborough, NJ 08844
Phone: (800) CSA-9447 or (908) 359-1471
E-mail: national.office@
costumesocietyamerica.com
Internet: www.costumesocietyamerica.com

Profile: Costume Designer

Name: Nan

Age: 55

Title: Costume Designer

Employer: Self-employed costume designer and Professor of Costume Design at DePaul University

Education: BA in Art, MFA in Costume Design

Years in Industry: 26 years

CAREER LADDER:

Assistant Designer to Costume Designer

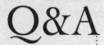

Which companies have the best internships in this field that are known to help launch a successful career?

There are many internship opportunities across the country. Internships are best for learning the ropes of the business and understanding how professional theaters operate. As for launching a successful career from an internship, it all depends on luck and opportunity, not on any particular internship.

Where are the best cities to live to find jobs like yours?

Although there are theater companies throughout the major cities of the United States, the best cities for the largest number of design opportunities are New York, Los Angeles and Chicago. New York and Los Angeles have television and film industries which employ costume designers as well.

What is your typical day like?

I shop for fabric, clothing and accessories, and I meet with the director and other designers and shop personnel. Additionally, I supervise actor fittings, I confer with the drapers/cutters, assistants and craftspeople who are building from my designs and I watch actor rehearsals and oversee costumes during the technical rehearsals through the preview process.

What are your job responsibilities?

I design the costumes for a production by analyzing the script and having discussions with the director and other designers about the artistic point of view of the production. I do research into the period or style of the production and then I design rough sketches which are subject to revisions until the designs are finally approved and budgeted. Then I do final costume plates which are presented to the actors, theater and costume staff. After that, I approve fabric samples, and do all that I've mentioned doing in a typical day.

Q&A

What is your favorite part of your job?

After we have finished and rehearsed with the costumes, I enjoy watching the show with an audience. It gives me a chance to see how effective my costume designs are in helping to tell the story of the play.

What do you dislike about your job?

There is usually a lot of travel and hotel living, which can be fun if you are single, but not so much fun if you have a family.

How did you know you wanted to pursue this career?

I started in fashion design but I didn't like designing for faceless customers. It was too much of a business. In *costume* design, you design for a specific character in a specific theatrical or filmic world. It is more satisfying artistically.

Describe how you got into this industry and how you got your most recent job.

I made contacts with my fellow students while I was still in school, and that led to my first jobs. I also worked for a professional costume shop in New York, which put me in contact with established designers whom I could later assist. Later on, my reputation as a designer led to job referrals. A costume designer is usually requested by the director of the production, so knowing and working well with a number of directors helps you to get work in the business.

What do you consider your greatest professional accomplishment?

I received an award for design collaboration which meant a lot to me because it was based on the recommendations of my peers.

To what professional associations do you belong and what do you read?

I belong to United Scenic Artists, and I stay on top of current events and literature because designers need to know about the world around them. I also keep track of the current fashion scene as well as developments in cultural and costume history.

Director

Job Description: Directors are responsible for the creative decisions of a production. They interpret scripts, express concepts to set and costume designers, audition and select cast members, conduct rehearsals, and direct the work of the cast and crew. They approve the design elements of a production, including the sets, costumes, choreography, and music.

Training and Educational Qualifications: There are no specific training requirements for producers and directors. Talent, experience, and business acumen are very important. An ability to deal with many different kinds of people while under stress is also essential. Many producers and/or directors begin as assistant directors; others gain industry experience first as actors, writers, film editors, or business managers. Formal training in directing and producing is available at some colleges and universities.

Job Outlook: Wage and salary employment in the motion picture and video industries is projected to grow 11 percent between 2006 and 2016, which is faster than the 14 percent growth projected for wage and salary employment in all other industries combined. Job growth will result from the explosive growth of demand for programming needed to fill an increasing number of cable and satellite television channels as well as the rising in-home demand for videos, DVDs, and films over the Internet.

Salary: The median annual earnings for salaried producers and directors are $56,310. The middle 50 percent earn between $37,980 and $88,700. Median annual earnings are $70,750 in motion picture and video industries and $47,530 in radio and television broadcasting.

Significant Facts:

- Keen competition is expected for the more glamorous jobs—writers, actors, producers, and directors—but better job prospects are expected for multimedia artists and animators, film and video editors, and others skilled in digital filming and computer generated imaging.

- Although many films are shot on location, employment is centered in several major cities, particularly New York and Los Angeles.

- Many workers have formal training, but experience, talent, creativity, and professionalism are the factors that are most important in getting many of the jobs in this industry.

INDUSTRY RESOURCES:

Screen Actors Guild
5757 Wilshire Boulevard
Los Angeles, CA 90036-3600
Phone: (323) 954-1600
Internet: www.sag.org

Directors Guild of America
Los Angeles Headquarters
7920 Sunset Boulevard
Los Angeles, CA 90046
Phone: (800) 421-4173
Internet: www.dga.org

Profile: Director

Name: Greg	**Employer:** @radical.media
Age: 27	**Education:** BFA Video/Film
Title: Commercial Director	**Years in Industry:** 4

CAREER LADDER:

Production Assistant on set   *Editor*
Freelance Assistant   *Staff Editor/Colorist*

Freelance Director:
I have directed commercials for companies such as Ameritrade, DHL, De Beers, Dewar's, Ford, Jack in the Box, Nike, and the Tube.

Where are the best cities to live to find jobs like yours?
Los Angeles or New York, depending on your personality.

What is your typical day like?
It's completely different every day. I spent the last two days helping Matthew Modine put together a short film, while also working on a project that I directed—a public service announcement for the Red Ribbon Foundation for the awareness of HIV/AIDS.

What are your job responsibilities?
After getting the concepts of a production from an ad agency, I write treatments which will be used to present ideas to the agency. If I am awarded the job, then we usually cast and choose all talent. On set, I direct the action, becoming a middle man between the set and the agency. I make sure they are happy and I am happy.

What is your favorite part of your job?
I love being on set.

What do you dislike about your job?
Conference calls. I'm much more effective in person.

Have you had any turning point or "light bulb" moments in your career that have helped you get to where you are today?
I took on the challenge of creating "bumpers" or interstitials for two years with a company called Cornerstone Promotion. I did it for free, but it led to most of the work I get today, including a short film commissioned by Nike.

How did you know you wanted to pursue this career?
I figured it out in school. I remember asking if I could hand in two commercials instead of one short film.

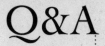

Profile: Director

Q&A

How did you get into this industry and how did you get your most recent job?

I got into the industry by being an on-staff editor for a sister company of @radical.media. Radical saw my work and soon started giving me low-budget, but creative, projects to direct. I got my latest job through @radical.media; it's a PSA for the Red Ribbon Foundation. I've also done recent projects for De Beers and Dewar's.

If you weren't doing this job, what similar careers might you consider?

Photography—it was originally my major, and I'm trying to pick it up again.

To what professional associations do you belong or would you like to belong?

I'd like to get into the Director's Guild of America.

What professional publications or Web sites do you read?

www.newstoday.com, www.videos.antville.org, www.gizmodo.com, and *Boards* magazine.

What advice do you have for others who would like to pursue this career?

Find a unique way in and always have something to show and talk about; your work is your best business card.

Profile: Documentary Filmmaker

Name: Ronit
Age: 29
Title: Founder/Director of Just Vision

Education: BA in Political Science, DEC Professional Theater Studies
Years in Industry: 6

CAREER LADDER:

Program Assistant, WITNESS, which at the time was a project of the Lawyers Committee for Human Rights
Program Associate, WITNESS, which became an independent organization Founder/Director, Just Vision

Did you have an internship in this field prior to starting your job?
Yes, I interned at B'Tselem: The Israeli Information Center for Human Rights in the Occupied Territories, which is in the same field as WITNESS. I also interned at the Dutchess County Criminal Court.

Which companies have the best internships in this field that are known to help launch a successful career?
There is no one trajectory. I work at the intersection of film/digital media advocacy/education/human rights and peace building. You can approach this field from many directions: journalism, community organizing, human rights internships, film company internships or study. Because there is no one path, the more interdisciplinary and serious the applicant, the better.

Where are the best cities to live to find jobs like yours?
I have been living in New York City since 2000 when I moved for my WITNESS job after college. Between 2000 and 2006, I spent time in Jerusalem, but on and off in four, six and eight-month chunks. New York has an incredibly diverse range of non-profits as well as sophisticated philanthropists to support this sector. It is a huge hub of creativity for this field. It is also the heart of documentary filmmaking in the United States; so for me, it was the ideal place to start.

What is your typical day like?
There is no typical day. Currently it consists mostly of telecommuting as some of my colleagues live in Jerusalem and DC. It involves responding to hundreds of emails daily, juggling fundraising, film distribution, legal matters and insurance for the film. I have to also consider staff management, outreach for our educational materials and board cultivation. My typical day could include attending film festivals and film screenings, strategizing about press outreach and reviewing interviews with Palestinian and Israeli peace builders which are published on www.justvision.org. At some points in my career development, my day involved pre-production, filming and working with my colleagues to edit the film.

Q&A

What are your job responsibilities?

- Raising support for the organization and keeping track of donors, donations, etc.

- Managing a staff of five from Jerusalem, New York and Washington, DC

- Managing a board of directors

- Reaching out to American secular, Muslim, Christian, Jewish, Arab, Israeli and Palestinian networks regarding our film and our Online Network for Peace at www.justvision.org

- Overseeing the direction of the organization

- Ensuring that our legal responsibilities are met

- Attending and promoting our film, Encounter Point, and supervising the creation of accompanying educational materials

- Seeking out new opportunities for Just Vision to further its mission of supporting grassroots Palestinian and Israeli peace builders

What is your favorite part of your job?

Working with my staff—they are the most amazing people. Also watching people respond and ask new questions about the Israeli-Palestinian conflict as they gain exposure to the content of our work.

What do you dislike about your job?

The administrative work and the financial insecurity of running a new organization. As the director, there is a constant stress to pay the bills and to increase our infrastructure.

Have you had any turning-point or "light bulb" moments in your career that have helped you get to where you are today?

When I was an intern at B'Tselem, I wanted to fuse my backgrounds in theater and political science. I felt that combining human rights work with filmmaking was the key. The rest followed from this realization.

How did you know you wanted to pursue this career?

It allowed me to be my whole self—creative, engaged on issues I care about, building bridges across sociopolitical divides in dynamic ways. I don't envy anyone—I really love what I do.

How did you get into this industry?

When I returned from my internship with B'Tselem, I kept talking about my dream to fuse human rights work and documentary filmmaking. A friend told me about WITNESS. I applied and got the job. That was the first step into the "industry" if you can call it that. It is more of

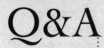

Profile: Documentary Filmmaker

Q&A an intersection of industries. After my first year at WITNESS, I began to think of applying the skills that I was acquiring to the Israeli-Palestinian conflict since it was about this that I found myself most knowledgeable and passionate. I then spent two years researching Just Vision while at WITNESS, and I finally landed a fellowship that enabled me to leave WITNESS and pursue Just Vision full-time.

What do you consider your greatest professional accomplishment?

Launching and sustaining Just Vision and gaining credibility with both Jewish and Arab audiences.

If you weren't doing this job, what similar careers might you consider?

There are many issues and areas that interest me so long as the entity engaged in the work is well managed and people interact in constructive ways. I have seen too many dysfunctional non-profits, and I now put a lot more stock in a well-run organization or operation. I am considering a few options, but they are in many different directions: politics, grassroots mobilizing through digital media, filmmaking and really immersing myself further in conflict resolution. I have several years to go with Just Vision before I explore these options with any seriousness.

To what professional associations do you belong?

I belong to Women in Film and International Documentary Association.

What professional publications do you read?

I read the *New York Times*, *Haaretz* and *Al Jazeera* every day. I read the *Economist*. I try to also read other Israeli press.

What advice do you have for others who would like to pursue this career?

Grow from experience. I think I was surprised to find how much my earlier experiences from CEGEP and college played into my work.

Lighting Designer

Job Description: Lighting designers plan, create, focus and plot theatrical and architectural lighting for homes, businesses, store displays, films, television and theater productions, and special events. In amateur theater, the lighting designer may also operate the lighting equipment during a production. Lighting designers work with the set and costume designers to capture the mood and dramatic effect envisioned by the director.

Training and Educational Qualifications: Lighting design is part of the larger industrial design occupation. A bachelor's degree in industrial design or theatrical or stage design is required for most entry-level commercial and industrial design positions. Many persons in industrial design also pursue a master's degree in order to increase their employment opportunities. Creativity and technical knowledge are crucial in this occupation. Designers in the lighting field also must have a strong sense of the esthetic—an eye for color and detail and a sense of balance and proportion. Those designers working for professional theaters or in film are usually expected to have specialized knowledge in those industries.

Job Outlook: Employment of commercial and industrial lighting designers is expected to increase at a rate comparable to the average projected for all occupations through 2016. The availability of more employment opportunities in this field will be the outgrowth of an expanding economy and a rise in consumer and business demand for new or upgraded products. However, competition for jobs will be keen because many talented individuals are attracted to the design field. The best job opportunities will be in specialized design firms, which are used by manufacturers to design products or parts of products. Designers with strong backgrounds in engineering and computer-aided design, as well as extensive business expertise, may have the best prospects.

Salary: The median annual earnings figure for commercial and industrial designers is $54,560. The middle 50 percent earn between $41,270 and $72,610. The lowest 10 percent earn less than $29,080, and the highest 10 percent earn more than $92,970.

Significant Facts:

- About 30 percent of commercial and industrial designers are self-employed. Many designers work for services firms.

- A bachelor's degree in industrial design, architecture, or engineering is required for entry-level positions. Some lighting design professionals have degrees in theatrical or stage design.

- Lighting designers who want to work in professional theaters or in film are usually expected to have specialized knowledge in those industries.

INDUSTRY RESOURCES:

Industrial Designers Society of America
45195 Business Court, Suite 250
Dulles, VA 20166-6717
Phone: (703) 707-6000
Internet: www.idsa.org

Profile: Lighting Designer

Name: John	**Employer: Cooper Lighting**
Age: 27	**Education: BFA, Industrial Design**
Title: Industrial/Lighting Designer	**Years in Industry: 3**

CAREER LADDER:

Merchandising Manager for Home Depot
Freelance Designer (graphic, furniture, and product design jobs)
Industrial/Lighting Designer for Cooper Lighting

Did you have an internship in this field prior to starting your job?
I was given the opportunity to do contract work for Cooper Lighting—building models and prototypes—with the chance that I might be given a full-time design gig. I've been here ever since then.

Which companies have the best internships in this field and are known to help launch successful careers?
In the Southeast, Ryobi/CCI and Electrolux are the best I know of. Interns get to work on a large variety of products and learn the latest tools and disciplines.

Where are the best cities to live to find jobs like yours?
Anywhere in Ohio, California, or New York is good because of the large creative presence of business HQ's. Most large cities are good as well, for example, Chicago, Los Angeles and Miami.

What is your typical day like?
I show up at 8:00 a.m. A normal part of my day is to spend a half hour or so doing trending and checking out new products. I also spend a good bit of time sketching and working in CAD. I've learned that too many meetings can be anti-productive.

What are your job responsibilities?
I basically work through the whole design process of bringing an idea into a sketch then into the computer and into a tangible product that can be made. We work very closely with marketing and engineering as we go through this cycle. I also do almost all of our in-house computer rendering and Photoshop work.

What is your favorite part of your job?
I like getting out of the office and doing research. I find it very gratifying to talk with customers and the people that deal with our products. There's no substitute for this work. Creativity blooms when you leave the office. When you lose the computer and the phone, it's almost Zen-like.

Profile: Lighting Designer

Q&A

What do you dislike about your job?

Meetings. I work in a corporate environment and we have meetings about the tiniest obscure details.

Have you had any turning point or "light bulb" moments in your career that have helped you get to where you are today?

I think I'm having one now. I've come to the point where I want to start my own business, either a consultancy or a manufacturer of a few products I've designed and really latched onto. I'll have to get back with you to see how the future pans out.

How did you know you wanted to pursue this career?

Growing up I loved drawing, working in my dad's shop, taking stuff and modifying my toys. I had always loved cars and as I looked into getting into that, I found this whole industry based on products. Before then, I thought engineers were the only ones to develop products. Now I see product design as the perfect career.

Describe how you got into this industry and how you got your most recent job.

As I was figuring out that "product designers" exist, my cousin told me about an art and design college. Within six months, I was enrolled and taking "Intro to Industrial Design."

If you weren't doing this job, what similar careers might you consider?

I've always liked the psychological aspect of creating products—that part of design that makes people become emotionally attached to their products—so ethnography and psychology would definitely be high on the list of alternate careers.

To what professional associations do you belong and what professional publications do you read?

I'm a member of Industrial Designers Society of America (ISDA). I read their newsletters and magazines. In fact, I'm a magazine hound so I look at everything I'm either interested in or draw inspiration from. Magazines are a sort of visual anthropology for me.

What advice do you have for others who would like to pursue this career?

Be aware that you are always working and thinking, whether you are at home, at the mall, or getting a latte. You constantly need to be subjectively looking at things for opportunities, inspiration, and direction. Always keep an open mind and try new things.

Producer (Film)

Job Description: Producers look for ideas that can be readily expressed on film. Then they work with the director to select the script, cast, and filming locations for that presentation. Producers are responsible for finding financing for a film's production, as well as seeing that production costs stay within the agreed-upon budget.

Training and Educational Qualifications: There are no specific training requirements for producers. Talent, experience, and business acumen are very important. Many producers start as assistant directors, actors, writers, film editors, or business managers. Formal training in producing is offered at some colleges and universities.

Job Outlook: Jobs in the motion picture and video industries are projected to grow 11 percent between 2006 and 2016, about as fast as average for all occupations. This job growth will result from the explosive demand for cable and satellite television programming. Also, more films will be needed to meet in-home demand for videos, DVDs, and films over the Internet.

Salary: Producers seldom have a set salary; they get a percentage of a show's earnings or ticket sales.

Significant Facts:

- Competition for producing jobs is keen and should be anticipated.

- Although many films are shot on location, employment is centered in several major cities, particularly New York and Los Angeles.

- Many producers have formal training, but experience, talent, creativity, and professionalism are the factors that are most important for making ones self marketable in this industry.

INDUSTRY RESOURCES:

International Federation of Film Producers Associations (FIAPF)
9, rue de l'Echelle 75001 Paris
E-mail: info@fiapf.org
Internet: www.fiapf.org

Independent Film & Television Alliance (IFTA)
10850 Wilshire Boulevard, 9th Floor
Los Angeles, CA 90024-4321
E-mail: info@ifta-online.org
Internet: www.ifta-online.org

Profile: Associate Producer

Name: Colleen	**Employer:** Lucky Duck Productions
Age: 23	**Education:** BFA Photography
Title: Associate Producer (television)	**Years in Industry:** 1.5

CAREER LADDER:

Intern
Production Assistant

Production Associate/Photo Editor
Associate producer

Did you have an internship in this field prior to starting your job?

I began at this company as an intern. I also was involved in an advanced (paid) internship program with Walt Disney World's Photo Imaging Department as a designer/developer of their latest system of photography currently used in the parks.

Which companies have the best internships in this field and are known to help launch successful careers?

I've been told Viacom is a great place to get an internship. If you're looking for journalism-related jobs, large networks are always impressive for a resume, but I've found that it's the smaller newsrooms or companies that truly let you get your hands dirty. So if you're looking to wow a future employer with your resume, a big corporation is for you. If you're looking to wow them with your knowledge, then you want a smaller company. You will truly find yourself with more hands-on experience in a more intimate atmosphere.

Where are the best cities to live to find jobs like yours?

I've had a lot of success in New York City. Los Angeles is more suited to producing movies if you're looking for that. I've also seen a lot of success in Wilmington, NC. But any and every town has local news stations and they will all have news-related production jobs.

What is your typical day like?

I am associate producer of a children's news show that airs on Nickelodeon called Nick News. We start our days around 10:00 a.m. I get to the office, check email and do typical office stuff. My job is a lot of technicalities. I'm in charge of finding footage that supports the story we are trying to tell. I'm also involved in finding the children and adults that we interview during our segments. Along the same lines, I set up the shoots that are needed to do said interviews. Any travel arrangements and crew calls that need to be made are part of my job. Once we choose what footage and photographs work best with our scripts, it is my job to license them and clear the minimum rights our show requires. My day consists of lots of phone calls, emails and faxing. On days that we are shooting, we are typically up and at the set by 6:00 a.m. I help prepare the breakfast table, keep the kids organized, keep my executive

Q&A

and senior producers happy and calm, and take care of a lot of the details that go into the day.

What is your favorite part of your job?

The people I work with. They're wonderful and I love my office. I also truly love the fact that I'm working on a television show that helps benefit our future children. It's not crappy entertainment. It's informative. It matters. As my boss says, "Life's too short to produce crap."

What do you dislike about your job?

Because I'm the associate producer, I tend to get thrown a lot of various and different tasks. It takes a very organized person to keep track of all the requests that come my way. I've also found that I reach a certain point where I have to learn to delegate. It's okay to ask our production assistant for help as well.

How did you know you wanted to pursue this career?

I honestly didn't plan this career—I sort of fell into it. I was at a writer's conference in May 2005. Linda Ellerbee, who owns the company that produces *Nick News*, was speaking at this conference. I grew up in a strict household where I wasn't allowed to watch much television. *Nick News* was one of the few shows I was allowed to see. When I met Linda, I mentioned this to her. She asked to see a sample of my writing, and after reading it, she offered me an internship. I accepted it.

If you weren't doing this job, what similar careers might you consider?

I've thought about going into editorial work, possibly working for a magazine or a publishing house. I think the premise behind these jobs is very similar.

What advice do you have for others who would like to pursue this career?

Television is a tough career to break into. If you're lucky enough to get an entry-level position or an internship, expect to work long hours. Any job worthwhile will be time-consuming. You may be doing anything from reorganizing their footage archive, to tracking down potential stories, to making coffee. My advice: Put in the time it takes to get the job done right and exceptionally well. Don't take short cuts. If your job is to make coffee for the office, make the best cup of coffee possible. Not only that, do it with a smile—because it truly does matter.

Profile: Senior Writer/Producer

Name: Merrill
Age: 29
Title: Senior Writer/Producer

Employer: Cartoon Network/Adult Swim
Education: BFA in Video/Film, BFA in Computer Art
Years in Industry: 6

CAREER LADDER:

Production Assist (Cartoon Network, commercials and print)
Associate Writer (Cartoon Network, commercials and print)
Writer/Producer (Cartoon Network, commercials and print)
Writer on adult swim show Stroker & Hoop
Creative Consultant on Harvey Birdman Attorney at Law (adult swim)
Freelance Comic Book writer (Spider-Man for Marvel, upcoming releases from Marvel and Virgin
   Comics. Co-creator of Indie book Tuff-Girl)
Senior Writer Producer (Cartoon Network)
Senior Writer Producer (adult swim and adultswim.com)

Did you have an internship in this field prior to starting your job?
I started interning for Cartoon Network between my 4th and 5th years at SCAD. The company was a little smaller back then and I had a chance to write some spots. My boss liked my stuff enough that he kept me on as a freelancer during my final year of education at Savannah College of Art and Design and hired me full time as soon as I graduated.

Which companies have the best internships in this field and are known to help launch successful careers?
An internship is like all schooling: the more you put into it, the more you get out. However, if you go to a really large company, you may find that you do not get to take the same chances or receive the same opportunities as someone who interns for a smaller company. Then again, bigger companies may be able to more readily hire you.

Where are the best cities to live to find jobs like yours?
Probably Los Angeles is the best city for my job. There are very few opportunities for television writers in Atlanta. I was one of the lucky ones.

What is your typical day like?
I am sure many people will say this, but there is no typical day. My creativity runs higher later in the day so I use the time before lunch to take care of clerical tasks. At the moment, I am working on adultswim. com. The morning is when I do the most producing. Then after lunch, I really get cranking on creative concepts. I sometimes will read something or listen to something and kind of zone out until I get ideas. I usually write my stuff down on a notebook and kind of just go crazy. In

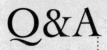

Profile: Senior Writer/Producer

Q&A

the late afternoon, I force myself to just pound it out—type it in a word processor and make it formal.

If I am working with a show staff that is currently in production, I usually take a day every other week to just come up with jokes or ideas. Because of the lead time in animation, it can take over a year to see the finished bit on TV. Because we are usually not constantly writing, we sometimes get to see a bunch of shows in several stages of production.

What are your job responsibilities?

It changes all the time. Currently, I am working as a senior writer for adultswim.com, which means that I am constantly creating new material for original shorts, games and existing show promotions. On a show, my only responsibility is to be funny. In comics, I want to make sure the story makes sense and is compelling and my artist understands what I want to see. And my biggest responsibility for every job is getting stuff done on deadline.

What is your favorite part of your job?

I like really nailing a joke. I like seeing something I wrote come to life. Occasionally, I get to write for an iconic character, like Spider-Man or Scooby-Doo or Robin, and that is a thrill all its own. In all honesty, nothing ever beat seeing my name on the Spider-Man cover or in credits for the first time. That's about equal.

What do you dislike about your job?

I don't like some of the extremely difficult people that I have to deal with. In a creative field, sometimes there are some bad personality clashes. I like 93 percent of the people I deal with, but then there is that other 7 percent. Also it is hard when you put everything you have into a project, and for some reason, it doesn't live up to your expectations.

Have you had any turning point or "light bulb" moments in your career that have helped you get to where you are today?

I remember being asked to write certain things, which I did, but also giving people additional choices that I liked better. The first time I did that—and it paid off—that was a huge moment. I was kind of fearful of presenting stuff when I first started. I guess I was afraid of falling flat. I still feel that way sometimes. The first time I presented a script and realized my knees weren't knocking and I was comfortable was a big moment.

How did you know you wanted to pursue this career?

I didn't know I would pursue a professional writing career but fell into it; although looking back, I think there were signs all along the way.

Q&A

How did you get into this industry?

I got in through interning and never really looked back. As soon as I was in, I fought for every opportunity I could get my hands on. I swung and missed a lot in the beginning, but each time I did, I learned a little something. Now I get most of my jobs from reputation or connections.

If you weren't doing this job, what similar careers might you consider?

I used to think I'd like to be an animator, but now I am not so sure. I think I would be interested in being a detective.

To what professional associations do you belong?

I am a member of the Association International du Film d'Animation (ASIFA).

What professional publications and Web sites do you read?

I read *Newsarama*, *Cynopsis*, *Aintitcoolnews*, *Cartoon Brew*, and Wizarduniverse.com. I also read *Write Now*.

What advice do you have for others who would like to pursue this career?

Read everything you can. Love what you are doing or you will be flattened quickly.

Profile: Supervising Producer

Name: Shannon
Age: 36
Title: Producer/Supervising Producer
Employer: Discovery Communications, Inc.

Education: BFAVideo/Art History, MAAA (ABT) Arts Administration
Years in Industry: 6

CAREER LADDER:

I began my career as administrative support for a talent placement agency and rose to regional manager in three years, running the Chicago area with a creative staffing service that brought in $7 million in revenue. I left that in 1999 to move back to the East Coast where I had the opportunity to break into television as a 2nd shift editor at Discovery's Technical Center. In two years, I progressed from 2nd shift to first shift, to lead editor for Discovery Channel U.S. I then moved from editing to producing in 2002, starting off in a support role. I became Producer and Supervising Producer in 2004.

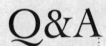

Which companies have the best internships in this field and are known to help launch successful careers?

Discovery has a good program—not in the technical end, but the business end definitely. I've also heard great things about Pixar.

Where are the best cities to live to find jobs like yours?

For television in general, it's all LA. For documentary programming, I'd say Washington, DC, New York City and Los Angeles domestically. London is the real capital of non-fiction television.

What is your typical day like?

Email, meetings, script review, writing, rushes review, conferences with outside production companies on programs we're working on together, network meetings. Did I mention meetings?

What are your job responsibilities?

I oversee programs that are scheduled to air on one of the nine Discovery networks in the United States. This includes budgeting, concept, pre-production, production, and basically shaping the program from start to finish. I work with two main groups: internal network executives and external production companies working under my guidance.

What is your favorite part of your job?

Variety. And I get to work with some of the best documentary companies in the world. Plus, I get to watch TV at work.

What do you dislike about your job?

It's only television. Although many people and executives feel differently, it's not that important. I'm thrilled to be in this industry but I do keep it in perspective. Oh, did I mention meetings?

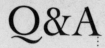

Have you had any turning point or "light bulb" moments in your career that have helped you get to where you are today?

I think that moment happened when I decided to have a career change at the age of 29. I had a good future in my previous "life" but it certainly wasn't fulfilling. I also had some family issues come up that put life and work in perspective. The "light bulb" moment was realizing that it wasn't about getting ahead—it was about feeling good about what you do. I've taken that attitude and have stood by it ever since.

How did you know you wanted to pursue this career?

I didn't. In fact, the one class I didn't take in college was documentary filmmaking. However, I've always wanted to learn and keep learning, so this career works very well. This career seems to fit me well.

How did you get into this industry and how did you get your most recent job?

Connections. Plain and simple. I happened to visiting my hometown and went to have a beer with a former classmate of mine/best friend. We talked about my desire to get back to the DC area and he remembered that I was pretty good at video editing. We talked some more and he offered me a job. In this industry, it's all about who you know. Period.

If you weren't doing this job, what similar careers might you consider?

Gallery or museum administrator. Non-profit administrator. I also definitely see myself teaching some day.

To what professional associations do you belong?

I belong to the Academy of Television Arts and Sciences.

What professional publications and Web sites do you read?

Variety, *Cable Weekly*, any newspaper articles regarding television trends, *Entertainment Weekly* and Cynopsis.com, a daily blog on the television industry.

What advice do you have for others who would like to pursue this career?

Be humble. Keep your connections from school and work. Things will never be given to you. You need to be your own cheerleader and be able to back up your boasts.

Set Designer/Scenic Artist

Job Description: Set designers design motion picture, television or theater production sets, signs, props, or scenic effects to establish the time period and mood of the story. They prepare scale drawings to guide the construction, modification, or alteration of their designs and usually oversee the production of their design plans.

Training and Educational Qualifications: While there is no set path to a career in set design, many designers have completed coursework in studio art, design, architecture and interior design. Many scenic designers also use computer software to create three-dimensional renderings.

Job Outlook: In 2004 there were 13,000 set designers in the United States. Through 2014, employment of set designers is projected to grow about as fast as the average for all industries.

Salary: Average earnings are $37,600 for set designers working for performing arts companies and $60,010 for set designers working in motion picture and video industries.

Significant Facts:

- Set designers design motion picture, television or theater production sets, signs, props, or scenic effects to establish the time period and mood of the story.

- Some scenic designers also use computer software to create design renderings in three dimensions.

- Many designers have completed coursework in studio art, design, architecture and interior design.

INDUSTRY RESOURCES:

United Scenic Artists
29 West 38th Street
New York, NY 10018
Phone: (212) 581-0300
Internet: www.usa829.org

Set Decorators Society of America
1646 N. Cherokee Avenue
Hollywood, CA 90028
Phone: (323) 462-3060
Internet: www.setdecorators.org

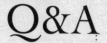

Profile: Set Decorator

Name: Sarah Stone
Age: 47
Title: Set Decorator

Employer: Various (Warner Brothers, Universal, Paramount, etc.)
Education: BFA
Years in Industry: 20

CAREER LADDER:

Graphic Designer
Freelance Set Decorator
Union Set Decorator

Q&A

Do you know which companies have the best internships in this field that are known to help launch a successful career?

The best way to get into the film business in the art department is to start at the bottom of the lowest budget production you can find, work for whatever they will pay you—even if it's in hamburgers—meet the production people, and get credits on your resume. The film industry is about who you know. Get to know as many people as you can (and hopefully have them like your work while you're at it!). Find listings for this type work in "the trades": *Variety, The Hollywood Reporter*; or online sources, or contact local film commissions.

Where are the best cities to live to find jobs like yours?

Los Angeles, New York, certain cities in Florida.

What is your typical day like?

Ten to 14 hours, lots of leg work, very exciting but hard. I get to meet a lot of directors, writers and celebrities, and I also get to work with a lot of very talented and fun people. Think "Studio 60" but with more lag time and fewer fascinating people. I do a lot of research on styles and designs, have a lot of meetings, do *a lot* of driving and shopping to find materials, and sometimes get very tired.

What are your job responsibilities?

A set decorator is responsible for delivering a finished and believable environment for the crew to shoot. The set decorator brings everything to the set that is literally not nailed down. That includes rugs, furniture, pictures, lamps, curtains, knickknacks, personal items that the characters might own, you name it. If you are shooting an exterior, a set decorator may bring tents, logs, wagons, farm implements, or other outdoor "decor." You never know what you might be working with from one shoot to the next.

What is your favorite part of your job?

The people who work on film crews are some of the hardest working, most diverse and creative people on earth. Some guy who is pounding

Q&A

nails for your set may turn out to also be a published author or a professional sitar player, or a pilot—you just never know who you are going to be working with. It's a really wonderful way to explode preconceptions about people. I also love the creativity of translating the script writer's words into a three dimensional visual which people look at and go "Wow!" That's when it all clicks.

What do you dislike about your job?

Not all of the people in the film business are nice. Some actually go way out of their way to be exceptionally cruel. You have to keep an eye out for those and watch your back.

Have you had any turning-point or "light bulb" moments in your career that have helped you get to where you are today?

Every day has a "light bulb" moment.

How did you get into this industry?

My first job was working as a graphic designer in New York City. I moved to Los Angeles and took a job as a receptionist at an ad agency before returning to graphic design once again. I met people who worked in movies and got an interview (based on my portfolio of paintings and illustrations) for a job opening to paint sets for a low budget feature and I got the job. I then worked as set painter/scenic designer for *Android* and later, I worked several jobs as a scenic artist for TV commercials. From there I moved into set design and then set decorating for various low budget features such as *Witchboard* and *Lady in White*. In 1989, I got hired as set decorator on a new TV series, *The Wonder Years*. I got into the International Alliance of Theatrical Stage Employees, Moving Picture Technicians, Artists and Allied Crafts of the United States, Its Territories and Canada (IATSE) as a set decorator, and I have now worked for 12 years as a union set decorator (*Article 99*, *Tales from the Crypt*, *Chicago Sons*, *Freaks and Geeks*, *The Bette Show*, and *The Hughleys*, which is my most recent job).

How did you know you wanted to pursue this career?

When I worked at the ad agency, I had to "dress for success" every day: tweed skirts, permanent-press shirts with the "non-threatening" bow at the neck, pantyhose, and pumps. When I had the interview at Roger Corman studio (which was called "New Horizon") to work on *Android*, I met the production team and they all looked like the "me" I was at home: creative/comfortable/eclectic. They loved my artwork (which was really dark and quirky) and were altogether positive about everything—just a fun bunch or people. I knew they were my lost tribe.

Profile: Set Decorator

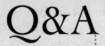

What do you consider your greatest professional accomplishment?

There is no single accomplishment I can point to as the best—there are many times that I look back on with satisfaction. I hope the best is yet to come.

If you weren't doing this job, what similar careers might you consider?

I'd run off to join the circus.

To what professional associations do you belong?

Set Decorator's Society of America and the International Alliance of Theatrical Stage Employees, Moving Picture Technicians, Artists and Allied Crafts of the United States, Its Territories and Canada (IATSE).

What professional publications and Web sites do you read?

Web sites and journals are too numerous to list. For the novice, I would recommend reading everything possible that has to do with film production—learn the lingo and find out who the players are: the production designers, set decorators, producers, directors, prop makers, special effects people—anyone who might be able to offer any information on a possible career. A lot of people like to give newcomers a few bits of advice. All of this information is on the Internet.

What advice do you have for others who would like to pursue this career?

The business has changed a lot in the last 20 years. It's a lot more corporate. The low budget "starter" niches like New Horizon and Concord Pictures are getting smaller and smaller. But they're still out there. Be tenacious.

Profile: Scenic Artist

Name: Susannah
Age: 38
Title: Scenic Artist
Employer: Intiman Theater

Education: BFA Painting and the Professional Artist Training Program of Seattle Repertory Theater

Years in Industry: 5 professionally but I've been involved in the field since 1990

CAREER LADDER:

Floral clerk, composite wing builder for radio controlled gliders, floral designer, decorative painter, actor on Shakespeare tour, art store clerk, Seattle Repertory Intern, decorative painter/ milestone artisan, scenic artist for Intiman Theater. I also do various scenic painting over-hire gigs in the off season, as well as pet portraitist, and specialty prop builder.

Did you have an internship in this field prior to starting your job?

Why, yes, I did, but it is not a requirement in Seattle. The Internship Program and the Rep allows one to apply for up to three different positions. I applied to paints, props, and costumes. Props called back first, so I worked with them for half a season and realized, again, that I am a painter not a builder.

Do you know which companies have the best internships in this field that are known to help launch a successful career?

I wasn't really looking to do an internship program when I saw the ad for the Rep's program. Scenic painting was something I had always been interested in but had no idea how to get into the field officially. (I had been working with fringe theaters for several years.) I believe that the program at the Rep is a really good one. I know that Yale has a great certificate program, which my boss attended.

Where are the best cities to live to find jobs like yours?

I chose a city to live in and happened to fall into a career field that I wanted. In Seattle, I know a number of scenics who are able to keep fairly steady work without having a "house" job at a theater or the opera. It is mostly union work. I also know someone who has kept very busy doing scenic work in New York (for theater, television, and film).

What is your typical day like?

The nice thing about my work is that it changes frequently. Depending on the show, there could be just my boss and I working or sometimes four extra people helping out. We could be starching a drop or carving Styrofoam; or we could be making up some crazy texture to trowel on some flats or painting wood to look like wood. Sometimes we have to spend all day working out budgets (time and money), or we are running about purchasing materials.

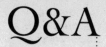

Profile: Scenic Artist

Q&A

What are your job responsibilities?

My main job responsibility is to assist my boss—the scenic charge artist—in any way she needs. That help can be in the form of working out square footage to figuring out how much material we will need; shopping for materials; working up samples based on the designer's elevations and research, and applying the sample techniques to the full scale set and altering it as necessary. Occasionally, my job includes being in charge of a small crew of over-hire painters. I also help touch up the set as it is installed, and I make sure those touch-ups are dry before actors get on stage to rehearse.

What is your favorite part of your job?

My favorite thing is the variety show to show. We get really excited when we get to trot out some of our traditional scenic artist skills. It can be a rare sight in theater these days, especially as digital projection becomes more prevalent in American theaters. I truly enjoy the process involved in creating a back drop—from sweeping the starch, to cartooning and painting the image, to folding it at the end. But playing in the muck and goo of a good texture, and getting to watch what the paint does on it, can be really pleasing also.

What do you dislike about your job?

The encroaching demise of scenic art in the wake of the digital revolution. Also, the financial struggles the non-profit regional theaters face can make for some frustrating cost constraints.

Have you had any turning-point or "light bulb" moments in your career that have helped you get to where you are today?

The first painting class I took was a "light bulb" moment. I was in my junior year in the wood department and I came to realize that I was willing to become a sophomore again in order to change my major to paint.

How did you know you wanted to pursue this career?

I was torn between theater and visual art when I entered college. I had painted one back drop (in totally ridiculous conditions—now that I know better) in high school, but I was thinking of acting at the time. After school, I toyed with set design. I worked with the Firehouse Theater Project in Richmond, VA, and I even did a couple of projects with the theater students at my former high school. But, ultimately, what I was always looking forward to (and what I watched during other performances) was the paint—to me, it's the fun part.

How did you get into this industry?

I got to paint a couple of things for plays that my husband was in at his college. Then when we moved back to Virginia, I started taking Meisner technique (acting) classes with the Firehouse Theater Project

Q&A

and I did some painting and set design for them. After we moved to Seattle, I saw an ad in a weekly paper for the Internship Program at the Seattle Rep. My internship was in props; I defected to the paint department. Basically it comes down to the people. I got small jobs here and there with people I met at the Rep. For my *job*, I worked with a decorative painting company. But, the work for them was even more sporadic, and to me, it was frustrating to make something really lovely that would only be seen in a tiny little powder room. I missed the collaboration of theater, being a part of a larger whole, and sharing my talents with a larger audience. I finally got fed up. I gathered photos of scenic work I had done to that point, put together a resume and sent out a bunch of packets letting theaters know I was ready and available to work. And shocker of shockers, I got calls. I got an over-hire gig at Intiman (the charge artist at the time had not received his mail from the theater, so he had not seen my portfolio. But he had been told about me by another charge in town who had one of my packets). There was another full time assistant at the time, but she was not working out and they offered me the position.

What do you consider your greatest professional accomplishment?

I was the charge artist for a brief time (interim, it is not a position I am interested in, at this time), and we had a big show for which I had a great crew working for me, and it was beautiful and fun. Getting to work at the Seattle Opera as over hire is always gratifying because it is so huge and such a great education. Also, I feel proud of the great working relationship that I have with my boss and with Intiman Theater.

If you weren't doing this job, what similar careers might you consider?

I really believe in theater, as hokey as that sounds. For all its shortcomings as a viable business (on the non-profit end) I believe in its potential to reach people, to entertain and educate. The hours and materials used are more reasonable than those of television and film. Perhaps teaching. There is always the dream of being able to do your own art (having the discipline) and only take over-hire gigs every now and then when you want to catch up with your friends—maybe one day.

To what professional associations do you belong?

I am a member of local Union 488 of International Alliance Theatrical Stage Employees, Moving Picture Technicians, Artists, and Allied Crafts of the United States, Its Territories and Canada (IATSE).

Q&A

What advice do you have for others who would like to pursue this career?

Really, people are the key in this industry. Niceness and a good core knowledge of scenic basics go a long way with most painters. You can learn a great deal along the way, but the networking potential involved in a training program of some sort can be invaluable. The degrees of separation in this business are low digits; production managers know people all over the country and can check a reference in an instant. It would be ill advised to burn bridges because you never know whom you will run into down the line.

Voice-Over Artists

Job Description: Voice-over actors read scripts for movies, internet voice files, CD-ROMs, and radio and television commercials. They may also narrate audio books, phone system hold messages, and corporate or industrial videos.

Training and Educational Qualifications: Most aspiring actors participate in high school and college plays, work in college radio stations, or perform with local community theater groups. Formal dramatic training, either through an acting conservatory or a university program, is generally necessary. Voice-over artists sometimes seek private coaching from experienced professionals in preparation for creating a recording of several voice samples to send to agents when seeking representation.

Job Outlook: Employment of actors is expected to grow about as fast as the average for all occupations through 2016. Competition for jobs will be stiff, in part because the large number of highly trained and talented actors generally exceeds the number of available parts. However, there are generally fewer voice-over actors than typical actors, so competition may not be as tough for voice-over artists as for actors of stage, screen, and television.

Salary: Median hourly earnings of actors are $11.61. The middle 50 percent earn between $8.47 and $22.51. The lowest 10 percent earn less than $7.31, and the highest 10 percent earn more than $51.02. The amount for median annual earnings is $16.82 in performing arts companies and $10.69 in motion picture and video industries. Annual earnings data for actors was not available because of the wide variation in the number of hours worked by actors and the short-term nature of many jobs, many of which may last for 1 day or 1 week. Voice-over artists who belong to a union get paid more per hour.

Significant Facts:

- Acting assignments typically are short term—ranging from 1 day to a few months—which means that actors frequently experience long periods of unemployment between jobs. Often actors, producers, and directors must hold other jobs in order to maintain a living.

- Employment in motion pictures and in films for television is centered in New York and Hollywood. However, small studios are located throughout the country.

- One of the largest markets for voice-over artists to do "industrials" is in Washington, DC.

- Many professional actors rely on agents or managers to find work, negotiate contracts, and plan their careers. Agents generally earn a percentage of the pay specified in an actor's contract.

INDUSTRY RESOURCES:

American Federation of Television and Radio Artists (AFTRA)
260 Madison Avenue
New York NY 10016-2401
Phone: (212) 532-0800
Internet: www.aftra.com

Voice123
130 7th Avenue #303
New York, NY 10011
Phone: (877) 275-8642
Internet: www.voice123.com

Profile: Voice-Over Performer

Name: Elisabeth

Age: Between 45 and Death (as Auntie Mame would say)

Title: Voice-Over and On Camera Performer

Employer: Self-employed

Education: BA in French Literature and Language. Years of training in Acting, Voice, Theater, Improvisation

Years in Industry: 35 years

CAREER LADDER:

I've done over 2,000 commercials and many network series shows—some of the most well known include the Bold and the Beautiful, Homicide, Law and Order SVU, Law and Order Criminal Intent, The Wire *and several other guest and co-star roles.*

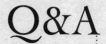

Did you have an internship in this field prior to starting your job?

The only internship was moving to NYC with $300 and my young son in a U-Haul. Then I just made calls.

Do you know of which companies have the best internships in this field that are known to help launch a successful career?

Most studios, theaters, film houses, and production companies sponsor internships for students. Also, actors are often looking for someone to help them with marketing and database entries. This is a great way to see what the "business of the business" is all about.

Where are the best cities to live to find jobs like yours?

With the advent of digital recording, the audio field is pretty much open to where you want to live. However, getting established is a whole other issue. The best training is still in New York City and Los Angeles.

What is your typical day like?

I often have audio auditions at my agent's office in Los Angeles. I get the copy from the receptionist that has been picked for me by the voice-over agents. I study the script and wait my turn to record it. Sometimes this wait can be as long as two hours in the waiting room. I also will get the scripts via email so that I can record the audition via my home studio and send it back to my agent's office if I have a conflict with a voice-over job, on camera or theater audition, etc.

What are your job responsibilities?

My responsibilities include some of the following: to be on time, to follow script direction, to listen to subtle changes. A voice-over artist must have the ability to analyze a piece of copy (script) quickly and then make changes according to a director's words. It's important to know different microphones and to understand how they affect my particular tone of voice, using a microphone to best service the kind of read I want to give. I've learned to be professional, courteous and not too

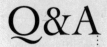

Profile: Voice-Over Performer

Q&A

chatty—that wastes producer's time and money. Likewise, it's appropriate to write short and sincere thank-you notes.

What is your favorite part of your job?
Standing in front of that microphone and creating a character I know is dead on!

What do you dislike about your job?
The uncertainty of the next job.

Have you had any turning-point or "light bulb" moments in your career that have helped you get to where you are today?
Every voice-acting coach I have ever worked with has always inspired some "light bulb" and that is such a gift to give a performer.

How did you know you wanted to pursue this career?
The first time someone hired me because they liked my voice—it happened in New York City with a producer who worked with me on camera.

How did you get into this industry?
I moved to New York City, hit the pavement and suffered poverty with my son until Angela Dipina from Cunningham, Escott, Dipina signed me, and I started working like crazy! Then it became a matter of marketing myself along with my agent and constantly improving the craft through study and practice.

What do you consider your greatest professional accomplishment?
A Regional Emmy for work on "Nicola Tesla, Master of Lightening," and voicing spots with former President Bill Clinton, Walter Cronkite and Morgan Freeman because of their dignity as human beings. Coaching others who have a dream of becoming voice-over performers and seeing them succeed is extremely satisfying to me.

If you weren't doing this job, what similar careers might you consider?
Creatively I would choose writing and photography.

To what professional associations do you belong?
Actors Equity Association (AEA), American Federation of Television Radio Artists, (AFTRA), Screen Actors Guild (SAG), Women In Film, and International Television and Video Associates.

Profile: Voice-Over Performer

Q&A

What advice do you have for others who would like to pursue this career?

Study the English language. Take acting classes. Learn different dialects. Get involved in theater. Take improvisation. Read and read some more. Read out loud, anything but the newspaper (it is too linear). Get yourself some inexpensive audio recording device and listen to the believability of your reads.

Drama Education: Drama Teacher (K-12)

Job Description: Drama teachers teach drama classes to students, sometimes in grade school, but usually at the high school level. They often hold auditions for student performers to appear in plays and musicals, direct rehearsals for performances, and organize performances.

Training and Educational Qualifications: Requirements for regular licenses to teach kindergarten through grade 12 vary by state. However, all states require general education teachers to have a bachelor's degree and to have completed an approved teacher training program with a prescribed number of subject and education credits as well as supervised practice teaching. Some states also require technology training and the attainment of a minimum grade point average. A number of states require that teachers obtain a master's degree in education within a specified period after they begin teaching.

Job Outlook: Through 2016, overall student enrollments in elementary, middle, and secondary schools—a key factor in the demand for teachers—are expected to rise more slowly than in the past as children of the baby boom generation leave the school system. This will cause employment of drama teachers to grow at a comparable rate with the average for teachers from kindergarten through the secondary grades. Projected enrollments will vary by region.

Salary: Median annual earnings of kindergarten, elementary, middle, and secondary school teachers range from $43,580 to $48,690; the lowest 10 percent earn $28,590 to $33,070; the top 10 percent earn $67,490 to $76,100.

According to the American Federation of Teachers, beginning teachers with a bachelor's degree earned an average of $31,753 in the 2004–05 school year. The estimated average salary of all public elementary and secondary school teachers in the 2004–05 school year was $47,602. Private school teachers generally earn less than public school teachers but may be given other benefits, such as free or subsidized housing.

Significant Facts:

- In addition to conducting classroom activities, teachers oversee study halls and homerooms, supervise extracurricular activities, and accompany students on field trips.

- Public school teachers must have at least a bachelor's degree, complete an approved teacher education program, and be licensed.

- Many states offer alternative licensing programs to attract people to teaching, especially for hard-to-fill positions.

INDUSTRY RESOURCES:

American Alliance for Theater and Education
7475 Wisconsin Avenue
Suite 300A
Bethesda, MD 20814
Phone: (301) 951-7977
Internet: www.aate.com

The Educational Theater Association
2343 Auburn Ave.
Cincinnati, OH 45219
Phone: (513) 421-3900
www.edta.org

American Federation of Teachers
555 New Jersey Ave. N.W.
Washington, DC 20001
Phone: (202) 879-4400
Internet: www.aft.org

National Education Association
1201 16th Street, NW
Washington, DC 20036-3290
Phone: (202) 833-4000
Internet: www.nea.org

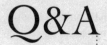

Profile: Drama Teacher

Name: Chris
Age: 40
Title: Middle Upper School Theater Teacher

Employer: Wakefield School
Education: BA, MA Theater History, MFA Directing
Years in Industry: 20+

CAREER LADDER:

Stage Manager
Lighting Designer
Set Designer
Producer
Artistic Director

Summer Camp Faculty
University Fellow
University Faculty
Playwright
Teacher (Independent K-12)

Q&A

Do you know of which companies have the best internships in this field that are known to help launch a successful career?

In theater that is a tough one because there are so many internships out there. One of the best I've seen is the McCarter Theater.

Where are the best cities to live to find jobs like yours?

Boston, Chicago, Milwaukee, New York, Seattle, and Washington, DC.

What is your typical day like?

I start at 8:00 a.m. preparing for a day of meeting with students and teaching classes. My first class starts at 8:30 a.m. Depending on the day of the week, it is either 6th grade moviemaking or upper-school acting. Our classes are 90 minutes long so I have a good long period to spend with students and the ability to go into strong detail about whatever aspect of drama I am addressing in each class. I teach only theater classes. On Monday I meet with all of the classes: 6th, 7th and 8th grade theater, plus introduction to theater and acting. The rest of the week the classes meet on a rotation.

After school, at about 3:30 p.m., I usually meet with students or hold rehearsals. When I am in production, my days always end with rehearsals. These can last until 6:30 p.m. one day or until 9:30 p.m. another day. I wake up in the morning looking forward to going to work because I spend the whole day teaching and working in my craft.

What are your job responsibilities?

I am the middle- and upper-school theater teacher. I teach all the theater related classes and direct and produce all of the school's middle and upper-school productions. We do two upper-school shows, one community musical, one eighth-grade show and one "all school" show each year.

What is your favorite part of your job?

Working with the students and watching them learn old ideas for the first time.

Q&A

What do you dislike about your job?

I am the only theater teacher at my school and am thus responsible for all aspects of a production. I have to find people to fill those jobs that I cannot, such as costume design and creation.

Have you had any turning-point or "light bulb" moments in your career that have helped you get to where you are today?

When I was in college, I realized that people actually made a living in theater, which had been a passion from a very early age.

How did you know you wanted to pursue this career?

I tried substitute teaching when I did not have any theater gigs, and I found that I actually liked it, so I became a drama teacher.

Describe how you got into this industry and how you got your most recent job.

When I was in high school, I was a miserable student barely passing. I had a mentor who took me under her wing and taught me that anything is possible if I spent enough time learning how to do it. Theater was my savior. I spent a good number of years as a professional after grad school, but I wanted to work with students either at a university or a private school. When I found that I could mix theater and teaching, I knew that theater education was the field for me.

What do you consider your greatest professional accomplishment?

I started looking at being a theater teacher because I have seen so much terrible high school theater. I knew I could do it better, and I have.

If you weren't doing this job, what similar careers might you consider?

Education outreach for a regional theater company.

To what professional associations do you belong?

American Alliance of Theater in Education, International Thespian Society, Virginia Association of Independent Schools.

What professional publications do you read?

Theater Review, Theater Journal, Art Search.

What advice do you have for others who would like to pursue this career?

Gain as much experience in the field as you can—then become a teacher. Those that have spent considerable time in the professional theater world will be able to better communicate their passion for the art form and to help students find their own path to artistic success.

Drama Professor (Postsecondary)

Job Description: Faculty in drama and theater departments teach in various sub-disciplines including acting, costume design, directing, drama/theater education, musical theater, playwriting, screenwriting, theater history and theater design. Many theater faculty members perform or have close ties to professional theaters or to the film and television industry.

Training and Educational Qualifications: Four-year colleges and universities usually consider PhD's for full-time, tenure-track positions, but they may hire master's degree holders or doctoral candidates for certain disciplines such as the arts, or for part-time and temporary jobs, including theater. Many professors in this field have a master's of fine arts (MFA) in acting, which is the terminal performance degree. Others have PhD's in other specialties like general theater, theater history, theater education, or performance studies. In two-year colleges, master's degree holders fill most full-time positions.

Job Outlook: Employment of postsecondary teachers is expected to grow much faster than the average for all occupations through 2016. A significant proportion of these new jobs will be part-time positions. Job opportunities are generally expected to be very good—although they will vary somewhat from field to field—as numerous openings for all types of postsecondary teachers result from retirements of current postsecondary teachers and continued increases in student enrollments.

Salary: Earnings for college faculty vary according to rank and type of institution, geographic area and field. According to a 2006-07 survey by the American Association of University Professors, salaries for full-time faculty averaged $73,207. By rank, the average was $98,974 for professors, $69,911 for associate professors, $58,662 for assistant professors, $42,609 for instructors, and $48,289 for lecturers.

Significant Facts:

- Opportunities for postsecondary teaching jobs are expected to be good, but many new openings will be for part-time or non-tenure positions.

- Prospects for teaching jobs will be better and earnings higher in academic fields in which many qualified teachers opt for nonacademic careers.

- Educational qualifications for postsecondary teacher jobs range from expertise in a particular field to a PhD, depending on the subject and type of educational institution.

INDUSTRY RESOURCES:

Association for Theater in Higher Education
P.O. Box 1290
Boulder, CO 80306-1290
Phone: (888) 284-3737
Internet: www.athe.org

American Association of University Professors
1012 Fourteenth Street, NW, Suite #500
Washington, DC 20005
Phone: (202) 737-5900
Internet: www.aaup.org

Profile: Drama Professor

Name: Kevin	**Employer:** Mason Gross School of the Arts, Rutgers University, BFA Program
Age: 46	
Title: Assistant Professor of Acting, Director of Performance Ensemble (BFA Program) and Head of BA Acting	**Education:** BS in Social Studies/ History, MFA in Directing
	Years in Industry: 25

CAREER LADDER:

High School Theater and Professional Workshop Teacher, Faculty Member at Oberlin Theater Institute, Director of Good Clean Fun (an educational theater company), Assistant Professor, director of plays in New York City and regionally over the last 20 years.

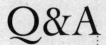

Did you have an internship in this field prior to starting your job?

I studied the Meisner Technique with Master teachers William Esper and Maggie Flanigan (they opened my eyes) for my basic understanding of the technique that I now teach. But it was Barbara Marchant, a Master Acting teacher of the Meisner Technique, who also has a real understanding of how to teach it to young people, who taught me how to teach the technique. I observed her in class at Rutgers and at Esper's private studio in New York City. She mentored me and gave me the courage to apply it for myself. I also studied directing with Harold Scott, Amy Saltz, and Michael Warren Powell at Rutgers, and they prepared me for a career in teaching directing and directing theater professionally.

Do you know of which companies have the best internships in this field that are known to help launch a successful career?

It's very difficult to secure an internship teaching acting. Most people who do this job have studied the practical application of the technique and then stay on and observe their teachers after they've graduated (if the teacher will take you on). It's not likely to just walk in off the street. Regarding directing, there are a few reputable companies or organizations that offer workshops or internships. New York Theater Workshop, Lincoln Center Theater Lab, and The Labyrinth Theater Company, all in New York City, come to mind.

Where are the best cities to live to find jobs like yours?

Teaching the art of acting, directing, or theater studies can be done anywhere. There are countless colleges, universities, high school programs, camps and summer institutes that offer such work. It is not necessary to live on either coast to do this job; there are some fine institutions in the middle of the country, and one must be willing to relocate because of the love of the work. The real trick is getting the job. It's not only what you know but also whom you know in this field. Theater is a collaborative art form and one is constantly meeting people. Be a good collaborator because you will meet those people again. Or you will meet someone who knows someone with whom you've worked. Don't

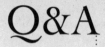

Profile: Drama Professor

Q&A

underestimate the power and importance of recommendation. When your friends are working, you're working.

What is your typical day like and what are your job responsibilities?

I teach in a conservatory so my students have three days a week when they are immersed in their field of study (the other two days are theater academics—history, dramatic literature, script analysis—or liberal arts requirements). I teach the Meisner Technique to the first-year students, and I direct the second-year students in a performance ensemble class in which they create their own performance pieces using theater games, improvisation, ensemble building, playwriting techniques, outside research, etc. I also teach a class called Actor/Director Relationship to the fourth-year students, I co-direct the fourth years in their Actor Presentation (Showcase) for the industry at the end of the year and I produce the festival of senior thesis productions. I am the head of the BA Acting program, so I have faculty workshops and meetings and I oversee the curriculum. On my two off-days from Rutgers, I am usually reading or watching something related to my field or I am working on a play I am directing professionally or working on a new script as a dramaturge. I do a lot of advising.

What is your favorite part of your job?

It's pretty hard not to feel like the whole thing is amazing. We're blessed to be doing our dream as our livelihood. I never understand people who work in the theater and still show up grumpy. I always want to say to them, "You're in the wrong job." You might as well go work in an office cubicle. Then you can be that guy who hates his job. But we get to do this magic for a living! I guess my favorite part is when my students don't need me anymore, as strange as that may sound. We really are working to make ourselves obsolete. I love showing up to observe my students in rehearsal and essentially saying, "Well, that's it. You're doing it. Nice job. Now I can go home."

What do you dislike about your job?

I hate writing evaluations. I am constantly in the process of evaluating my students, critiquing them, giving them notes, holding face-to-face evaluation meetings with them. I have no problem with this and they actually crave it. But, when it comes to writing it down, something just balks in me, maybe because of the permanency of it. Acting, and the process of learning, are fluid and flexible and want to be left alone. I hate having to track every single movement of the journey. But it must be done.

Profile: Drama Professor

Q&A

Have you had any turning-point or "light bulb" moments in your career that have helped you get to where you are today?

Like all kids who fall in love with the theater, I thought I wanted to be an actor. That's because when you go to the theater all you see is the actor. It doesn't occur to you that someone lit the thing, or wrote it, or is backstage pulling on ropes, etc. Later, when I started doing theater, I became fascinated by all that goes into it and I knew I was more drawn to directing. I wanted to be responsible for the whole story. Later still, doing theater in the schools, I saw the audience response and realized how powerful theater can be as a teaching tool. It was a short jump to knowing that I was a teacher or director, not an actor.

How did you know you wanted to pursue this career?

This will sound awful, but I originally went to a college that had a terrible theater department and our acting training was bad. So after hours, we students used to stay in the building and I would teach in the little black box theater (I was eighteen!). I had been studying Viola Spolin's theater games with a wonderful teacher named David Braucher, who was a professional actor. I would simply do at night with my fellow disgruntled students the games he had taught me during the day. Everybody loved it, we felt the joy of acting freely, and I realized I had some aptitude for teaching. I knew I wanted to do it as my career and I've always managed to do some form of teaching in my work since then.

How did you get into this industry?

Like all actors, I auditioned for roles and won the parts. So I was an actor for a while. Community theater, small professional jobs, whatever. But I also always found a way to teach: church groups, synagogues, high schools, and colleges. I worked with an educational theater company wherein we would not teach theater, but teach *through* theater. We'd use plays as a way of getting the students to analyze social situations. There were a lot of different learning styles being employed there. I was always fascinated by the way different individuals process information. I knew, however, I could not be taken seriously as an educator unless I got an advanced degree. Consequently, I went to Rutgers and got an MFA, which I knew was necessary to teach acting in a conservatory program. While I was in my final year, I made it known to the director of the BFA Acting program that I was interested in teaching. She saw something in me, took me under her wing, and mentored me. I observed her class and once she let me sub for her. That was a big step. I graduated, got some very valuable experience in the world of professional directing, and a year later, a position opened up in the BFA Acting program at Rutgers. I was offered the job. It should be said, however, that during that year, I sent my teaching resume out to hundreds of organizations and was rejected by each and every one. It is extremely difficult to land a college teaching job cold.

Profile: Drama Professor

Q&A

What is your greatest professional accomplishment?

We've had quite a few students go on to do extraordinary work professionally. Our students have film, television, and Broadway careers—award winners who are seen by millions. However, I am equally proud of my students who go on to have careers in what would be characterized as Indie Theater, what was once called downtown or off-off Broadway. They are less interested in the commercial world and are more concerned with developing a theater community that speaks in a challenging way to an audience of one hundred people at a time. I've also had students who, after training in this particular discipline, leave it for other things. I recently wrote a letter of recommendation for a former student who joined the Peace Corps.

If you weren't doing this job, what similar careers might you consider?

I have no aptitude for anything else. If I didn't do this, I'd be dead.

To what professional associations do you belong and what do you read?

I am not in any professional arts unions like Actors Equity or the SSDC. I am in my union at Rutgers-the AAUP (American Association of University Professors). I read *American Theater* and www.NYTheater.com.

What advice do you have for others who would like to pursue this career?

Study. Study. Study. You must be well versed in everything, especially the history, sociology, psychology, etc. of the human species and of this particular art form. Eastern Theater. Western Theater. African Theater. You must know it all. You must remain curious for your entire life. You must bring wonder, fascination, and awe to your daily existence. Also, you must have diligence and fortitude because this is not a job for the weak-hearted. You will meet with many rejections and disappointments. People will put you down so you must be good at lifting yourself up. Finally, to paraphrase Peter Brook who answered a young director asking him how to become a director, "There is no such thing as an out-of-work director. Unlike actors who must beg people to let them be in their play, a director must simply get a script, get some actors, and direct them. Do it in your basement if you must." There is no reason not to be practicing your craft if your craft is teaching acting. Get some actors and work on something. Do it in your basement if you must.

Chapter 2

Careers for Artists

Among all of the creative jobs, artists have the most opportunities for fulfilling careers in a variety of fields. Aside from being a self-employed professional artist who sells his or her own work, there are a multitude of occupations in art that enable artists to work full-time in various industries. These include general business, entertainment, government, fashion, museums, non-profits, publishing and technology.

Designers of many types have viable careers in art. Specifically, vocations for designers in the art field include the following: fashion designers, commercial and industrial designers (such as those who work with furniture and lighting), floral arrangers, interior designers, jewelry designers, and many others. Additionally, many businesses employ graphic artists to create visually appealing promotional materials or publications to provide information to clients and consumers.

Some artists specialize in one artistic form and devote their careers to it, for example, photographers and illustrators. Architects and landscape architects use their artistic skills to design spaces in which people will live, work and play; however, the career path to becoming an architect requires the honing of other advanced skills in addition to utilizing a creative vision.

Some artists choose to share their love of art in the classroom setting by becoming art teachers or art professors at colleges and universities or they work in museums as educators. Additional careers in museums that may be attractive to artists include becoming an art conservator or museum curator. Art therapy is another career option available to artists who are interested in combining art with learning or improving lives through art; it is similar to teaching in that the therapist works in an artistic space and utilizes many of the genres of art to help people evoke feelings.

Other careers incorporate technological skills with artistic ability, producing occupations such as digital animation, Web design and Web user interface design. With the growing use of technology in our everyday lives, opportunities for artists with technological skills should continue to multiply in the coming years.

Animator

Job Description: Animators draw by hand and use computers to create the large series of pictures that form the animated images or special effects seen in movies, television programs, and computer games. Some draw storyboards for television commercials, movies, and animated features.

Training and Educational Qualifications: Postsecondary training is recommended for all artist specialties. Many colleges and universities offer programs leading to a bachelor's or master's degree in fine arts. Independent schools of art and design also offer postsecondary studio training and award students with certificates in specialty areas or associate's and bachelor's degrees. In many instances, formal educational programs in art also provide training in computer techniques, which are used widely in the visual arts.

Job Outlook: Multi-media artists and animators should have better job opportunities than other artists, but they will still experience competition. Demand for these workers will increase as consumers continue to expect more realistic video games, movie and television special effects, and 3D animated movies. Additional job openings will arise from an increasing demand for Web site development and for computer graphics adaptation from the growing number of mobile technologies.

Salary: The median annual earnings of salaried multi-media artists and animators are $51,350. The middle 50 percent earn between $38,980 and $70,050. The lowest 10 percent earn less than $30,390, and the highest 10 percent earn more than $92,720. Median annual earnings are $57,310 in motion picture and video industries and $48,860 in advertising and related services.

Significant Facts:

- About 63 percent of artists and related workers are self-employed.

- Keen competition is expected for both salaried jobs and freelance work; the number of qualified workers exceeds the number of available openings because the arts attract many talented people with creative ability.

- Artists usually develop their skills through a bachelor's degree program or other post-secondary training in art or design.

INDUSTRY RESOURCES:

Animators Unite, Inc.
525 85th Street
Brooklyn, NY 11209
Internet: www.animatorsunite.com

ASIFA-Hollywood (Association Internationale Du Film D'animation)
2114 Burbank Boulevard
Burbank, CA 91506
Phone: (818) 842-8330
Internet: www.asifa-hollywood.org

Profile: Animator (Entry-Level)

Name: Brian
Age: 23
Title: Animator

Employer: Radical Axis
Education: BFA, Computer Art
Years in Industry: 1.5 years

CAREER LADDER:

Intern, animator

Did you have an internship in this field prior to starting your job?

I had an internship with the Redmoon Theater build shop in Chicago, which is the third largest theater in the Chicago area, primarily known for found-object puppetry. It was an unpaid internship that involved everything from sweeping floors to helping to design props. Being on build crew for the length of two productions, another part of my job was to help micromanage fellow interns newer than I. It was a rewarding experience all around.

Which companies have the best internships in this field and are known to help launch successful careers?

I have had several friends who have successfully interned at larger studios (Nickelodeon, Cartoon Network), and they all find it amazingly helpful as an "in" to put on their resumes as well as helpful practical studio experience. An important thing to note is that internships in California tend to be more of a "production assistant" type internship rather than an artistic one, due to union issues.

Where are the best cities to live to find jobs like yours?

For animation, the choices mostly limit themselves (within the U.S.) to California, New York, and Atlanta, perhaps in that order of opportunity. Having started out in Chicago, I am familiar with many other studios spread throughout other larger cities (Chicago, of course, but Boston as well), but I'm certain most would agree that the first three I listed are the main areas.

What is your typical day like?

As a small team of about seven (animators) responsible for a show, my day usually starts out animating, picking up the scene I left off the previous night. Perhaps I am more fortunate than animators in some other studios, because I am pretty much animating all day long with a few minor (30 minutes a week total) meetings with respective supervisors.

What are your job responsibilities?

Everyone on our smaller team is responsible for scene set-up, lip sync and animation (both keys *and* tweens). There is some design work maybe one day out of the week, which is usually assigned based on our strengths or availability.

Profile: Animator (Entry-Level)

Q&A

What is your favorite part of your job?

My favorite part of my job is honestly best exemplified when I realize that I am doing what I truly love to do—all day long. I work with a small team and can point out which parts of a televised episode constitute my work. Making a sustainable wage while creating something out of nothing is a powerful feeling, one that I feel wouldn't be as great working anywhere else.

What do you dislike about your job?

My biggest job woes are probably trends that face the industry as a whole. I take solace knowing that those whom I idolize in my field are probably downtrodden over the same issues I deal with daily.

Have you had any turning point or "light bulb" moments in your career that have helped you get to where you are today?

I suppose my biggest epiphany that paid off came when I realized that you had to already be in the area a prospective studio is hiring to actually work there. Certain career guides will give you a lofty view that if a studio likes you enough, they'll fly you in for an interview and a test and whatnot, but the reality of the industry is that is not at all the case. Simply being in the right place at the right time has done the most for my career.

How did you know you wanted to pursue this career?

I think the awe of watching animated films as a child more or less set me on a permanent track at an early age.

Describe how you got into this industry and how you got your most recent job.

I started in the industry by looking for internship postings while in Chicago. Ultimately, going with unpaid work on the weekend helped to proverbially get my "foot in the door" and at least let me spend my time doing semi-professional artistic work. As far as my most recent job, blind luck happened to help, as a former college contact knew to mention me when it came time to hire at her studio. Showing that I wasn't remaining stagnant after graduating probably worked heavily in my favor.

If you weren't doing this job, what similar careers might you consider?

I had a fairly promising academic background prior to my college days; but I enjoy being in the arts so much that if I weren't specifically working as an animator, I'd probably search for some sort of equivalent design position somewhere else.

Profile: Animator (Entry-Level)

Q&A

What professional magazines/newspapers/journals/Web sites do you read?

I frequently find Cartoonbrew.com to be a great source for all things pertinent to animation present and past. John Kricfalusi has an amazing, yet rarely updated, blog that I always find myself returning to. Between the two of them, I feel relatively well informed about the happenings in my industry.

What advice do you have for others who would like to pursue this career?

Don't be afraid to ask questions. Do anything you can to keep yourself from being disenchanted. Your current set of skills isn't your only selling point, and hopefully it is something you're working on, even if you're not in your current field of choice. Art isn't a race that is full of snares and things you can necessarily do wrong. A lot can be said about being in the right place at the right time.

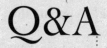

Profile: Animator

Name: Rob	**Employer:** Neversoft Entertainment
Age: 24	**Education:** BFA Animation
Title: Animator	**Years in Industry:** 1.5

CAREER LADDER:

Intern, animator.

Q&A

Did you have an internship in this field prior to starting your job?

Yes, I got lucky and was called by a production house in San Diego out of the blue. I took a year off from school and started what was supposed to be a three-month internship in animation. The internship had full-time animator responsibilities, so I worked more like a staff member then an intern. After three months, I was hired as a full-time temp (temp because I returned to school to graduate). During my time there, I worked on 15 minutes of cinematics for the video game "LA Rush" and two CG commercials for Kellogg's. Honestly, I would never have had the opportunities given to me had it not been for this internship. It basically enabled me to pick and choose job offers after school because of my experience.

Which companies have the best internships in this field and are known to help launch successful careers?

Small production houses enable you to work completely on a project and work on different aspects of that project. Bigger feature studios have good internships as well and look great on a resume but you will never gain the same sense of knowledge because you generally always wear one hat. Smaller production houses enable you to wear multiple hats, learn from a tightly knit team, and work up the ladder faster. However, any internship in animation is vital—experience speaks more then anything else, especially when you are competing with all your classmates who have graduated at the same time as you.

Where are the best cities to live to find jobs like yours?

Los Angeles is the leader, San Francisco is a close second, and I'd say New York is third. Other cities are popping up like Dallas, Chicago, and even Austin, Texas.

What is your typical day like?

I walk into work, pass the skateboard half pipe, get some breakfast then start working diligently on my assigned sequences. Generally this is what I will do all day, taking a break for lunch to eat on our outside patio with some of my co-workers. About once a week, we'll have reviews with the director, lead, and producer to see the progress of the cut scene animator's assigned shots and to discuss what could be improved.

Q&A

What are your job responsibilities?

I am responsible for creating the game cinematics you see in our video game products; those are the parts that advance the story. I work with motion capture data and implement animation on top of it. Also I am responsible for the overall look and feel of the game. I use various cameras and cuts to create a film-like experience in the game.

What is your favorite part of your job?

Everything...the people, the way I am treated and taken care of at work, and waking up every day excited to go to work—plus, you can't beat the free lunches either every day.

What do you dislike about your job?

The lack of windows. The last studio that I had, looked into Balboa Park in downtown San Diego, but this studio is a converted warehouse that has no natural light filters. It's a small gripe but there it is, nevertheless.

How did you know you wanted to pursue this career?

Since I was in first grade, I fell in love with video games. Then by meeting the right people who told me to pursue what I was good at and enjoyed most, I basically stumbled into animation and never looked back.

Describe how you got into this industry and how you got your most recent job.

I am a lucky one. It's a cut-throat industry and very hard to get into. In my case I never had to look for a job and always was choosing between job offers from various companies. It all started with the company who granted me an internship after seeing my work on my Web site—they called me up out of the blue. After my experience in the industry and a return to school, potential employers started calling and emailing, setting up interviews and what not. Needless to say, I feel very fortunate because the hard work and *very* long hours I put into school paid off incredibly and I never found myself actually looking for a job. In fact, I had one lined up before I graduated.

If you weren't doing this job, what similar careers might you consider?

Working in film or designing Web sites.

What professional Web sites do you read?

The site www.gamasutra.com is the leader in video game industry news, www.awn.com animation world network is a leader in news for animation and www.cgtalk.com is a forum/news source for all things having to do with computer graphics.

Profile: Animator

Q&A

What advice do you have for others who would like to pursue this career?

Be passionate! You should be spending every waking minute animating. Trust me, it's a tough industry to get into. You will be competing with the best of the best—industry pros who are also looking for jobs. Give yourself some time to have fun in school but go above and beyond the requirements of the class. Work on your own stuff and never stop animating. Also meet and surround yourself with the best students at school. Work with them and ask for critiques. I found that the best people in the classes worked in groups and challenged each other rather than working alone at home. School is the time to get critiques, learn from others, and develop a tough skin. When you get into the industry, they are not going to fluff critiques for you because you are expected to be able to perform by then.

Profile: Creative Manager for Universal Studios

Name: Paul Sessa

Age: 32

Title: Creative Manager, Entertainment

Employer: Universal Studios Hollywood (NBC Universal)

Education: BFA, Animation/Film

Years in Industry: 8

CAREER LADDER:

Data entry temp for The Writers Guild of America; Character Escort, Universal Studios Hollywood (Theme Park); Character Designer, Anteye.com; Production Coordinator of Special Events, Universal Studios Hollywood; Supervisor of Design and Brand Placement, Universal Studios Hollywood; Creative Manager of Entertainment, Universal Studios Hollywood

Do you know which companies have the best internships in this field that are known to help launch a successful career?

Probably Walt Disney Theme Parks/Universal Studios Theme Parks (CA/FL).

Where are the best cities to live to find jobs like yours?

Cities in California and Florida are good, plus other theme parks around the country.

What is your typical day like?

I am usually working on designs for the next big entertainment event for the Theme Park—that can be anything from a parade (designing floats) to the overall park decor look (Holiday/Halloween) to prop window displays (promoting Universal Films) to designing photo spots or environments for our costumes characters (Dora the Explorer, SpongeBob, Shrek). We then take those designs and execute them in the park.

What are your job responsibilities?

I am responsible for tracking a budget per project, conceptualizing designs and then implementing them. Art directing scenic houses and vendors. Art directing signage and graphics.

What is your favorite part of your job?

Working in a kids' environment—I get to go to a theme park every day!

What do you dislike about your job?

The corporate bottom-line reality end of things.

Have you had any turning-point or "light bulb" moments in your career that have helped you get to where you are today?

Somewhere along my journey, I realized I didn't have the passion to do animation, and I think that unlikely path led me to something I really enjoy and is a huge creative outlet for me.

Profile: Creative Manager for Universal Studios

Q&A

How did you know you wanted to pursue this career?

I really didn't. I always loved theme parks but never knew jobs like this existed. They are not exactly listed in the "Help Wanted" section of the newspaper. . .

How did you get into this industry?

I was pursuing working for an animation company while doing some of my temp jobs when I happened to fall into special events at Universal. I gained much production experience and started getting requests to do creative assignments for our clients as well. By making my artistic talents visible, I was able to get the leads to my current job. Who knew a job like this existed? In a way, a lot of my job responsibilities have been created as I go.

What do you consider your greatest professional accomplishment?

Creating a niche for myself and really defining what I bring to the company in the way of creativity.

If you weren't doing this job, what similar careers might you consider?

I would probably be an activities director at a retirement community! Who knows, it may be my second career!

To what professional associations do you belong?

I am an Executive Leader for our in-house affinity group called Out@NBCU.

What professional magazines/newspapers/journals/Web sites do you read?

I read *Variety* and a whole slew of Web sites. I love Youtube.com—you can type in anything and see some sort of clip regarding the subject.

What advice do you have for others who would like to pursue this career?

Don't be scared to take a longer path to get where you want to be. You may find some unexpected surprises along the way.

Profile: Digital Filmmaker

Name: Matthew	**Employer:** Ice Blink Studios
Age: 30	**Education:** BFA Computer Art/Film-Video
Title: Pre-visual Animator/Layout Artist	**Years in Industry:** 9

CAREER LADDER: INTERN;

Production Assistant; Previsualization Artist; Previsualization Lead; Previsualization Supervisor; Previsualization/Layout Lead

Did you have an internship in this field prior to starting your job?
Yes, I interned at Industrial Light & Magic where I helped in many departments. I was constantly learning a post-production pipeline as it was in motion (not in theory or planning). Most of all, I met people, *lots* of people, and learned other opportunities in the industry to which I could apply my goals.

Which companies have the best internships in this field and are known to help launch successful careers?
Industrial Light & Magic, Disney, Pixar, Tippett Studios, Digital Domain, WETA Digital.

Where are the best cities to live to find jobs like yours?
As much as I hate to admit it, being in LA opens up the most opportunities—direct access to the studios, directors, etc. A *lot* of post-work, however, is also located in the San Francisco Bay Area. Being in or close to California helps get things started, but it's not necessarily mandatory.

What is your typical day like?
Everyday I work with the director of the film I'm working on and help him/her lay out sequences shot by shot.

What are your job responsibilities?
I work with directors, usually during pre-production, to help them plan their film prior to its being made. I think about story-telling techniques, camera angles and character performance, budgetary issues and continuity problems and much, much more. Once execution of these decisions starts, it's my job to see them through, overseeing layout of the film (how the film is structured shot by shot, sequence by sequence).

What is your favorite part of your job?
Working, learning, and collaborating with some of the greatest directors of our time.

What do you dislike about your job?
The hours limit outside projects and late nights are very common. The further into production we are, the later the nights tend to be.

Profile: Digital Filmmaker

Q&A

How did you know you wanted to pursue this career?

I had always loved to draw and had always loved movies, so those around me assumed I would set my sights to be a Disney Animator. But when I interned at ILM, I learned about the new field of Animatics, combining animation and film to help pre-plan a movie. I fell in love with the idea and spent my last year in school developing a reel that catered to film-making and pre-visual layout. I always knew I wanted to make films and I figured animation was the best way for me to do so. It turns out that it was the best way to get myself into the industry of making movies.

Describe how you got into this industry and how you got your most recent job.

I got into this industry via a bet with my roommate in school. We both bet each other that we wouldn't meet the deadline for the ILM internship. I got mine in the day before it was due and—after a long interview process—I actually got the job. I met people doing Animatics and Pre-visualization and realized that this is what I wanted to do, so I geared my reel to reflect that and sent Lucasfilm my first copy. It was because of one of those short animation films that I did in college that I was hired.

During my work at Lucasfilm, I met Doug Chiang, the production designer on the Star Wars prequels. Doug and I became good friends and ended up leaving Lucasfilm around the same time. He hired me to work on *The Matrix* sequels, and I've been with him ever since. Doug later founded the current company I am employed with, Ice Blink Studios, currently exclusive to Robert Zemeckis projects.

If you weren't doing this job, what similar careers might you consider?

Ultimately, I'm a director, and that's my goal in the end. I direct short films and music videos on the side, where I am able to learn from the directors that I work with. I can apply the knowledge and skills that I acquire in these situations to my own films. If I were not doing this, I'd be directing—basically what I'm doing now—or co-directing, to a degree.

What professional publications do you read?

Magazines: *Cinefex, Filmmaker, Variety.*

Web sites: Variety.com, HollywoodReporter.com, Aintitcoolnews. com (for fun).

What advice do you have for others who would like to pursue this career?

If you want to be a filmmaker, then *make films*. It's really that simple. You'll learn more through experience in this industry than by other

Profile: Digital Filmmaker

Q&A

means, and it's better to learn on simple at-home (so to speak) productions versus getting your feet wet in the big leagues. Use any tools you can get your hands on, no matter how primitive. Your work will only get better with each project. With the endless avenues of ways to get your film in front of an audience, it's only a matter of time until the right person is watching at the right time.

Profile: Video Game Animator

Name: Michael Casalino
Age: 34
Title: Senior Environment Modeler (Video Game 3D Artist)
Employer: EA Sports

Education: BFA Computer Animation
Years in Industry: 7

CAREER LADDER:

Assistant Texture Artist
Associate Texture Artist
Associate Environment Modeler

Environment Modeler
Lead Environment Modeler
Senior Environment Modeler

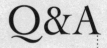

Did you have an internship in this field prior to starting your job?

I did have an internship, but it was not in a 3D environment. I was at MTV, working on MTV Downtown (traditional animation), Helter Skelter (a traditional animation that did not air but was being animated by Bill Plympton) and I made some background characters for Celebrity DeathMatch.

Which companies have the best internships in this field and are known to help launch successful careers?

EA Sports, of course. We bring the top students in, and if they really shine while they are here, we have no problem adding them to our team. Movie companies are good to work for as well, but it's tough to find places in that industry that have job security.

Where are the best cities to live to find jobs like yours?

Instead of talking cities, we will just talk California. There are so many game companies there that if you turn the corner, there will be another one ready for you if you like that kind of stuff. Austin, Texas has been really booming lately with game companies. And New York is slowly coming onto the market.

What is your typical day like?

Since I am a senior artist, I work closely with the development manager and art director on tasks for the day/week. The day could consist of modeling, scheduling, mentoring junior artists, attending meetings and doing any other tasks that affect the team/project. The days are usually pretty busy, but the time goes fast when you stay so involved.

What are your job responsibilities?

I am a part of asset creation, and I help create visual targets with the art director. I also work with the development director to make the schedule and the overall project plan. I am involved in staffing decisions and hiring, and I assist in the career development of junior artists.

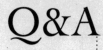

Profile: Video Game Animator

Q&A

What is your favorite part of your job?

To be very cliché, everything. I love what I do and I am always having fun doing it. I guess when the day comes that I am not having fun anymore, it is time to go.

What do you dislike about your job?

Politics, but you will find that everywhere.

How did you know you wanted to pursue this career?

When I first graduated from college, I took some little jobs freelancing and I did not have job security. I knew I was not getting any younger and I needed to settle down with a *career* and not just a job. I saw a commercial one day for EA Sports and I said to myself, that is what I want to do. Here I am seven years later.

Describe how you got into this industry and how you got your most recent job.

I sent EA Sports the reel I did during college and they loved it. But keep in mind that 3D work nowadays has come a long way from almost eight years ago, so the requirements that I met at that time were much different from what they would be today.

If you weren't doing this job, what similar careers might you consider?

Probably graphic design or architecture.

To what professional associations do you belong and what professional magazines/newspapers/journals/Web sites do you read?

International Game Developers Association (IGDA), National Association of Photoshop Professionals (NAAP), and SIGGRAPH, the Association for Computing Machinery's Special Interest Group on Graphics and Interactive Techniques.

What Web sites do you visit?

www.3dtotal.com
www.highend3d.com
www.cgchannel.com

What advice do you have for others who would like to pursue this career?

Work hard. Learn everything you can learn at school and then some. This industry is growing rapidly and advancing every day. Remember that what you learn today might be obsolete tomorrow. Keep up with technology and never be afraid to learn.

Architect

Job Description: Architects are licensed professionals trained in the art and science of building design. Architects design the overall aesthetics of buildings to suit a client's needs, ensuring that it is functional, safe and economical.

Training and Educational Qualifications: All states and the District of Columbia require individuals to be licensed before they may contract to provide architectural services. Licensing requirements include a professional degree in architecture, a period of practical training or internship, and a passing score on all divisions of the Architect Registration Examination (ARE). The majority of all architectural degrees are from 5-year bachelor of architecture programs. In addition, a number of schools offer 2-, 3- and 4-year master of architecture programs.

Job Outlook: Employment of architects is expected to grow 18 percent between 2006-2016, which is faster than the average for all occupations. Internship opportunities for new architectural students are expected to be good over the next decade, but more students are graduating with architectural degrees than in past decades, and some competition for entry-level jobs can be anticipated. Prospective architects who have had internships while in school will have an advantage in obtaining intern positions after graduation.

Salary: Median annual earnings of wage and salary architects are $64,150. The middle 50 percent earn between $49,780 and $83,450. The lowest 10 percent earn less than $39,420, and the highest 10 percent earn more than $104,970. Those just starting their internships should expect to earn considerably less.

Significant Facts:

• About one in four architects are self-employed—more than three times the proportion for all professional and related occupations.

• Licensing requirements include a professional degree in architecture, three years of practical work training, and passing scores in all divisions of the Architect Registration Examination.

• Architecture graduates may face competition; opportunities will be best for those with experience working for a firm while still in school and for those with knowledge of computer-aided design and drafting technology.

INDUSTRY RESOURCES:

The American Institute of Architects
1735 New York Avenue NW
Washington, DC 20006
Phone: (800) AIA-3837 or (202) 626-7300
Email: infocentral@aia.org
Internet: www.aia.org

Intern Development Program
National Council of Architectural Registration Boards
1801 K Street NW, Suite 1100K
Washington, DC 20006-1310
Phone: (202) 783-6500
Email: customerservice@ncarb.org
Internet: www.ncarb.org

Profile: Architect

Name: Don Chapman

Age: 40

Title: Architect

Employer: Chapman Design Group, Inc.

Education: BA Interior Design, MA Architecture

Years in Industry: 21

CAREER LADDER:

Technical Illustrator Roper Power Equipment

Architectural Intern: Hanson Architects

Architectural Intern: Joseph Hall Architects

Architectural Intern: VGR Architects

Architectural Intern: Design Partnership, Inc.

Architectural Intern: Interpretive Design Architects

Architectural Intern: F.J. Clark Architects

Architect and President: Chapman Design Group, Inc.

Developer and Builder: Stonebridge @ Rankin's Lake

Q&A

Which companies have the best internships in this field and are known to help launch successful careers?

Working for Joseph Hall as an intern was my real inspiration in starting my own business, so I recommend that firm.

Where are the best cities to live to find jobs like yours?

I would generally suggest most anywhere in the South due to the migration of people seeking to reside where they will have four mild seasons and a growing economy.

What is your typical day like?

Very busy—generally 7:00 a.m. to 7:00 p.m.

What are your job responsibilities?

Architect and design coordination of homes ranging 2,000 to 15,000 square feet, developer and builder of a 107-home subdivision located in Anderson, SC.

What is your favorite part of your job?

Clients—most of them become great friends!—and creating something new for each of them.

What do you dislike about your job?

Time. My days just don't seem to be long enough to get everything done. I also dislike collecting fees—I never enjoy asking for money, even though I've earned it.

How did you know you wanted to pursue this career?

I just knew, but it was probably due to the encouragement of my parents, friends, and teachers.

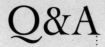

Profile: Architect

Q&A

How did you get into this industry?

I knocked on doors until I was hired and worked for a variety of firms until I started my own firm. I wanted to be in control of my destiny.

If you weren't doing this job, what similar careers might you consider?

I don't know... I thank God he pointed me in the right direction.

To what professional associations do you belong?

The American Institute of Architects (AIA), Home Builders Association (HBA), National Council of Architectural Registration Boards (NCARB).

What advice do you have for others who would like to pursue this career?

Be a sponge. Learn all that you can from your employers, associates, and even competitors. Establish a great reputation and never deviate from your standards.

Landscape Architect

Job Description: Landscape architects are often involved with the development of a site from its conception. Working with architects, surveyors, and engineers, landscape architects help determine the best arrangement of roads and buildings. They also collaborate with environmental scientists, foresters and other professionals to find the best way to conserve or restore natural resources. Once these decisions are made, landscape architects create detailed plans indicating new topography, vegetation, walkways and other landscaping details, such as fountains and decorative features.

Training and Educational Qualifications: A bachelor's or master's degree in landscape architecture usually is necessary for entry into the profession. A bachelor's degree in landscape architecture takes 4 or 5 years to complete. There are two types of accredited master's degree programs: a 3-year first professional master's degree that is designed for students with an undergraduate degree in another discipline, and a 2-year second professional degree program for students who already have a bachelor's degree in landscape architecture.

Job Outlook: Employment of landscape architects is expected to increase faster than the average for all occupations through the year 2016. The expertise of landscape architects will be highly sought after in the planning and development of new residential, commercial and other types of construction in order to meet the needs of a growing population.

Salary: Median annual earnings of landscape architects are $55,140. The middle 50 percent earn between $42,270 and $73,240. The lowest 10 percent earn less than $34,230 and the highest 10 percent earn over $95,420.

Significant Facts:

- More than 26 percent of all landscape architects are self-employed—more than 3 times the proportion of all professionals.

- A bachelor's degree in landscape architecture is the minimum requirement for entry-level jobs; many employers prefer to hire landscape architects who also have completed at least one internship.

- Landscape architect jobs are expected to increase due to a growing demand for incorporating natural elements into man-made environments, along with the need to meet a wide array of environmental restrictions.

INDUSTRY RESOURCES:

American Society of Landscape Architects
Career Information
636 Eye Street NW
Washington, DC 20001-3736
Phone: (202) 898-2444
Internet: www.asla.org

Council of Landscape Architectural Boards
144 Church Street NW, Suite 201
Vienna, VA 22180-4550
Phone: (703) 319-8380
Internet: www.clarb.org

Profile: Landscape Architect

Name: Mike	**Education: BA Environmental**
Age: 46	**Studies, MLA Landscape**
Title: Landscape Architect	**Architecture**
Employer: Self-employed	**Years in Industry: 17**

CAREER LADDER:

Draftsperson, design draftsperson, designer, directeur d'études, architecte-paysagiste, dessinateur. Newest: landscape architect/principal landscape architect.

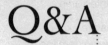

Did you have an internship in this field prior to starting your job?

I had two internships: one in campus planning and another in designing and building a garden at the university arboretum.

Do you know of which companies have the best internships in this field that are known to help launch a successful career?

Smaller companies tend to give broader experience at less (or no) pay, while large companies get you up to speed and allow you to make more contacts for the future. So small companies probably better prepare you to practice on your own, but large firms prepare you to work on big projects as part of a team—it depends on what form you want your career to take.

Where are the best cities to live to find jobs like yours?

Judging by membership information in the American Society of Landscape Architects (ASLA), urban areas of California are probably the best place to get a job since California has the most landscape architects of any state. However, you can probably find a job in any major urban area if you possess the necessary skills. You can use the ASLA Web site to research firms and read job postings.

What is your typical day like?

It varies. Sometimes I spend a lot of time on the computer doing technical drawings for construction, compiling data, working with databases, spreadsheets, processing digital images and doing graphic design for presentations. Others times I design, sketch, photograph projects or meet with clients and give the computer a rest.

What are your job responsibilities?

We're a small firm, so I have to do a bit of everything. Tasks include designing exterior spaces with their associated features and systems, Computer Aided Design (CAD), 3D modeling, accounting, database maintenance, illustration, photography, client relations, equipment maintenance, construction administration and research.

Profile: Landscape Architect

Q&A

What is your favorite part of your job?

In the office, designing and illustrating new projects is a lot of fun. It's especially so when I think of something new that works really well for a given situation. Out of the office, walking through things our firm has designed and watching them mature is fun. Nothing beats going to a party in a space that you've imagined and seeing everyone enjoying it.

What do you dislike about your job?

Sometimes I have to work long hours doing things like specifications or revisions. Discussing construction costs is difficult because everyone expects landscaping to cost less than it does.

Have you had any turning-point or "light bulb" moments in your career that have helped you get to where you are today?

When I was in France and realized that it was time to start my/our own firm. I suppose there were some design "ah-ha's" that resulted in interesting things being built that led to more work.

How did you know you wanted to pursue this career?

When I was looking for work with an environmental studies degree, I realized that landscape architecture would combine environment, art and a bit of geekiness. It would also make me more employable since people would at least know what I studied. I also hoped it would be less dull and more creative than my other options, like writing Environmental Impact Reports (EIRs) and preparing planning documents.

How did you get into this industry?

I got two simultaneous internships in planning and designing/building while doing undergrad studies. I worked at a large landscape architecture firm while pursuing my MLA.

What do you consider your greatest professional accomplishment?

Hopefully, it's still in the future. Just getting this business to work well enough to pay the bills was probably my longest sustained effort. International projects in Monaco, Addis Ababa, Jakarta and Jordan were great adventures, but I don't know if they were really personal accomplishments.

If you weren't doing this job, what similar careers might you consider?

Illustrator, writer, photographer, comedian, filmmaker.

To what professional associations do you belong?

American Society of Landscape Architects (ASLA), International Federation of Landscape Architects (IFLA).

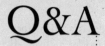

Q&A

What do publications do you read?

Landscape Architecture magazine, *Scientific American*, International Federation of Landscape Architects (IFLA) newsletter, *Topos* magazine, *Wired*, *Food & Wine*, *Sunset*, *Dwell*, *Fine Homebuilding*, *Western Interiors & Design*. The technology, food and architecture magazines are great places for ideas since they show new spaces and what people are doing in them.

What advice do you have for others who would like to pursue this career?

Swear a vow of poverty and be ready to do a lot of boring, non-creative work hunched over a computer before you can begin to steer yourself towards artistic or creative work. There is a pretty nasty licensure test called the LARE to pass before becoming a landscape architect. In California, you must first complete two years of apprenticeship under a licensed landscape architect, unless this has changed since I took the test.

Art Gallery Director

Job Description: Art gallery directors can also be called art dealers and are sometimes gallery owners themselves. The job of an art gallery director is to arrange exhibitions and events for a gallery or galleries, developing a schedule, contacting exhibitors, and researching artists and their work to ensure that exhibits are compatible with the gallery.

Training and Educational Qualifications: Most art gallery directors have a college degree in art or art history. Some management positions require a master's degree.

Job Outlook: Employment of artists and related workers is expected to grow faster than average. Competition for jobs is expected to be keen for both salaried and freelance jobs in all specialties, because the number of qualified workers exceeds the number of available openings. Also, because the arts attract many talented people with creative ability, the number of aspiring artists continues to grow. Employers in all industries should be able to choose from among the most qualified candidates.

Salary: Salaries vary depending on the budget of the gallery. Exact salaries for art gallery directors could not be obtained; however, within the larger category of art-related careers, generally "directors" can expect to earn in the high end of the field.

Significant Facts:

- Jobs in art galleries require a degree in art; management positions often require a master's degree in art or art history.

- Jobs in art galleries can be found in commercial galleries as well as in non-profit environments such as museum galleries and galleries at colleges and universities.

INDUSTRY RESOURCES:

Art Dealers Association of America, Inc.
575 Madison Avenue
New York, NY 10022
Phone: (212) 940-8590
Internet: www.artdealers.org

Profile: Art Gallery Director

Name: Kelly
Age: 36
Title: Art Gallery Director

Employer: Owings-Dewey Fine Art, Santa Fe, NM
Education: BA Art History, MFA Art History
Years in Industry: 11

CAREER LADDER:

Associate Director to Director

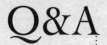

Did you have an internship in this field prior to starting your job?
Yes, an internship at a gallery in Palm Springs, CA where I assisted in sales, curating an exhibition and researching the provenance and history of particular works of art.

Which companies have the best internships in this field and are known to help launch successful careers?
Private galleries with an established history and reputation. Consider markets outside of New York City and LA for more hands-on and direct experience, such as Santa Fe, Chicago or Scottsdale, AZ.

Where are the best cities to live to find jobs like yours?
New York and Santa Fe.

What is your typical day like?
It changes day to day, depending on where we are in the exhibition schedule. Working with clients always comes first, but some days I could be installing a show or designing an ad in *Art News*. I could meet with an artist to review a portfolio or travel to New York for auctions at Sotheby's and Christie's. There are also less glamorous days spent updating inventory, painting bases or organizing a sculpture delivery with truck drivers and crane operators.

What are your job responsibilities?
Running all aspects of the gallery operation: curate, install and promote all exhibitions; assist clients with sales, appraisals and consignments; inventory acquisition via auction, private party purchase or artist representation; design and create all ads and promotional material; research and write artist biographies and text for exhibition catalogues; develop and maintain Web site and digital image inventory; hire, train and manage all personnel; conduct gallery tours and educational lectures.

What is your favorite part of your job?
Auction bidding or meeting with artists to review portfolios.

What do you dislike about your job?
Dealing with shipping artwork, especially importing sculpture from overseas and having to navigate customs.

Profile: Art Gallery Director

Q&A

Have you had any turning point or "light bulb" moments in your career that have helped you get to where you are today?

When I one day realized that I was holding a Georgia O'Keeffe painting in one hand and a John Marin in the other—both artists that I studied in school and admired at museums but was never able to touch or examine closely.

How did you know you wanted to pursue this career?

I started out studying painting in college. While I had talent, I soon realized that my passion was studying other people's art. I was fascinated by how much you could learn about history, culture and society just by studying the art from a particular period.

Describe how you got into this industry and how you got your most recent job.

Right out of graduate school I knew that New York was too big a city for me. I therefore chose Santa Fe for its large and diverse art market, but smaller community life. Through a family connection, I submitted a resume to the largest gallery in Santa Fe, Nedra Matteucci's Fenn Galleries. The result was that I was hired as an associate director. After three and a half years at this gallery, I was hired by Owings-Dewey Fine Art as Director of their sculpture department. Two years later, I opened a new gallery for Owings-Dewey and have been directing this gallery ever since.

If you weren't doing this job, what similar careers might you consider?

Museum Curator or Advertising/Print Designer.

To what professional associations do you belong?

Museum of New Mexico Foundation and Fine Art Dealers Association (FADA).

What publications and Web sites do you read?

Print publications I read are *Art News, Art and Antiques, The Art Newspaper, El Palacio, Southwest Art*, and the *Santa Fean*. On the Web, I read Art Net, Ask Art, and Collector's Guide.

What advice do you have for others who would like to pursue this career?

It can be as glamorous and idealized as you envision, but be prepared for the reality as well. Just like any business, there are the day-to-day activities that must be dealt with. Be prepared to roll up your sleeves and get dirty minutes before the exhibition reception where you're drinking a glass of wine and hobnobbing with a celebrity.

Art Therapist

Job Description: Art therapy incorporates art media, images, the creative art process and patient/client responses that are reflections of an individual's development, abilities, personality, interests, concerns, and conflicts. An art therapist may work as part of a team that includes physicians, psychologists, nurses, mental health counselors, marriage and family therapists, rehabilitation counselors, social workers and teachers.

Training and Educational Qualifications: Entry into the profession of art therapy is at the master's level. Graduate level art therapy programs include the following: master's degree in art therapy, master's degree with an emphasis in art therapy, or 24 semester units in art therapy coursework with a master's degree in a related field.

Job Outlook: Art therapy is an expanding field and employment continues to increase as art therapy becomes recognized by professionals and clients, and in work settings.

Salary: Entry level income is approximately $32,000, with a median income of $45,000. Top earning potential for salaried administrators ranges between $50,000 and $100,000. Art therapists with PhDs, state licensure, or who qualify in their state to conduct private practice, have an earning potential of $75.00 to $150.00 per hour in private practice.

Significant Facts:

- Art therapists work in a wide variety of settings, including hospitals and clinics, (both medical and psychiatric), residential treatment centers, halfway houses, domestic violence and homeless shelters, schools, colleges, and universities, correctional facilities and elder care facilities.

- An art therapist must have sensitivity, empathy, emotional stability, patience, interpersonal skills, insight into human behavior, and an understanding of art media.

- Entry into the profession of art therapy is at the master's level.

INDUSTRY RESOURCES:

American Art Therapy Association, Inc.
5999 Stevenson Avenue
Alexandria, VA 22304
Phone: (888) 290-0878 or (703) 212-2238
Email: info@arttherapy.org
Internet: arttherapy.org

Art Therapy Credentials Board
3 Terrace Way, Suite B
Greensboro, NC 27403-3660
Phone: (877) 213-2822 or (336) 482-2856
Email: atcb@nbcc.org
Internet: www.atcb.org

American Art Therapy Association, Inc.
5999 Stevenson Avenue
Alexandria, VA 22304
Phone: (888) 290-0878
Internet: www.arttherapy.org

Art Therapy Credentials Board
3 Terrace Way, Suite B
Greensboro, NC 27403-3660
Phone: (877) 213-2822
Internet: www.atcb.org

Salary Source: American Art Therapy Association, Inc. Web site: www.arttherapy.org.

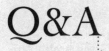

Profile: Art Therapist

Name: Jessica

Age: 32

Title: School-based art therapist

Employer: Community Reach Center; Thornton, CO

Education: BFA Painting, MA Counseling Psychology and Art Therapy

Years in Industry: 3

CAREER LADDER:

Early childhood therapist; school-based therapist

Q&A

Did you have an internship in this field prior to starting your job?

Completing an internship was a part of the three-year master's program. Students pick their own internship site, usually unpaid. My site was at Project Self-Sufficiency, a low-income housing project, mostly for women with children who were attempting to go back to school. I was the on-site art therapist and worked men, women, children, and families. I also ran some art therapy groups. My internship was 20 hours per week from September through June.

Which companies have the best internships in this field and are known to help launch successful careers?

Many art therapy internships are part of a master's program and fulfill a portion of the requirements for eventual licensure and certification as an art therapist. Hospices are good sites, as are hospitals, schools, counseling centers, day treatment centers, addiction recovery centers and community mental health centers.

Where are the best places to live to find jobs like yours?

East Coast and West Coast, especially the states of New York, Pennsylvania, Delaware, Maryland, and California.

What is your typical day like?

I work 8:00 a.m. to 4:00 p.m., doing therapy with kids in grades 6-12, either as regular clients or when there is a crisis. Art therapy is a major modality in my work, although I don't use it with every client. For some clients, I do family therapy and run groups.

I also work part-time directing an art therapy program in the mountains of Colorado. This is a culture camp for kids who are international adoptees. During the summer months, there is a Korean Camp, China Camp, Vietnamese Camp, East India Camp, Latin American Camp and Russia Camp. The art therapy program provides children ages 3-12 with an opportunity to process thoughts and feelings around adoption and to identity issues.

Profile: Art Therapist

Q&A

What are your job responsibilities?

My day job responsibilities are to maintain a caseload of 15 kids and to run four groups per week. I work to support kids' healing and well-being.

What is your favorite part of your job?

Seeing a kid who begins to trust again after a childhood of abuse and neglect, and having the opportunity to be a part of that. Seeing how the art process has inherent healing potential, and how art can reveal us to ourselves.

What do you dislike about your job?

Paperwork and negotiating the current failures in the health care system.

Have you had any turning point or "light bulb" moments in your career that have helped you get to where you are today?

On September 11, 2001, I was in my second week of a three-year program, and that day, I arrived at my art therapy class, frightened, confused, and overwhelmed. I experienced first-hand that day how engaging with the art process allowed me to access and release the jumble of feelings that had already started to freeze inside me.

How did you know you wanted to pursue this career?

I found that being an art therapist allowed me to both actively engage my identity as an artist, as well as be of service to others in the world.

Describe how you got into this industry and how you got your most recent job.

Going through a graduate program and then applying for jobs upon graduation. Knowing people at the center at which I applied helped.

To what professional associations do you belong?

Art Therapy Association of Colorado.

What professional magazines/newspapers/journals/Web sites do you read?

Journal of the American Art Therapy Association.

What advice do you have for others who would like to pursue this career?

Volunteer first (I did this by doing art with kids at a homeless shelter in Savannah) to see if working with others is a good fit for you. Being a therapist also requires acknowledging painful aspects of one's own history, so a clear understanding of one's own wounding is essential.

Artist

Job Description: Fine artists typically display their work in museums, commercial art galleries, corporate collections and private homes. Some of their artwork may be commissioned but most is sold by the artist or through private art galleries or dealers. Only the most successful fine artists are able to support themselves solely through the sale of their work.

Training and Educational Qualifications: Postsecondary training is recommended for all artist specialties. Many colleges and universities offer programs leading to a bachelor's or master's degree in fine arts. Independent schools of art and design also offer postsecondary studio training which typically leads to a certificate in the specialty or to an associate's or bachelor's degree, while formal educational programs in art also provide training in the computer techniques that are used widely in the visual arts.

Job Outlook: Employment of artists and related workers is expected to grow faster than the average. Competition for jobs is expected to be keen for both salaried and freelance jobs in all specialties, because the number of qualified workers exceeds the number of available openings.

Salary: The median annual earnings of salaried fine artists, including painters, sculptors, and illustrators, are $41,970. The middle 50 percent earn between $28,500 and $58,550. The lowest 10 percent earn less than $18,350, and the highest 10 percent earn more than $79,390. Earnings data for many self-employed fine artists is not available.

Significant Facts:

- About 62 percent of artists are self-employed.

- Artists usually develop their skills through a bachelor's degree program or other post-secondary training in art or design.

- Earnings for self-employed artists vary widely; some well-established artists earn more than salaried artists, while others find it difficult to rely solely on income earned from selling art.

INDUSTRY RESOURCES:

The Art Network
P.O. Box 1360
Nevada City, CA 95959
Phone: (800) 383-0677 or (530) 470-0862
Email: info@artmarketing.com
Internet: www.artmarketing.com

Profile: Artist

Name: Tiffani Taylor
Age: 27
Title: Artist

Employer: Self-employed (LLC business with site at www. tiffaniart.com)
Education: BFA Painting, MA Art History
Years in Industry: 11

CAREER LADDER:

From 1996 to 1999, I painted my first commissioned mural in a hospital and subsequently painted murals in private homes; 1999-2000, I worked in a pottery shop during my second year of college where I sold my finished pieces in the window and assisted others in learning pottery painting techniques; 2000-2001 I worked as a gallery assistant. I learned a great deal about galleries and art patronage during this time. From 2001 until now, I have worked as a self-employed artist. I paint murals, paintings and pottery.

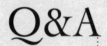

Where are the best cities to live to find jobs like yours?

Artists can work anywhere. I do believe that it may be easier to make a living in some cities than others. For example, growing up in Ogden, Utah, I know that there were not many art galleries, but many individuals commissioned murals. Savannah, Georgia is a great place to thrive as an artist. There are many galleries, the Savannah College of Art and Design, and people who love and support the arts, as well as the Telfair Art Museum.

What is your typical day like?

There truly is no typical day—especially living in such a magical city as Savannah! —you never know what opportunity will greet you that day or what (or who!) will inspire you. For example, one day I will go to a private home or business and paint large-scale murals on thirty-foot tall scaffolding; and the next, I will paint pottery composed of bird motifs that are inspired by a beautiful vintage card I received from my grandmother in the mail. My only constant is knowing that I will paint each day, whether it is a mural, pottery or canvas.

What are your job responsibilities?

Time management is very important in keeping up with the business portion of being an artist, so every morning I look over my goals and responsibilities, including gallery shows, mural work, and other commissions. I then go into my studio and paint on pottery or canvas, whichever I am inspired to do. My paintings have many layers and I like to live with each one for awhile, rotating each canvas and adding layers on daily. Like most creative people I know, I work best at night. I often paint until 4:00 a.m. Since I was fifteen years old, I have painted or drawn almost every day of my life. I paint because I have to.

From a business perspective, I find that the structure necessary to function as a self-employed artist includes the following: forming an entity (i.e., LLC), setting up a retirement plan (i.e., SEP or 401 K),

Q&A

finding and maintaining health insurance (for me, it is Blue Cross Blue Shield), having an accountant, and finally, hiring a lawyer to negotiate contractual agreements.

What is your favorite part of your job?

Some of the best parts about being an artist are expressing my thoughts and feelings; for example, when art is the result of being filled with overwhelming emotion and then I am able to later stand in a gallery, or meet with a client, and see their reaction to what I have created. When emotions are evoked through art that is shared, it makes the interconnectedness of all things and persons in life more apparent and you feel deeply embedded in the vein of life.

I have always loved the process and tools for creating art. Every time I squeeze a fresh tube of paint onto my palette, I feel such happiness, a fluttering in my heart, and gratitude for the moment I am in. The times of fear and uncertainty are outweighed by the end result: I truly feel I am living my dream. Many times a week I recite in my mind the quote by Henry David Thoreau, "Go confidently in the direction of your dreams. Live the life you have imagined."

What do you dislike about your job?

There is nothing I dislike about my job.

I believe fear is a major factor that stops most art careers—the fear of putting oneself out in the world for others to see. Additionally, artists are faced with the problem solving of being self-employed.

How did you know you wanted to pursue this career?

To answer this question, I must first describe my grandmother. She always taught me to seek beauty and notice the details in nature. While camping in the mountains of Star Valley, Wyoming, we picked wild flower bouquets and she pointed out how brilliantly red the Indian Paintbrush was, the delicate billows of the dandelion, and the hummingbirds that so touched her heart. As far as I know, I am the only visual artist in the family, but my mom and sister have always written poetry and I would describe my maternal grandparents as aesthetic souls. I think I always somehow knew I was meant to be an artist.

Have you had any turning point or "light bulb" moments in your career that have helped you get to where you are today?

When I was sixteen years old, I saw a poster for the Savannah College of Art and Design and knew at that moment that I was meant to attend the college. Savannah was the most beautiful city I had ever seen—dripping Spanish moss accentuating majestic oaks in front of historic facades. While looking at the poster, I remember thinking, what could be more incredible than to study and create art in such a beautiful city?

Q&A

It was very difficult to leave Utah to attend college in Savannah, especially because my family was all in Utah—I was, and continue to be, so close to my mom, a single mother of three. My family could not support my education and college seemed a distant dream. But from the moment I saw that poster, I began working toward obtaining scholarships to make my dream a reality. I was awarded a Presidential Scholarship from the President of Savannah College of Art and Design without which I never could have afforded my education.

At the Savannah College of Art and Design, I studied with Joy Flynn, Darrell Naylor-Johnson, and Sandra Reed (three stand-outs among many other great professors). These three individuals provided me the entrepreneurial and technical knowledge, as well as encouragement, to truly begin my career as a full-time artist. I began supporting myself with my artwork during my junior year of college and have done so ever since. Much to my delight, in May 2005, my mom, sister, and nephew moved to Savannah.

Describe how you got into this industry and how you got your most recent job.

I painted every day of my life and did not let fear stop me. Time management, dedication and love for what I do have all helped me along my path. I've learned that as an artist, it is very important to have a business card and Web site. With these two tools, you can provide others with immediate access to what you do; it is very effective in gaining commissions, selling current work, and spreading word of your talent.

If you weren't doing this job, what similar careers might you consider?

More than anything, I would love to teach. It is my hope that in a few years I will teach Professional Practices in Art at the collegiate level, as well as general painting and art history courses. I would also be interested in art director positions, owning and running a gallery, and working at a museum. Anything to do with art!

What publications do you read?

I wake up every day and read the *Savannah Morning News*, and then I read through CNN.com. Literature is an important inspiration to my work. I love the classics and new literature.

What advice do you have for others who would like to pursue this career?

Don't let fear of the unknown stop you. Take it a day at a time and live the life you have imagined. Work each day toward "self-actualizing;" become the best person you know you can be. Don't listen to "dream squashers." Surround yourself with positive people who inspire you and believe in you. Ask for advice from people you admire.

Illustrator

Job Description: Illustrators typically create pictures for books, magazines, and other publications and for commercial products such as textiles, wrapping paper, stationery, greeting cards, and calendars. More and more, illustrators are working in digital formats, preparing work directly on a computer.

Training and Educational Qualifications: Postsecondary training is recommended for all artist specialties. Although formal training is not strictly required, it is very difficult to become skilled enough to make a living without some training. Many colleges and universities offer programs leading to the bachelor's or master's degree in fine arts.

Job Outlook: The growth in computer graphics packages and stock art Web sites is making it easier for writers, publishers, and art directors to create their own illustrations. As the use of this technology grows, there will be fewer opportunities for illustrators. One exception is the small number of medical illustrators, who will be in greater demand to illustrate journal articles and books as medical research continues to grow.

Salary: The median annual earnings of salaried fine artists, including painters, sculptors, and illustrators, are $41,970. The middle 50 percent earn between $28,500 and $58,550. The lowest 10 percent earn less than $18,350, and the highest 10 percent earn more than $79,390.

Significant Facts:

- Evidence of appropriate talent and skill displayed in an artist's portfolio is an important factor used by art directors, clients, and others in deciding whether to hire an individual or to contract out work.

- Artists employed by publishing companies, advertising agencies, and design firms generally work a standard work week. During busy periods, they may work overtime to meet deadlines.

- Self-employed artists can set their own hours, but they may spend much time and effort building a reputation and selling their artwork to potential customers or clients.

INDUSTRY RESOURCES:
The Society of Illustrators
128 East 63rd Street
New York, NY 10021-7303
Phone: (212) 838-2560
Email: info@societyillustrators.org
Internet: www.societyillustrators.org

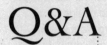

Profile: Illustrator

Name: Ken	**Employer: FOX TV**
Age: 37	**Education: BFA, Illustration**
Title: Design Manager	**Years in Industry: 6**

CAREER LADDER:

Graphic Artist to Broadcast Designer/Animator

Q&A

Did you have an internship in this field prior to starting your job?
I started working part-time and weekends.

Which companies have the best internships in this field and are known to help launch successful careers?
Almost every news station has an internship program, including FOX. Some are paid. There are thousands of internship possibilities in this career; in fact, this is one of the art fields in which you can get a definite job and benefits, or freelance any way you like.

Where are the best cities to live to find jobs like yours?
Any metropolitan area.

What is your typical day like?
Jumping from one project to another. Fixing, and critiquing animations and designs. Managing multiple deadlines while also designing.

What are your job responsibilities?
Motivating employees, critiquing, managing deadlines, finding creative approaches to animations and design. Pulling together long-term promotions. Integrating graphics into other departments, software and systems.

What is your favorite part of your job?
Designing new animations.

What do you dislike about your job?
Paperwork.

How did you know you wanted to pursue this career?
I wanted a career in design. Then I saw what was happening in this area and decided it was for me.

How did you get into this industry?
I started part-time without a real portfolio. I was able to prove myself and went full-time within weeks. I hardly knew how to use a computer but had a great design background; I knew that I could learn the tech side, although it's harder to teach someone the design side if they are not designers. I paid attention and acted the part of the position I

Q&A

wanted before I received it (in attire, attitude, professionalism, good design, and "pushing the envelope").

If you weren't doing this job, what similar careers might you consider?

Anything artistic. Sculpting, movies, commercials.

To what professional associations do you belong?

Broadcast Design Association, Promax, and the local design directors club.

What professional Web sites do you read?

Many computer and 3D design magazines: *Mac world, STASH video magazine, Computer Graphics World, 3D World,* and *Computer Arts.* Future Publishing from the UK has several magazines that are the best.

What advice do you have for others who would like to pursue this career?

Build up a great reel. Learn to do the graphics that news needs (i.e., stingers, bumps, opens). Even though a person might not know the terminology, he or she can tape a news show and mimic every animation, thereby literally learning all these types of animations. It's easy to learn the terminology later. Text-oriented design and animations are crucial—3D is going to help. Look into Zaxwerks for After Effects; it's easy 3D to learn, plus AE is the standard de facto program to know in this career.

I didn't even know that a career in broadcast design existed until a friend got into the business. Sometimes I see this as a secondary listing under animation or graphic design, but there are a lot of jobs in the industry. This field is a perfect in-between for editors, compositors, animators, and graphic designers. The animation here is definitely different than standard movie animation. These animations are text based and the learning curve is a lot less than for traditional character animation. It can lead to careers in the movies, post houses, commercials, news, corporate design and the Web.

Profile: Magazine Illustrator

Name: Christopher
Age: 36
Title: Graphic Designer/Illustrator
Employer: *Southern Living Magazine*

Education: Bachelor's in Graphic Design
Years in Industry: 10

CAREER LADDER:

Floral designer, freelance graphic designer/illustrator, associate designer (Slaughter Hanson Advertising), designer/illustrator (Southern Living Magazine)

Where are the best cities to live to find jobs like yours?
Growing cities in the southeast. Some rather unassuming cities may be a great outlet for design jobs.

What is your typical day like and job responsibilities?
Design magazine page layouts, several info-graphic illustrations, logo and icon designs for special projects and meetings with art directors and story editors

What is your favorite part of your job?
Illustration.

What do you dislike about your job?
I have to be more conservative with design than I'd like sometimes.

Have you had any turning point or "light bulb" moments in your career that have helped you get to where you are today?
Managing a florist shop and helping make its highest profits ever, treating pro bono work the same as paid projects, seeing the vast difference between advertising and editorial, going to an art school with professors who have been in the field.

How did you know you wanted to pursue this career?
I always enjoyed and was interested in ads and design. I wanted to know how ads worked, influenced, and affected the public. Also, I realized that sometimes graphic design could be just as artistic as fine art.

How did you get into the industry?
I applied to editorial and advertising positions when I graduated. In fact, my first job out of school was a year in advertising, which was more fast-paced than an editorial job. It prepared me for working quickly and efficiently at a monthly magazine. I worked hard on my portfolio before applying to make sure I had samples that displayed I could make the transition from advertising to editorial.

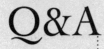
Profile: Magazine Illustrator

Q&A

If you weren't doing this job, what similar careers might you consider?

Furniture design, cartoonist, advertising, or the entertainment industry.

What professional publications do you read?

I read *Communication Arts, How Magazine, Lürzer's Archive,* and *Wallpaper.*

What advice do you have for others who would like to pursue this career?

Along with being a good designer, you must always keep in mind that you deal with people who may or may not have your vision, your best interests at heart, and varying opinions on how a project should be executed. This includes bosses that supposedly know more than you and clients whom you supposedly know more than they. Figuratively speaking, the human element is our bread and butter—the bane of our existence—and can never be ignored.

Remember to be thick-skinned, slow to judge, and not too easily offended when judged. The visual arts field is a subjective, opinionated and varied career to enter. You'll have designs someone's going to love or hate or be indifferent to. Prepare for the negative but always strive for the positive. Have a good understanding of people and what they want and need, along with good design skills, and you'll do well.

Photographer

Job Description: Photographers produce and preserve images that paint a picture, tell a story, or record an event. To create commercial-quality photographs, photographers need both technical expertise and creativity. Producing a successful picture requires choosing and presenting a subject to achieve a particular effect and selecting the appropriate equipment.

Training and Educational Qualifications: Employers usually seek applicants with a "good eye," imagination, and creativity, as well as a good technical understanding of photography. Entry-level positions in photojournalism or in industrial or scientific photography generally require a college degree in photography or in a field related to the industry in which the photographer seeks employment. Freelance and portrait photographers need technical proficiency gained through a degree program, vocational training, or extensive photography experience.

Job Outlook: Employment of photographers is expected to increase about as fast as the average for all occupations through 2016. The number of individuals interested in positions as commercial and news photographers usually is much greater than the number of openings. Growth of Internet versions of magazines, journals, and newspapers will require increasing numbers of commercial photographers to provide digital images.

Salary: The median annual earnings of salaried photographers are $26,170. The middle 50 percent earn between $18,680 and $38,730. The lowest 10 percent earn less than $15,540, and the highest 10 percent earn more than $56,640.

Significant Facts:

- Related work experience, job-related training, or some unique skill or talent—such as a background in computers or electronics—are beneficial to prospective photographers.

- More than half of all photographers are self-employed; the most successful are adept at operating a business and able to take advantage of opportunities provided by rapidly changing technologies.

- Because most freelance photographers purchase their own equipment, they incur considerable expense acquiring and maintaining cameras and accessories. Unlike news and commercial photographers, a few fine arts photographers are successful enough to support themselves solely through their art.

INDUSTRY RESOURCES:

American Society of Media Photographers, Inc.
150 North Second Street
Philadelphia, PA 19106
Phone: (215) 451-2767
Internet: www.asmp.org

National Press Photographers Association
3200 Croasdaile Drive, Suite 306
Durham, NC 27705
Phone: (919) 383-7246
Email: info@nppa.org
Internet: www.nppa.org

Profile: Assistant Fashion Photographer

Name: Jake
Age: 26
Title: Assistant Fashion Photographer/Digital Technician

Employer: The Bon-Ton Inc./CPS Photo Studios
Education: BFA Photography
Years in Industry: 4

CAREER LADDER:

Photo Assistant
Photographer
Digital Photographer

Freelance Photographer
Fashion Photo Assistant/Digital Technician

Q&A

Where are the best cities to live to find jobs like yours?
New York City, Los Angeles, Miami, Chicago.

What is your typical day like?
Assistant photographer on all aspects of digital capture of on-figure fashion merchandise for adverts in/on billboards, newspapers, direct mailers, broadsheets, etc.

What are your job responsibilities?
Pre- and post-productions of photo sets, lighting, set-up, digital capture procedures and file management, among other things that good assistants should do.

What is your favorite part of your job?
Getting paid to travel on location: Puerto Rico, New York City, Miami, Chicago.

What do you dislike about your job?
The chain of command (e.g., working in a corporate environment).

Have you had any turning point or "light bulb" moments in your career that have helped you get to where you are today?
I've learned to be persistent and confident of my abilities and then prove it to potential employers. I dream big! Anything is possible.

Describe how you got into this industry and how you got your most recent job.
I freelanced after graduation. Getting gigs was slow at first, but I never gave up. I sent out numerous resumes, cover letters, and promos to potential clients, internships, employers, agencies, studios and production companies. About one out of every 15 would materialize. I played those odds and ended up with a job in my field.

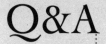

Profile: Assistant Fashion Photographer

Q&A

To what professional associations do you belong and what professional publications do you read?

I belong to Advertising Photographers of America (APA) and the American Society of Media Photographers (ASMP). I read *Communication Arts*, *Picture*, *Blackbook*, and *Workbook*.

What advice do you have for others who would like to pursue this career?

Traditional photography is not "now." Concentrate on becoming digitally savvy. Know a lot of software and digital capture systems. Get familiar with both PC and MAC. Film is for the fine artist—it's great to know but it's not used in the field. You have to be a digital tech to be a good assistant anymore unless you get with a photographer that still shoots film, but that's rare.

Art Education: Art Teacher (K-12)

Job Description: Art teachers teach various artistic techniques (drawing, painting, photography, etc.) to children of all ages in private and public school settings. Art teachers may also arrange exhibitions of students' work.

Training and Educational Qualifications: Requirements for regular licenses to teach kindergarten through grade 12 vary by state. However, all states require general education teachers to have a bachelor's degree and to have completed an approved teacher training program with a prescribed number of subject and education credits as well as supervised practice teaching. Some states also mandate technology training and the attainment of a minimum grade point average. A number of states require that teachers obtain a master's degree in education within a specified period after they begin teaching.

Job Outlook: Through 2016, overall student enrollment in elementary, middle, and secondary schools—a key factor in the demand for teachers—is expected to rise more slowly than in the past as children of the baby boom generation leave the school system. Projected enrollments will vary by region.

Salary: The median annual earnings of kindergarten, elementary, middle, and secondary school teachers range from $43,580 to $48,690; the lowest 10 percent earn $28,590 to $33,070; the top 10 percent earn $67,490 to $76,100.

According to the American Federation of Teachers, beginning teachers with a bachelor's degree earned an average of $31,753 in the 2003–04 school year. The estimated average salary of all public elementary and secondary school teachers in the 2004–05 school year was $47,602. Private school teachers generally earn less than public school teachers but may be given other benefits, such as free or subsidized housing.

Significant Facts:

- In addition to conducting classroom activities, teachers oversee study halls and homerooms, supervise extracurricular activities and accompany students on field trips.

- Public school teachers must have at least a bachelor's degree, complete an approved teacher education program and be licensed.

- Many states offer alternative licensing programs to attract people into teaching, especially for hard-to-fill positions.

INDUSTRY RESOURCES:

National Art Education Association
1916 Association Drive
Reston, VA 20191-1590
Phone: (703) 860-8000
Internet: www.naea-reston.org

American Federation of Teachers
555 New Jersey Avenue NW
Washington, DC 20001
Phone: (202) 879-4400
Internet: www.aft.org

National Education Association
1201 16th Street, NW
Washington, DC 20036-3290
Phone: (202) 833-4000
Internet: www.nea.org

Profile: Art Teacher

Name: Jes

Age: 35

Title: Art Educator

Employer: Fulton County School System and Georgia State University

Education: BFA Illustration, MA Ed Art Education; Specialist in Educational Leadership

Years in Industry: 10

CAREER LADDER:

Architectural illustrator, freelance illustrator, set designer, middle school art teacher, high school art teacher and department chair for school system, part-time college professor

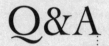

Did you have an internship in this field prior to starting your job?

I student taught for 16 weeks in the public school system where I am now employed.

Which companies have the best internships in this field and are known to help launch successful careers?

I chose Fulton County Schools for my internship because I was the most impressed by that school system's dedication to Fine Arts when I moved to Atlanta. Depending on where you go to college or plan to teach, your internship opportunities will differ.

Where are the best cities to live to find jobs like yours?

Teaching is universal; part of its appeal is that you can live around the world and still share your love of art with students.

What is your typical day like?

I teach sculpture and ceramics for half of my regular work day and then spend the afternoon doing my administrative duties as department chair of 14 secondary art teachers. In the evening, I teach art education and a computer-based graphic arts class to future art educators.

What are your job responsibilities?

I teach 150 students per day in my day position and then manage the art departments of seven schools and twenty teachers. I order supplies, create instructional materials, write curriculum and act as a mentor to other teachers.

What is your favorite part of your job?

I enjoy all of it. The students are wonderful and I would like to continue teaching foundation courses for college.

What do you dislike about your job?

Long hours and a general lack of understanding about why the arts are so important to education in the United States.

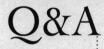

Q&A

Have you had any turning point or "light bulb" moments in your career that have helped you get to where you are today?

I got a job in illustration as soon as I graduated from college but grew tired and bored with it after the second year. I had begun training new employees for the company and enjoyed showing them how we operated as a company. Then one day it just struck me that I preferred the "teaching" part of my day to the illustrating part. I quit shortly after that and spent the next year getting certified to teach art in the state of Georgia. I also earned my master's degree. It was the best decision I ever made and I have never looked back.

Describe how you got into this industry and how you got your most recent job.

I student taught in the school system where I currently am employed. At the time, I was so impressed with the art program—and the support for the arts—that I applied for a position and was hired. I recently was promoted to department chair based on curriculum writing experience, mentorship and leadership certification.

If you weren't doing this job, what similar careers might you consider?

I would be a college professor full time or a graphic designer.

To what professional associations do you belong?

I am a member of the National Art Education Association, the GA Art Education Association, the Professional Association of GA Educators and the International Sculpture Society.

What advice do you have for others who would like to pursue this career?

Student teaching is the most important and influential part of the certification program. Learn all that you can during this part of your education.

Art Professor (Postsecondary)

Job Description: Art professors usually specialize in one particular aspect of art (such as painting, sculpture or art history) and teach at professional art institutes, community colleges, four-year colleges and universities. Art faculty also keep up with new developments in their field and may consult with non-profit and community arts organizations.

Training and Educational Qualifications: The terminal professional degree in creating art is the master of fine arts (MFA); most art professors have an MFA and have experience in exhibiting their artwork. However, professors of art education may have a master's of education (MEd) in addition to an MFA or PhD. Art history professors normally have a PhD in art history and are expected to publish scholarly articles on topics in art history.

Job Outlook: Employment of postsecondary teachers is expected to grow much faster than the average for all occupations through 2016. A significant proportion of these new jobs will be part-time positions. Job opportunities are generally expected to be very good—although they will vary somewhat from field to field—as numerous openings for all types of postsecondary teachers result from retirements of current postsecondary teachers and continued increases in student enrollment.

Salary: Earnings for college faculty vary according to rank and type of institution, geographic area, and field of study. According to a 2006-07 survey by the American Association of University Professors, salaries for full-time faculty averaged $73,207. By rank, the average was $98,974 for professors, $69,911 for associate professors, $58,662 for assistant professors, $42,609 for instructors and $42,609 for lecturers.

Significant Facts:

- Opportunities for postsecondary teaching jobs are expected to be good, but many new openings will be for part-time or non-tenure track positions.

- Educational qualifications for postsecondary teacher jobs range from expertise in a particular field to an MFA or PhD, depending on the subject being taught and the type of educational institution.

INDUSTRY RESOURCES:

American Association of University Professors
1012 Fourteenth Street, NW, Suite #500
Washington, DC 20005
Phone: (202) 737-5900
Internet: www.aaup.org

National Art Education Association
1916 Association Drive
Reston, VA 20191-1590
Phone: (703) 860-8000
Internet: www.naea-reston.org

Profile: Art Professor

Name: Therese
Age: 49
Title: Assistant Professor
Employer: The School of the Art Institute of Chicago

Education: BFA, Studio Arts, MEd Instructional Leadership, PhD Curriculum
Years in Industry: 5 in current position

CAREER LADDER:

Assistant Professor of Art Education
Director of BFA with Emphasis in Art
    Education Program
Charter School Summer School Director
Associate Director for the Center for Youth
    and Society

Associate/Museum Consultant
Museum Exhibit Developer
Exhibit Researcher
Media Research Assistant

Q&A

Did you have an internship in this field prior to starting your job?
I was a co-op student while an undergrad at the School of the Art Institute. This was in the media research department at the Field Museum of Natural History. This led to my first "real" job at Field, doing media research, which then led to an assistant exhibit development job. That position, in turn, led to an exhibit development job at Field on the Africa Exhibit. And that led to my work in museums with youth, which in the end led to my return to grad school and work in art education.

Do you know of which companies have the best internships in this field that are known to help launch a successful career?
It's not one field, but several. Field Museum always has great internships, as do other area museums. But to end up in art ed, you also need experience in schools.

Where are the best cities to live to find jobs like yours?
Many cities have programs for art education. I'd recommend looking for art education professors who present at conferences, write in the field of art education and also the wider field of education, and who are attuned to issues of public education nationally. Professors who address those issues are found most often in big cities.

What is your typical day like?
I have no typical day. One day each week I teach a group of field-work students. We meet in a seminar and at their placement sites or at other schools in Chicago. Another day I meet with students and interview undergraduates who are interested in entering art education at SAIC. And on a third day I work on projects related to the Multicultural Arts High School, a Chicago Public School that is also a partner of SAIC. Other days I work on writing and related projects; this can range from developing a blog about education to lobbying the Illinois State Board

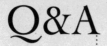

Q&A

of Education to include sexual orientation, social justice, and gender identity in the Professional Standards for teacher preparation.

What are your job responsibilities?

I teach, I direct an undergraduate teacher education program and I engage in creative and professional work in the field of art education.

What is your favorite part of your job?

Making visits in schools across the city of Chicago is my favorite job task. I love meeting the children and youth. I value deepening my understanding of the issues facing public education, and I am energized by witnessing the wonderful projects my own students prepare for the children in their placement schools.

What do you dislike about your job?

I don't like seeing that so many public schools are poorly funded, and many of the students in these schools are suffering from the effects of poverty—hunger, bad teeth, exhaustion. Teachers are badly affected by the poverty of their students too, of course. It's a huge social problem, and it has become much worse in recent years.

Have you had any turning-point or "light bulb" moments in your career that have helped you get to where you are today?

I think education is the key to everything, but my understanding of how poverty limits access—and ultimately often achievement, as well—was sparked by my years as a graduate student visiting urban schools.

How did you know you wanted to pursue this career?

I wasn't always sure art education was the field for me—this was a gradual awakening. But I realize that art has always given me a way to connect in school, even when I felt out of step with the mainstream. And I wanted to be able to pass on that feeling to children in public schools. This is more and more difficult because the No Child Left Behind Act has had the effect of scaring many schools away from art because it only charts achievement in traditionally academic fields like math and English.

How did you get into this industry?

I was an art major as an undergrad and then I ended up working in museums. I met an education professor who was helpful to me, encouraged me to enter grad school, and then mentored me. He isn't an artist, but he encouraged me to bring my art to education. I did that and wrote a dissertation about how young urban youth use museums. Also as a graduate student, I taught on a part-time basis at my present place of employment. This led to my position. My field of study was not art education, but curriculum, a broader field. I'm more interested in generalization than specialization.

Profile: Art Professor

Q&A

What do you consider your greatest professional accomplishment?

Perhaps two—being the exhibit developer for the science sections of the Africa Exhibit at Field Museum, and more recently, acting as co-editor for the Handbook of Social Justice in Education, due for publication by Lawrence Erlbaum Press in 2007.

If you weren't doing this job, what similar careers might you consider?

Exhibit development, or museum directorship, or even school directorship.

To what professional associations do you belong?

I belong to the American Educational Research Association (AERA), the National Art Education Association (NAEA) and the Movement for a New Museology (MINOM).

What professional publications do you read?

Some of my favorite journals are the *International Journal of Qualitative Studies in Education*, the *Harvard Educational Review*, and *Teachers College Record*.

What advice do you have for others who would like to pursue this career?

Think big; don't "boxify" yourself; refuse marginalization. I mean, read widely, stay aware of social issues, think of the pig picture. Always ask: Who benefits from this? Who's getting the biscuits and who's getting the crumbs? And do your best to make this place better for more people—we need concerned individuals in all professions who are focused on social justice.

Design: Art Director (Advertising and Publishing)

Job Description: Art directors in advertising and publishing develop design concepts and review material that is to appear in periodicals, newspapers, and other printed or digital media. They decide how best to present the information visually, so that it is eye catching, appealing, and organized. Art directors decide which photographs or artwork to use and oversee the layout design and production of the printed material. They may also direct workers engaged in artwork, layout design, and copywriting.

Training and Educational Qualifications: Art directors usually begin as entry-level artists in advertising, publishing, design, and motion picture production firms. An artist may be promoted to art director after demonstrating artistic and leadership abilities. Some art schools offer coursework in art direction as part of postsecondary training. Depending on the scope of their responsibilities, some art directors may elect to enhance their training by pursuing a degree in art administration.

Job Outlook: Art directors work in a variety of industries, such as advertising, public relations, publishing and design firms. Despite an expanding number of opportunities, competition will continue to be keen for available openings.

Salary: Median annual earnings of salaried art directors are $68,100. The middle 50 percent earn between $49,480 and $94,920. The lowest 10 percent earn less than $37,920, and the highest 10 percent earn more than $135,090. The median annual earnings for persons in advertising and related services are $70,630.

Significant Facts:

- In 2004, there were 71,000 art directors in the United States.

- Art directors work in a variety of industries, such as advertising, public relations, publishing and design firms.

- Despite an expanding number of opportunities, art directors will experience keen competition for any available openings.

INDUSTRY RESOURCES:

The Art Director's Club
106 West 29th Street
New York, NY 10001
Phone: (212) 643-1440
Email: info@adcglobal.org
Internet: www.adcglobal.org

Profile: Art Director – Magazine

Name: John
Age: 45
Title: Art Director
Employer: *HR Magazine*

Education: BFA Communication Art and Design
Years in Industry: 24

CAREER LADDER:

Freelance illustrator, graphic artist and designer, art director

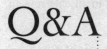

Where are the best cities to live to find jobs like yours?

There are publications or creative service jobs available in most cities. Obviously, the best paying ones are at larger companies.

What is your typical day like?

Surf the net for news and visual images. Read my emails. Make my "to do" list. Meet with my staff. Take care of administrative work such as contracts, bills and calendar. Attend various department meetings, including talking to the editor. Brainstorm on art concepts, commission artists and photographers, design pages and make corrections as needed.

What are your job responsibilities?

I am responsible for art concepts, designing and managing a staff to produce a monthly trade magazine. This includes establishing the work flow and standards, overseeing staffing projects, scheduling design resources, supervising associate designers, including outside vendors, and managing budgets—effectively managing multiple projects from initial concept through final completion with extensive interaction at senior management levels. I also direct photo shoots, provide digital imagery support and attend press checks.

What is your favorite part of your job?

Designing covers and creating art for the magazine.

What do you dislike about your job?

The administrative part of managing people, budget and schedules.

How did you know you wanted to pursue this career?

I've always loved art so it only made sense to work in an area that I love.

Describe how you got into this industry and how you got your most recent job.

My roommate in college got a job at the local newspaper and told me about the opportunities. I wanted to be an illustrator but things were slow at the time. After a few years, I got a job at *The Washington Times*, then later at the *Baltimore Sun*, followed by *The Washington Post*. After a

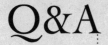

Q&A

number of years, I accepted a position with *National Geographic Magazine*. They began cutbacks so I left to join *HR Magazine* in 2003.

What do you consider your greatest professional accomplishment?

Staying employed after all these years and being able to adapt to change. I started as a traditional artist. As computers became popular in my field, I switched gears and became a computer graphic artist. Then as those opportunities dried up, I began to design and finally became an art director.

If you weren't doing this job, what similar careers might you consider?

Web design or advertising.

To what professional associations do you belong?

The Art Director's Club.

What professional magazines/newspapers/journals/Web sites do you read?

I scan several sites that include snd.org, adcmw.org, spd.org and aiga.org.

What advice do you have for others who would like to pursue this career?

Study and learn as much as you can about the field. Practice your craft every day. Stay in tune with others in the field for contacts and don't get comfortable.

Profile: Art Director – Film & Television

Name: Angie
Age: 45
Title: Art Director and Propmaster
for "Dinner and A Movie",
"Movie and a Makeover" and
Cartoon Network's "Cartoon
Fridays"

Employer: TBS, Inc. (Turner
Broadcasting Service, Atlanta,
Georgia)
Education: BFA Photography
Years in Industry: Photographer, 5;
Film Experience, 17

CAREER LADDER:

Staff photographer for an advertising firm in NY; Photographer for music videos in Atlanta, GA; Co-owner of photography studio in Atlanta, GA; assistant propmaster on films; Props Department for Broadway Films at Savannah Civic Center; decorator on national commercial spots; art director PBS documentaries; art director for music videos; art director "Dinner and a Movie" TBS; propmaster "Movie and a Makeover" TBS; propmaster "Cartoon Fridays" Cartoon Network; propmaster TNT; art director TCM; art director "Iraq's Most Wanted" CNN

Did you have an internship in this field prior to starting your job?
No, I sent out lots of resumes and made a lot of phone calls.

Do you know of which companies have the best internships in this field that are known to help launch a successful career?
Turner Broadcasting Services in Atlanta has one of the best internships that I know of.

Where are the best cities to live to find jobs like yours?
New York; Los Angeles; Wilmington, NC; and Atlanta, GA.

What are your job responsibilities?
It depends on what show I am doing. But basically I am responsible for the creative look of the show.

What is your favorite part of your job?
I love to bring to life a writer's script, especially when I am working on the Cartoon Network's show "Cartoon Fridays." I bring a lot of cartoons to life by creating their props and sets. It can be lots of fun.

What do you dislike about your job?
Sometimes I have to get up very early and work a lot of hours to meet the show deadlines. That is one of the most important points of this kind of career—you have to be able to meet every deadline.

Have you had any turning-point or "light bulb" moments in your career that have helped you get to where you are today?
In 1988, I was working for an advertising agency while living in New York City. One night a "Twelve K" (one of the largest lights used by the film industry to illuminate a set at night) shined right through my living room window. I ran to the window and saw a lot of commotion

Q&A

going on in the street, so I decided to go downstairs and take a look. I asked the doorman and a lady with curly hair what was going on. The lady answered, "We are making a movie with Amy Irving called *Crossing Delancey*."

I said, "That's very cool. Where is she?"

And the woman replied, "That's me and you are about to get in trouble because we are getting ready to film and you are in the shot." She told me to go across the street and tell them that I could watch the monitor from her director's chair. It was a great night. I wanted to be part of creating films. And that was my new goal: to go from two-dimensional to three-dimensional creations.

How did you get into this industry?

In 1990, a friend of mine was working on a Hallmark Hall of Fame movie and asked me if I could drive some of the crew members around the locations. I agreed to help and was driving the art director who asked me to tell her about my background because I recognized that some of the furniture she was using was Queen Ann era. I told her I graduated from Savannah College of Art and Design, which prompted her to respond that I shouldn't be driving—I should be helping her. So I got my first job in the film business. The photographs used in the frame were mine.

In 1991 I was interviewed and hired by Scott Stephens, the propmaster on a television series in Atlanta called "I'll Fly Away." Little did I know that one of his credits was *Dances with Wolves*. And one of his closest friends was the decorator who gave me my first job on that Hallmark movie. She recommended me for the assistant position with Scott Stephens. He taught me a lot about the film business—and I went on to work on many films

What do you consider your greatest professional accomplishment?

What I do now. I am allowed to have as much creative freedom as I want in order to accomplish the look and the feeling the writers want to see come to life.

If you weren't doing this job, what similar careers might you consider?

I would consider designing scenery and props for Broadway plays.

To what professional associations do you belong?

I belong to the International Alliance of Theatrical Stage Employees, Moving Picture Technicians, Artists and Allied Crafts of the United States, Its Territories and Canada (IATSE) local 491 and to the Savannah Film book.

Profile: Art Director – Film & Television

Q&A

What professional magazines/newspapers/journals/Web sites do you read?

I read everything and anything from decorating books and magazines to Money Market and history books since I work with Cartoon Network, CNN, TCM, TBS, and now Court TV. I need to be well rounded in my knowledge.

What advice do you have for others who would like to pursue this career?

Networking is very important!

Commercial & Industrial Designer

Job Description: Commercial and industrial designers combine the fields of art, business, and engineering to design the products used every day by businesses and consumers. These designers are responsible for the style, function, quality, and safety of most manufactured goods. Usually these designers will specialize in one particular product category such as automobiles, appliances, technology goods, medical equipment, furniture, toys, tools or housewares.

Training and Educational Qualifications: A bachelor's degree in industrial design, architecture, or engineering is required for most entry-level commercial and industrial design positions. Many candidates in industrial design also pursue a master's degree in order to increase their employment opportunities. Creativity and technical knowledge are crucial in this occupation. People in this field also must have a strong sense of the esthetic—an eye for color and detail and a sense of balance and proportion. Designers must understand the technical aspects of how the product functions.

Job Outlook: Employment of commercial and industrial designers is expected to grow about as fast as average for all occupations through 2016. Employment growth will arise from an expanding economy and from an increase in consumer and business demand for new or upgraded products. However, competition for jobs will be keen because many talented individuals are attracted to the design field. The best job opportunities will be in specialized design firms which are used by manufacturers to design products or parts of products. Designers with strong backgrounds in engineering and computer-aided design, as well as extensive business expertise, may have the best prospects.

Salary: Median annual earnings for commercial and industrial designers are $54,560. The middle 50 percent earn between $41,270 and $72,610. The lowest 10 percent earn less than $31,510, and the highest 10 percent earn more than $92,970.

Significant Facts:

- About 30 percent of commercial and industrial designers are self-employed.

- A bachelor's degree in industrial design, architecture, or engineering is required for entry-level positions; however, many commercial and industrial designers choose to pursue a master's degree in either industrial design or business administration.

- Manufacturers have been outsourcing design work to design services firms in order to cut costs and to find the most qualified design talent.

INDUSTRY RESOURCES:

Industrial Designers Society of America
45195 Business Court, Suite 250
Dulles, VA 20166-6717
Phone: (703) 707-6000
Internet: www.idsa.org

Profile: Industrial Design - Furniture Designer

Name: John Jaqua
Age: 38
Title: Director of Design and Engineering

Employer: Bretford, Inc.
Education: BFA Furniture Design, MFA Furniture Design
Years in Industry: 12

CAREER LADDER:

Product Engineer
Product Designer
Director of Design
Sales and Marketing Director

Director of A&D Marketing (Architects & Interior Designers)
Director of A&D New Business Development
Manager of Engineering
Director of Design and Engineering

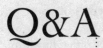

Did you have an internship in this field prior to starting your job?

I interned at Karges Furniture in Evansville, Indiana. It is a world-famous furniture company, primarily residential, noted as one of the most expensive in the world because of the beautiful craftsmanship, artisansal finishes, and uncompromised quality and perfection. I was an intern in the design and engineering department and worked on several designs for King Hussein of Jordan and for the Fall High Point furniture show in High Point, NC. It was a summer internship and was unpaid, which was difficult at the time. Now looking back on it, it was worth more than gold.

Which companies have the best internships in this field and are known to help launch successful careers?

Bretford, INC., Herman Miller, Paoli Furniture, Bernhardt Furniture, Baker Furniture, Knoll, Charles Alan Furniture.

Where are the best cities to live to find jobs like yours?

Chicago; Grand Rapids, MI; New York; Dallas/Ft. Worth; High Point, NC; Southern Indiana; Rochester/Buffalo; Charlotte, NC; Milan, Italy; and Como, Italy.

What is your typical day like?

Meetings all day, on the phone constantly. Including my commute, I work 6:00 a.m. to 5:00 p.m.

What are your job responsibilities?

Managing and directing new product development with a staff of 18 direct reports.

What is your favorite part of your job?

Traveling and getting in front of the customers.

What do you dislike about your job?

Butting heads with stubborn engineers! Too many hours yet still not enough time to get things done.

Profile: Industrial Design – Furniture Designer

Q&A

Have you had any turning point or "light bulb" moments in your career that have helped you get to where you are today?

I discovered that being a director of design is a very specialized position in that it combines many specific skills, yet it really may be best described as a "Renaissance Man" Entrepreneurial Visionary-type position. It's definitely critical for creating great products in nimble companies with a clear future vision.

How did you know you wanted to pursue this career?

I worked on yachts, picked up woodworking in the process, and I started building furniture out of necessity.

Describe how you got into this industry and how you got your most recent job.

I totally focused and concentrated on the contract office furniture market. I got my current job by being recommended for it by a president of another company.

If you weren't doing this job, what similar careers might you consider?

Consumer product development, fashion industry, importing products from Europe, or hotel/commercial real estate design and development.

To what professional associations do you belong?

American Institute of Architects, Chicago Furniture Designers Association, Industrial Design Society of America (IDSA), International Interior Design Association (IIDA).

What professional publications you read?

I read *Interior Design, Contract, Metropolis, Abitare, Frame, Architectural Digest, Graphis, ID, Crains Business, Core77,* and Herman Miller's Web site.

What advice do you have for others who would like to pursue this career?

Work hard and smart, take business courses, and be persistent.

Profile: Industrial Design – Toy Designer

Name: David Silva
Age: 27
Title: Toy Sculptor/Designer

Employer: McFarlane Toys
Education: BFA, Sequential Art and Illustration
Years in Industry: 3

CAREER LADDER:

Toy designer; toy sculptor

Where are the best cities to live to find jobs like yours?
New York/New Jersey area or San Diego.

What is your typical day like?
I pretty much just sculpt all day—and play with toys a little.

What are your job responsibilities?
Produce a product consistent with the reference and information given and, of course, create accurate and functional sculpted pieces.

What is your favorite part of your job?
Seeing my sculpt (or design) in the final packaging. It's very gratifying to know that my work will be bought by millions around the world. The free toys aren't bad either.

What do you dislike about your job?
A lot of times I don't feel challenged enough. I like big projects that I can really get into. I don't like the small, quick stuff.

Have you had any turning point or "light bulb" moments in your career that have helped you get to where you are today?
I guess the turning point was when I moved to New Jersey after working freelance for over a year as a designer in Savannah. Because of this, I was able to work in-house and become a sculptor.

How did you know you wanted to pursue this career?
I was a big fan of Todd McFarlane as a kid. I'd always draw the character that made him famous, Spawn. It was Spawn that really got me interested in comics initially and influenced me to create my own characters and plots. This led me to study sequential art in college. I wanted to be a comic book artist at first but decided that I liked to design and sculpt better, so I geared my education toward a conceptual illustration path. I was an admirer of McFarlane toys throughout college and strove to make my own sculptures and characters as detailed and impressive as those. My college education got me a job working for my childhood influence as a toy designer, which led to me being a toy sculptor. It's very exciting. I feel inspired by my job, and the knowledge I've gained at this company has been invaluable.

Profile: Industrial Design – Toy Designer

Q&A

How did you get into this industry?

I got the design job just three weeks after graduating with my BFA. I had sent out my portfolio to several toy companies and was very happy when McFarlane Toys showed interest since they were at the top of my list. The design president got in contact with me and seemed to be impressed with my concept art. This got me a job as a toy designer. Several sculptors had left the company at the time that I moved to New Jersey, and they were shorthanded. I was asked to come in and help out temporarily as a sculptor. I liked sculpting more than designing because there was more work involved and there was a greater opportunity to grow. Six months later, I was hired full-time as a sculptor, which is the position I really wanted in the first place but didn't think I was good enough to get. I'm still asked to design from time to time, but I mostly just sculpt. I'm the only sculptor there who also designs for them.

If you weren't doing this job, what similar careers might you consider?

I would love to do concept art for movies, which is still on the agenda after I learn all I can in this field. I'd also love to work as a paleo-artist (an artist who reconstructs prehistoric animals as sculptures, drawings, or paintings) for museum reference books or other appropriate media. I'm a huge fan of prehistoric animals.

What professional Web sites and magazines do you read?

I just check the toy news Web sites such as 16bit.com and figures.com and toy magazines such as *ToyFare*, *Tomarts*, and *Lee's Toy Review* to keep up to date on the toy industry.

What advice do you have for others who would like to pursue this career?

Learn your anatomy, pay close attention to detail, and don't be afraid to play with lots of toys!

Profile: Industrial Designer/Firm Owner

Name: Stephanie
Age: 33
Title: Industrial Designer and Owner of Laf, Inc. and Moss05

Employer: Self-employed
Education: BFA Industrial/Product Design
Years in Industry: 5

CAREER LADDER:

In 2003, I started Laf, Inc., which specializes in soft goods, print, and package design, and I could not be more delighted that I did it. Then in 2005, I started Moss05, which specializes in casual footwear for men and women.

Did you have an internship in this field prior to starting your job?

Yes, I interned at a company called Navigator Biometric LLC, an England-based company that had offices in Savannah and Canada. I worked for this company for over a year while I was in school. It was a fantastic experience and introduction to designing, developing, manufacturing and inventing a product/idea from start to finish.

Where are the best cities to live to find jobs like yours?

I would love to be in New York; in fact, I moved there right after college about six months before I started my company. It was an amazing experience. There were lots of opportunities, but it was competitive and expensive. I chose to move home after a summer so I could start my own company.

What is your typical day like?

I start my workday at 9:00 a.m. I have about 30 clients that I design mostly in the graphic design area, (corporate identity branding, packaging, event design print, advertising, marketing, and apparel design). I am still the only employee, but do have alliances with many other local designers in the surrounding areas. I hit the ground running every a.m. and I don't stop until about 10:00 p.m. almost every day. I still work from home, and it has been a fantastic experience. I have had the opportunity to learn what I am really good at, before growing too fast and having to take work just to survive.

What are your job responsibilities?

I own the company, so I have a lot to do. My responsibilities include design, marketing, freelancing, markets, sourcing, billing, and much more. Plus I do a lot of volunteer work in my community—that helps me stay well rounded—and I love to give to people!

What is your favorite part of your job?

To able to design and work for myself.

Profile: Industrial Designer/Firm Owner

Q&A

What do you dislike about your job?

That I do not have sources and mentors—I would love to find more people that do what I do, so that I could bounce ideas off someone else. I am in Ft. Myers, Florida and industrial design is kind of out of the box for most of my local clients and alliances. Starting a company out of school with hardly any experience was probably one of the more risky things I have ever done, but truly one of the most inspiring.

How did you know you wanted to pursue this career?

When I started failing business school, and started researching what I truly wanted out of my career, I discovered industrial design. I knew this would be the career that would keep me stimulated for the rest of my life. Being only three years in my profession, I am going to have to say I still have mountains to climb; but I am so excited about the journey ahead, I can hardly wait.

If you weren't doing this job, what similar careers might you consider?

Musician, professional athlete, publicist, marketing and media.

To what professional associations do you belong and what publications do you read?

I belong to Industrial Designers Society of America and I read *Dwell*, *How*, *Print*, *I.D.*, *Core 77*, and *Cool Hunting*.

What advice do you have for others who would like to pursue this career?

Just go for it, never give up....

Floral Designer/Florist

Job Description: Floral designers—or florists—cut live, dried, or silk flowers and other greenery and arrange them into displays of various sizes and shapes. They design these displays by selecting flowers, containers, and ribbons and arranging them into bouquets, corsages, table centerpieces and wreaths for weddings, funerals, holidays, and other special occasions.

Training and Educational Qualifications: Floral design is the only design occupation that does not require formal postsecondary training; most floral designers learn their skills on the job. Employers generally look for high school graduates who have creativity, a flair for arranging flowers, and a desire to learn. Many florists gain their initial experience working as cashiers or delivery personnel in retail floral stores. The completion of formal design training, however, is an asset for floral designers, particularly those interested in either advancing to chief floral designer or opening their own businesses.

Job Outlook: Despite the projected decline in employment, job opportunities are expected to be good because of the need to replace workers who leave the occupation. Job opportunities should be good because of the relatively high replacement needs in retail florists that result from comparatively low starting pay and limited opportunities for advancement. The demand for floral designers will continue to grow as flower sales increase as a result of the increasing population and lavishness of weddings and other special events that require floral decorations.

Salary: Median annual earnings for wage and salary floral designers are $21,700. The middle 50 percent earn between $17,690 and $27,330. The lowest 10 percent earn less than $15,040, and the highest 10 percent earn more than $33,650. Median annual earnings differ slightly between grocery store and florist shop employees with a figure of $23,990 for grocery stores and $21,210 for florist shops.

Significant Facts:

- Floral design is the only design specialty that does not require formal postsecondary training.

- Many floral designers work long hours on weekends and holidays, filling orders and setting up decorations for weddings and other events.

- About one-third of floral designers are self-employed.

INDUSTRY RESOURCES:

American Institute of Floral Designers
720 Light Street
Baltimore, MD 21230
Phone: (410) 752-3318
Internet: www.aifd.org

Society of American Florists
1601 Duke Street
Alexandria, VA 22314
Phone: (800) 336-4743
Internet: www.safnow.org

Profile: Floral Designer

Name: Tom **Age:** 53 **Title:** President and CEO	**Employer:** Self-employed, Three Bunch Palms Productions **Education:** Three years of college **Years in Industry:** 25 +

CAREER LADDER:

Delivery driver, part time designer, designer, wedding coordinator, retail floral shop manager, director of retail operations, event planner and manager, and now owner and CEO of my company.

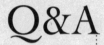

Do you know of which companies have the best internships in this field that are known to help launch a successful career?

There are quite a few large retail floral operations throughout the United States, many in suburban areas as well as large cities. Some offer different programs and learning curves dependent on skill level.

Where are the best cities to live to find jobs like yours?

Cities that are usually very diversified with lots of arts and cultural centers, while attracting influential consumers who thrive on trends as well as tradition. Examples include Seattle, San Francisco, Miami, Los Angeles, Chicago, New York, Dallas, Houston, Boston, Topeka, Atlanta, Denver, Santa Fe, and Portland.

What is your typical day like?

Appointments with clients, site inspections and diagrams with clients, procuring products from wholesale floral suppliers and other vendors that are needed for a particular event, coordination with other services for events, staffing and scheduling for events and functions.

What are your job responsibilities?

All aspects ranging from client meetings and consultations, designs, planning, personnel, financial and execution of function—an owner should know how to do it all well.

What is your favorite part of your job?

Bringing to life a creative thought and vision after collaborating with the client.

What do you dislike about your job?

Dealing with taxes.

Have you had any turning-point or "light bulb" moments in your career that have helped you get to where you are today?

I love giving educational seminars about different aspects of the floral industry and sensing the need that the audience (or students) has for learning more about this wonderful business. The passion I have for

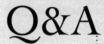

Profile: Floral Designer

Q&A

what I do is very relevant when I know I am getting their attention and they want to hear more. Empowerment!!

How did you get into this industry?

I needed a part-time job in college, so driving for a florist was an easy start. And then I wanted to give more: to offer assistance to those (consumers) who wanted something a little special and unique, from a small floral design for a special birthday to creating an event which would make people say, "*Wow!!!*" "*Amazing!!!*" I learned that it also meant sharing these talents with others who would like to pursue this career. I love teaching.

What do you consider your greatest professional accomplishment?

Becoming an accredited member of The American Institute of Floral Designers and becoming the President of the Association (which will be 2007-2008).

To what professional associations do you belong and what professional publications do you read?

I belong to American Institute of Floral Designers, California State Floral Association, Society of American Florists, and Teleflora Educational Specialists. I read *Florists' Review*.

What advice do you have for others who would like to pursue this career?

Focus, be determined, read all type of articles relating to the field, work part-time, volunteer to work at retail or event companies, and stay current with all types of technology.

Graphic Designer/Graphic Artist

Job Description: Graphic designers—or graphic artists—plan, analyze, and create visual solutions to communications problems in print, electronic, and film media. To do this, they must use a variety of methods such as color, type, illustration, photography, animation, and various print and layout techniques. Graphic designers develop the overall layout and production design of magazines, newspapers, journals, corporate reports, and other publications. They also produce promotional displays, packaging, and marketing brochures for products and services, and they may design logos for products and businesses.

Training and Educational Qualifications: A bachelor's degree is required for most entry-level and advanced graphic design positions although some entry-level technical positions may only require an associate's degree. Graphic designers also need to be familiar with computer graphics and design software. A good portfolio—a collection of examples of a person's best work—often is the deciding factor in getting a job.

Job Outlook: Employment of graphic designers is expected to grow about as fast as average for all occupations through the year 2016, as demand for graphic design continues to increase from advertisers, publishers, and computer design firms. Graphic designers are expected to face keen competition for available positions; therefore, individuals with a bachelor's degree and knowledge of computer design software—particularly those with Web site design and animation experience—will have the best opportunities.

Salary: The American Institute of Graphic Arts reported in 2005 that entry-level designers earned a median salary of $35,000, while staff-level graphic designers earned $45,000. Senior designers earned $62,000. Freelance designers reported median earnings of $60,000. Design directors, the creative heads of design firms or in-house corporate design departments, earned $98,600.

Significant Facts:

- Graphic designers with Web site design and animation experience will have the best opportunities for employment.

- A bachelor's degree is required for most entry-level positions; however, an associate's degree may be sufficient for technical positions.

- About 25 percent of designers are self-employed; many do freelance work in addition to holding a salaried job in design or in another occupation.

INDUSTRY RESOURCES:

American Institute of Graphic Arts (AIGA)
164 Fifth Avenue
New York, NY 10010
Phone: (212) 807-1990
Internet: www.aiga.org

Graphic Artists Guild
90 John Street, Suite 403
New York, NY 10038-3202
Phone: (212) 791-3400
Internet: www.gag.org

Profile: Graphic Designer – Non-profit Organization

Name: Christina
Age: 27
Title: Graphic Designer

Employer: Institute for Private Investors
Education: BFA in Graphic Design
Years in Industry: 5

CAREER LADDER:

Freelance graphic designer; design intern; graphic designer

Did you have an internship in this field prior to starting your job?

I worked as a design intern for Ink & Co., an advertising and design firm in NYC. Some days I cleaned and organized the studio, and some days I worked on designs for big-name products and fashion lines. I discovered that the advertising field was not for me, and that I wanted to focus more on identity and print design. This led me to graphic design.

Where are the best cities to live to find jobs like yours?

The majority of the best graphic design jobs are in New York City. Most other big cities like Atlanta and San Francisco have good markets, but NYC has the widest range and the most competitive pay.

What is your typical day like?

I run down my list of priorities and begin on the projects with the closest deadlines. Before starting a new project, I meet with the team of content developers, editors, the web programmer and my supervisor to determine what we're designing, its function, our goals for the piece and the audience we're trying to reach. Then there is round after round of thumbnail sketches, roughs, drafts, comps and approvals; that usually takes a few weeks. Eventually we go on press (both in-house and out) and the project is completed. In between the big projects, I sketch ideas for new projects.

What are your job responsibilities?

I manage the identity of my company which includes our logos, fonts, trademarks, copyrights and color standards. I maintain brand consistency over all printed and digital media: corporate stationery, brochures, handouts, newsletters, applications, forms, invitations, annual reports, posters, conference displays, signage, etc. I coordinate with the web programmer to create digital graphics, icons and banners for our Web site, and I design all corporate advertising for trade publications. I manage and oversee print production for corporate conferences and events, as well as handle some light administrative design work.

What is your favorite part of your job?

I never do the same thing every day. It's always different and fresh.

Profile: Graphic Designer – Non-profit Organization

Q&A

What do you dislike about your job?

The corporate dress code! I can't tell you how many times I get called in by the conformist fashion police.

How did you know you wanted to pursue this career?

Graphic design is just so much a part of me. I do it in my sleep, I dream in designs, I sketch on the backs of envelopes and napkins, I lay out ideas on the train home, I get inspired by the colors and patterns while window shopping. I design at work all day and I come home and work on projects there too. I've always been drawing, sketching, and organizing things. I entered and won my first art competition at age five. It's something that just lives in me.

Describe how you got into this industry and how you got your most recent job.

I was working freelance out of art college to make ends meet and looking for employment in New York City. I had a decent portfolio of freelance projects from clients that I lugged around the city looking for work. I interned and interviewed for over a year before I finally found what I was looking for. I used Internet job listings and the local newspapers as a resource for openings and answered every one that I found. Most were not the right fit either for me or for them. But eventually I came across a great opportunity and it was a good match of skills for the position.

If you weren't doing this job, what similar careers might you consider?

I'd consider designing upscale invitations, or working in the music industry designing CD/DVD packaging. I'm also an amateur Web site designer, so I think that would be a lot of fun as a career as well.

What professional magazines do you read?

I read *Communications Arts*, *HOW Magazine* and *Graphic Design Magazine*.

What advice do you have for others who would like to pursue this career?

Never stop learning. Find networking opportunities with other designers and keep on top of the latest technology and attend design conferences.

Profile: Graphic Designer – Television News

Name: Collin Pissara
Age: 27
Title: Nightly News Assistant
  Lead Graphic Designer

Employer: NBC
Education: BA Video/Film
Years in Industry: 4

CAREER LADDER:

In-Studio Cameraman, Comcast
Assistant to Children's Department Manager,
  Penguin Publishing

Last Call with Carson Daly Graphic Artist
Today Show Graphic Artist
NBC Nightly News Assistant Lead Artist

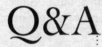

Did you have an internship in this field prior to starting your job?
Yes, I interned in the NBC New Media department. It was a small four-man operation within NBC that handled the needs of clients with a range of digital projects.

Which companies have the best internships in this field and are known to help launch successful careers?
NBC's internship program is pretty darn good. You have to have a strong GPA to be considered. The program is called the Page Program and it's nationally known.

Where are the best cities to live to find jobs like yours?
I live in New York, and I pay a fortune for rent, but it's worth it. I'm in the thick of it and I work in the thick of it. I love it. It can be taxing though—both financially and emotionally—so can commuting two hours to live on a farm though. Many graphic design jobs in television are in the major markets like Los Angeles, Chicago, Boston, and New York, but they're consolidating all the time and the local guy, and even the minor-major markets are being grouped into regional areas to cover an entire network's sister stations.

What is your typical day like?
My day starts at 2:00 p.m. I spend the first half hour catching up on emails and preparing the work station for the day. Then I spend four hours designing graphics for *Nightly News*. Between 3:30 p.m. and 7:00 p.m. are the most pressure-packed times each day. My partner and I are creating graphics for that night's broadcast. From 8:00 to 10:00 pm, I work on graphics for the next morning's *Today Show*.

What are your job responsibilities?
Create graphics for *Nightly News* with Brian Williams—everything from story titles and series animations, anything you see could be my work. I also work for the *Today Show* a couple hours a week in a similar environment, but it is more entertainment based as opposed to news.

Q&A

What is your favorite part of your job?

Problem solving. Having to figure out how to get some bizarre format converted to another format so that some editor across the country can use it in his piece. I love creating title animations when I'm pressed for time. I also love that every day I have different graphics to work on. It's rare that I'm working on any one graphic for more than a few days. My interest in my job stays fresh this way.

What do you dislike about your job?

I work with a lot of older people—many whom are in their forties and fifties who are not extremely comfortable in the Mac environment. I find myself tutoring many times, which I actually enjoy, but at times I wish I had others to tutor me. I wish I worked with more people my age. I am "the kid."

Have you had any turning point or "light bulb" moments in your career that have helped you get to where you are today?

My first involvement with news designers (*Today Show* and *Nightly News*)—besides those I worked with on my internship—came in an overnight session I did a few years back, where I was scheduled to assist artists in adapting to the new Mac environment. I thought I would be treated as "the kid" and figured most people knew more about it than I did anyway. Once I learned people were eager to learn from me, I realized I was worried about nothing, and that I could be of value to the company and grow as an artist and a teacher and moreover, as a person.

How did you know you wanted to pursue this career?

I always grabbed the video camera. I always owned a Mac. I put the two together. It was easy.

How did you get into this industry?

I received the internship from a friend that I met at a summer camp in 8th grade. We were counselors. We coincidentally ended up going to the same college. He was a few years older and graduated first, then offered me an internship around 1998 or so. I knew nothing of the digital design environment then, so I interned there every break I could until I graduated from college. I was about to leave for a trip to Switzerland when they called me up out of the blue and offered me a job working on the *Carson Daly Show*.

If you weren't doing this job, what similar careers might you consider?

I'm a huge sports fan, and I think working for a minor league baseball team would be fun. I would also absolutely love to work for a small documentary film organization or even become a travel assistant on shoots for the Travel Channel.

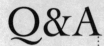

Profile: Graphic Designer – Television News

Q&A

To what professional associations do you belong?
New York Motion Graphics Artists.

What publications do you read?
Videographer Magazine and *Layers* magazine. I also listen to several podcasts, including CNET Buzz out Loud Podcast, Inside Mac Podcast, MacCast Podcast, *New York Times* Podcast.

What advice do you have for others who would like to pursue this career?
Find somebody who works in the field. Don't be scared to walk right into a network and have a demo reel (just finish the demo reel—it doesn't have to be perfect). Have knowledge about a show and show a dedicated desire to work for that show. You might get the job or at least be seriously considered. You'd be surprised how many times NBC is looking for workers and they don't even post job openings.

Profile: Graphic Design – Television

Name: Amanda	**Employer: HGTV**
Age: 25	**Education: BFA Motion Graphics**
Title: Designer	**Years in Industry: 2**

CAREER LADDER:

This is my first job in the industry.

Where are the best cities to live to find jobs like yours?

There are always the major cities like New York, Los Angeles and Atlanta that have a lot of design vendors or TV networks. But you don't have to live in a big city if you don't want to. Quality of life is a number one priority with me, and I did not want to live in a big city. You can find something that you want to do anywhere. I ended up in Knoxville, TN, and I love it. I have every luxury that I could possibly want in a city, and I also have lakes and mountains just a few minutes from my house. So I would say, decide where you want to live first and the job will come.

What is your typical day like?

I work with several producers to visually interpret their ideas, and then we collaborate to put together promos for new shows. Sometimes those promos have money behind them and we can travel and put together a shoot, and sometimes we have no money to work with and we design and edit in-house. I also work with programming directors to create graphic packaging for all shows on the air. We have so many shows that four designers are not enough to go around. Many times we send show packaging to outside vendors. In these instances, I act as the liaison art director with the outside vendor and our in-house design director. If the show package is not sent out of house, I create a story board for approval and then move on to the design and animation for the show opening and all other visual elements within the show.

What are your job responsibilities?

I design and animate graphics for show promos and show graphics. I also help brainstorm and create visuals to better brand the network.

What is your favorite part of your job?

Creative collaboration.

What do you dislike about your job?

The approval process.

Have you had any turning point or "light bulb" moments in your career that have helped you get to where you are today?

I have learned a better way of creating storyboards for show animations. I used to try to figure out how it would animate and create a show logo first. Now I put that aside and start with how I want it to look: I

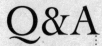

Profile: Graphic Design – Television

Q&A create style frames, rather than storyboard frames, and it gives me a whole new perspective. I also started creating the show logo after I create the style frames. The animation of the elements comes much easier once I know what it will look like.

How did you know you wanted to pursue this career?

I went to college knowing that I wanted to be an artist. I didn't know how I would make a living as an artist because I saw myself as a practical artist rather than a "freedom artist." By freedom artist, I mean someone that strives to see the world in all ways possible and create art from anything and everything. The more I thought about it, the more I realized the world needs practical artists as much as they need freedom artists. Look around you: everything is designed, whether it's your car, or your favorite chair, or even your refrigerator. So I decided to get into the computer side of design. I didn't fit in with the 3D animators because I didn't sketch *Star Wars* characters on my notebook all day, but I did start to fit in with the motion graphics designers. So that is what I do for my career; I am a motion graphics or broadcast designer.

How did you get into this industry?

I went to a job fair at my college and met my current boss. I sent him my demo reel afterward and was later contacted for an interview. I did not know that I was the only candidate that they decided to interview. In fact, I did not understand that my boss was not allowed to give me any information on whether or not they were interested in hiring me. They told me that they had other candidates to interview and they would be in touch. I actually thought it was "over" at that point. I figured that if they wanted to hire me, they would have done it then and there—at my interview—because it had taken me seven months to get an interview. If I can offer any advice to those out there looking for a job, it's to not get discouraged when you don't receive an answer concerning a job right away. There was so much paperwork to be filled out on their end and there was nothing they could say to me. Finally, about a month later, I was offered the job.

If you weren't doing this job, what similar careers might you consider?

When I graduated college, I would have done any job just to get into the industry, and I think anyone should be willing to do that. You can always take another job that comes along down the road. If I were not doing my current job, I would like to work for a small company and work in graphic design. Any job that involves creativity is fine for me.

What professional publications and Web sites do you read?

I like to keep up with Adcritic.com and Adland. Also, I watch TV to see what else is out there and what else is overdone. Knowing the

cutting edge is always a good thing because I work in television. I also like to search other design company Web sites to see what they are doing. That way I find potential companies to work with, or just to get inspiration for my own work.

What advice do you have for others who would like to pursue this career?

Have confidence in yourself and really market yourself. The only way your dream job is going to find you is if you go looking for it. Don't get discouraged. I've been turned down many times, and now I realize it was for the best.

Profile: Senior Graphic Designer – Fashion Industry

Name: Ashley	**Employer: Coach**
Age: 28	**Education: BFA, Graphic Design and BFA, Fashion Design**
Title: Senior Graphic Designer	**Years in Industry: 4**

CAREER LADDER:

Art director; assistant designer; associate designer; senior graphic designer

Did you have an internship in this field prior to starting your job?

During college I interned with a small advertising agency where I was exposed to all aspects of the business: design, marketing, account management, securing new business, etc. It helped me tremendously in figuring out quickly which parts of the business I enjoyed and which parts I didn't.

Which companies have the best internships in this field and are known to help launch successful careers?

I think it varies on what the individual is looking for. Any internship is a good one in helping you define what you want and don't want to do for a living. Experience is invaluable!

Where are the best cities to live to find jobs like yours?

With my background being in fashion design, New York was a logical and important choice. With other design fields, I would suggest researching companies and seeing where they are located. Generally, if you want to pursue a serious career in design and work with big accounts, you might want to look at larger cities like New York, Chicago, Boston, and Los Angeles as choices.

What is your typical day like?

A typical day for me involves reading email, managing and organizing schedules, meeting with different teams to anticipate and discuss upcoming projects, and of course designing!

What are your job responsibilities?

I design in-house merchandising guidelines distributed to all Coach retail and factory stores. We start with a photo shoot where we set up our showroom to look like our stores and take upcoming product and merchandise it. Then I take the images and design a monthly guideline that is distributed to all the stores. These guidelines show stores how to display and arrange their newest product and help ensure a consistent brand message for Coach nationwide.

What is your favorite part of your job?

Working with good people is extremely important and something I highly value. I also enjoy the ownership and autonomy I am given to do my job. It is very rewarding to be able to work in a creative environment where what you are designing has tangible impact.

Q&A

What do you dislike about your job?

Sitting in front of a computer day after day can be tiring and both mentally and physically challenging.

Have you had any turning point or "light bulb" moments in your career that have helped you get to where you are today?

Early on, I realized that it is easy to produce good-looking design but much harder to articulate why good design works or explain how you ended up where you did. In big business and corporate environments, being able to articulate your right-brained message to a left-brained audience is key. In graphic design the bottom line is always about improving communication. If the end product is beautiful but fails to make the message clear to your target audience, then the piece has failed. The challenge always lies in being able to produce work that achieves results for your clients and keeps you challenged creatively.

How did you know you wanted to pursue this career?

I was getting a fashion design degree and thoroughly enjoyed the graphic aspect of mood boards and editorial design. Six weeks before graduating with a BFA in fashion design, I decided to declare a double major and pursue graphic design. Four years later I found the ideal mix of being a graphic designer for a fashion company.

How did you get into this industry?

Immediately after school I was referred by a professor to an ad agency in DC where I got a job as an art director. Then I moved to New York unemployed where a friend working at a fashion company told me about an assistant design position in outerwear design. Two years later I applied for a graphic design position for Coach where I've been ever since.

If you weren't doing this job, what similar careers might you consider?

Work for myself doing high-end freelance.

What professional publications do you read?

I belong to the American Institute of Graphic Arts (AIGA). I read all fashion magazines as well as *Communication Arts, Surface, Nylon, Paper, Women's Wear Daily* and *Print.*

What advice do you have for others who would like to pursue this career?

When you pay attention to what you enjoy doing and why you enjoy it instead of focusing on what you don't want or like, then you start to define who you are and what you are looking for. Being able to define who you are allows you the freedom to clearly pursue goals while also attracting opportunities that are best suited to you.

Interior Designer

Job Description: Designers are involved in planning the interior spaces of buildings, and interior designers draw upon many disciplines to enhance the function, safety, and aesthetics of these spaces. Interior designers are concerned with how different colors, textures, furniture and lighting work together to meet the needs of a building's occupants.

Training and Educational Qualifications: Postsecondary education—especially a bachelor's degree—is recommended for entry-level positions in interior design. In addition, 24 states, the District of Columbia and Puerto Rico register or license interior designers. The National Council administers the licensing exam for Interior Design Qualification (NCIDQ). To be eligible to take the exam, applicants must have at least six years of combined education and experience in interior design, of which at least two are for postsecondary education in design.

Job Outlook: Employment of interior designers is expected to grow 19 percent from 2006-16, which is faster than the average. Economic expansion, growing homeowner wealth and an increased interest in interior design will increase demand for designers. However, interior designers are expected to face keen competition for available positions because many talented individuals are attracted to this profession.

Salary: Median annual earnings for interior designers are $42,260. The middle 50 percent earn between $31,830 and $57,230. The lowest 10 percent earn less than $24,270, and the highest 10 percent earn more than $78,760.

Significant Facts:

- Keen competition is expected for jobs in interior design because many talented individuals are attracted to the field.

- About 26 percent of interior designers are self-employed.

- Postsecondary education—especially a bachelor's degree—is recommended for entry-level positions in interior design; licensure is required in 24 States, the District of Columbia and Puerto Rico.

INDUSTRY RESOURCES:

Council for Interior Design Accreditation
146 Monroe Center NW, Suite 1318
Grand Rapids, MI 49503-2822
Phone: (616) 458-0400
Email: info@accredit-id.org
Internet: www.accredit-id.org

National Council for Interior Design Qualification
1200 18th Street NW, Suite 1001
Washington, DC 20036-2506
Phone: (202) 721-0220
Email: info@ncidq.org
Internet: www.ncidq.org

Profile: Interior Designer

Name: Anne
Age: 26
Title: Interior Designer
Employer: Alt Breeding Schwarz Architects

Education: BA Art History and Classics, MA Interior Design
Years in Industry: 2

CAREER LADDER:

Junior Designer to Staff Designer/Interior Designer

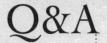

Where are the best cities to live to find jobs like yours?
Washington DC, New York, Chicago, San Francisco.

What is your typical day like?
Every day is different. I spend some time at the computer drawing construction documents and updating orders/emailing to coordinate with engineers, contractors, vendors, etc. I also spend time on site, in the field, measuring and inspecting progress. Some days I spend with clients in meetings to discuss concepts, progress of design and selection of finishes and fabrics. Lastly, I spend a lot of time in the design library, sketching and putting together materials and palettes for projects.

What are your job responsibilities?
I am often the only interior designer on a specific job, so I work hand in hand with the architects in the firm and with the clients. I am responsible for my construction drawings on the interiors from start to finish (applying for building permit and receiving it). I am the head contact person for interiors for my jobs (sometimes dealing with large companies, owners, contractors, engineers). For the residential work I do, I sometimes work in partnership with another designer. In residential work, we are responsible for procurement and delivery of all furniture/fabrics, etc. I am also responsible for selecting, ordering and approving samples of all finish materials for the project.

What is your favorite part of your job?
I enjoy the diversity of projects—no two projects are the same. I enjoy that I get to be creative and it is satisfying to see something built that I worked on.

What do you dislike about your job?
I dislike having to do bookkeeping and tracking orders (the administrative part of it). There is no job in interior design that allows you to be creative *all* of the time.

Have you had any turning point or "light bulb" moments in your career that have helped you get to where you are today?
I realized that I needed to trust my instinct and not be afraid to throw my ideas out there. Sometimes they work and sometimes they

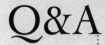

Q&A

don't, but I'll never get anywhere with the ideas that do work if I never put them out there.

Describe how you got into this industry and how you got your most recent job.

I introduced myself to my current boss as soon as I moved to town. She was not hiring at the time, but I asked for an informational interview as I had seen her firm's work and thought it was great. I accepted another job with a different firm. A year later, I noticed on the ASID (American Society of Interior Designers) Web site that my current boss was hiring. I called her again, and she remembered me from our first meeting the year before. I came back for an interview and told her that I still wanted to do work for her. She hired me on the spot.

If you weren't doing this job, what similar careers might you consider?

Architecture or graphic design.

To what professional associations do you belong and what professional publications do you read?

I belong to the American Society of Interior Designers (ASID). I read *Interior Design* magazine, *Architectural Digest*, and *Architectural Record*. I also keep up with current interior design, architecture and art books that are published every year. While it is good to know what your peers are doing, it is important not to just read books/publications in your specific field. Sometimes a painting or a landscape can inspire and influence my design more than a particular "style" of interior design.

What advice do you have for others who would like to pursue this career?

Understand that you will have to be well rounded. You need to have skills in technical, creative areas as well as interpersonal skills—a lot of time is spent dealing with clients, engineers and other professionals. Working as a team or group is a must.

Web Designer and Web User Experience Designer

Job Description: Web Designers create graphics and plan overall design for Web sites; other similar titles include Web Director or Webmaster. User Experience Designers develop electronic environments that provide users with an intuitive, consistent experience. User Experience Designers also conduct usability tests on existing environments. Combining their design knowledge and experience with their collected user data, designers then propose solutions to usability problems.

Training and Educational Qualifications: Occupations in the computer systems design field require varying levels of education. However, most Web User Experience professionals have a bachelor's degree, and many hold a master's degree. Growth in the number of qualified workers, as well as shrinking of the technology job market from its peak earlier in the decade, has allowed employers to become more selective, hiring those candidates with the most education and experience.

Job Outlook: The computer systems design and related services industry grew dramatically throughout the 1990s, and employment more than doubled. Despite recent job losses in certain sectors, this remains one of the 20 fastest growing industries in the nation. As a result, wage-and-salary employment is expected to grow 38 percent by the year 2016, compared with only 11 percent growth projected for the entire economy.

Salary: Employees in the computer systems design and related services industry generally command higher earnings than the national average. All production or non-supervisory workers in the industry averaged $1,265 a week in 2006, significantly higher than the average of $568 for other industries. This reflects a concentration of professionals and specialists who often are highly compensated for their specialized skills or expertise.

Significant Facts:

- The computer systems design and related services industry is expected to experience rapid growth, adding 489,000 jobs between 2006 and 2016.

- Professional and related workers enjoy the best prospects, reflecting continuing demand for the higher level skills needed to keep up with changes in technology.

- Computer specialists account for 54 percent of all employees in this industry.

INDUSTRY RESOURCES:

American Association of Webmasters
7017 Litchfield Road #331
Glendale, Arizona 85307
Phone: (623) 202-5613
Internet: www.aawebmasters.com

Usability Professionals' Association
140 N. Bloomingdale Road
Bloomingdale, IL 60108-1017
Phone: (630) 980-4997
Email: office@usabilityprofessionals.org
Internet: www.upassoc.org

Profile: Web Designer/Director

Name: Richard
Age: 46
Title: Web Director

Employer: Thomas M. Cooley Law School
Education: BFA Industrial Design
Years in Industry: 22

CAREER LADDER:

Designer, Graphtec Industries, Ltd.
Project Coordinator, Graphtec Industries, Ltd.
Director of Design and Research, Graphtec Industries, Ltd.
Business Owner/Creative Director, Automation Graphics and Design, Inc.
Information Technology Specialist, State of Michigan, Department of Management and Budget
Internet Coordinator, State of Michigan, Department of Management and Budget
State of Michigan Webmaster, State of Michigan, Michigan.gov
Web Director, Thomas M. Cooley Law School

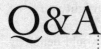

Did you have an internship in this field prior to starting your job?
I worked summers for Graphtec Industries, Ltd. on projects for GM Design Staff and GM Technical Center in Warren, Michigan.

Where are the best cities to live to find jobs like yours?
The opportunities are world-wide.

What is your typical day like?
New project development, meetings, design supervision/direction with staff, email, web coding, photography.

What are your job responsibilities?
I am responsible for all Internet and Intranet activities for Cooley Law School, the largest law school in the nation.

What is your favorite part of your job?
Prototype development/research.

What do you dislike about your job?
Report writing.

Have you had any turning-point or "light bulb" moments in your career that have helped you get to where you are today?
Yes, I've realized that most everything is about design in initial perception—it is what individuals bring with them when they try to look at something or perceive what it is.

How did you know you wanted to pursue this career?
I toured CCS after I had an opportunity to show some of my early work to someone at GM Design Staff. I saw that I was not the only one in the world who was obsessed with drawing cars all day long, as I was accepted at CCS.

Profile: Web Designer/Director

Q&A

How did you get into this industry?

The Internet found me. I started drawing things by hand, with paper and colored markers, which is what I was taught to use. A couple of years after I graduated from CCS, I saw my first ray-traced 3D model in the basement of GM Design Staff on an SGI Indigo. From that moment on, I threw away all my markers. I gained experience with Apple software and a variety of digital editing software. That led to the Internet in 1994 and digital multimedia. I have been immersed in the digital world ever since.

What do you consider your greatest professional accomplishment?

Inventing technical documentation that was designed, developed, and delivered in a 100% digital format in multiple languages.

If you weren't doing this job, what similar careers might you consider?

Computer graphics, print media of some kind; I would definitely explore games and the movie industry.

To what professional associations do you belong and what professional publications or Web sites do you read?

The Internet has made associations kind of passé. You can get any information about almost anything that is known to the human race on the Internet, both good and bad. I read a lot of information on-line. I do attend annual conferences. One that I recommend is the annual Nielsen Norman Group Usability Week.

What advice do you have for others who would like to pursue this career?

Immersion is the best learning environment. Try it for yourself and explore technology. Always read, read, read, and remain humble when speaking to others. Never, ever be the one-man show (boat).

Profile: User Experience Designer

Name: Samantha
Age: 30
Title: User Experience Designer
Employer: Corel

Education: BFA Art History, MHCI
Years in Industry:
2 years in this type of role; I have more years of experience in related positions.

CAREER LADDER:

Communications Manager (entry-level post-grad position)
Design Consultant/User Interface Designer (early career design position)
Quality Assurance Analyst (mid-career analysis position)
User Experience Designer (mid-career design position)

Did you have an internship in this field prior to starting your job?
I did not have an official internship in this field, but I worked in a "student work" classification as a user interface designer and design consultant on real world projects to gain experience in my field.

Which companies have the best internships in this field and are known to help launch successful careers?
Google
Microsoft
IBM
NASA

Where are the best cities to live to find jobs like yours?
Atlanta, Boston, Chicago, New York, San Jose and the surrounding San Francisco Bay Area.

What is your typical day like?
There is no typical day. Some days involve putting out fires, so to speak—just getting important problems solved quickly—while others adopt a more relaxed pace, taking time to do competitive analysis or brainstorm on future designs. I have the ability to telecommute from home quite often and do not have set work hours. I choose to work a general schedule of 8:00 to 4:00, but I can also work a little later at home one day and take an afternoon off now and then. During the day, I communicate with other designers within my team, as well as with software engineers, quality assurance engineers, and marketing staff. Much of this communication is done via email or in meetings.

What are your job responsibilities?
I must research and understand the user and apply this information to user interface designs. I create mockups and interaction flows, conduct competitive analysis, and work with a team of software engineers and quality assurance professionals to create an amazing product.

Profile: User Experience Designer

Q&A

What is your favorite part of your job?

Getting the chance to think about future concepts, brainstorming new designs and solving major problems. I also love working with such a talented group of people. It doesn't get any better than this.

What do you dislike about your job?

Sometimes it gets hard to think long-term when handling many short-term problems.

Have you had any turning point or "light bulb" moments in your career that have helped you get to where you are today?

When working as the communications manager for a non-profit organization, I dealt with advertising and other media on a daily basis. It was then I realized that my background in art history combined with my passion for computers might lead to something new. Thinking about the customer (the advertising target audience) guided me to recognizing this person as a user instead of a consumer. Although they are the same person, it means looking at design from a new angle. From that point, I aimed high for an excellent graduate school and used that to advance my career as a designer.

How did you know you wanted to pursue this career?

I have always had an eye for what is usable—from products like cellular phones and car stereos to software and Web sites. It was just a matter of finding that there was a career out there that mixed usability with design.

How did you get into this industry?

Graduate school was the link between me and user interface design. Because my undergraduate degree was in liberal arts, it would have been hard to break into the user experience design field had I not used most of my electives in studio art and interaction work to provide a foundation to launch me into this career. I found my most recent job while searching many job boards for related positions. The description for this job sounded quite intriguing and interviews were very enticing. I was a definite match for this position.

If you weren't doing this job, what similar careers might you consider?

I would consider graphic design as a career. I love the challenge of design work and I enjoy spending my day using digital imaging software. Even if I were in another career, I imagine I would still do this on the side for fun.

What professional publications do you read?

I read a lot of published papers, so most of my reading stems from scouring the ACM digital library. I also read magazines related

Profile: User Experience Designer

Q&A

to digital photography, user experience, and web blogs from industry professionals.

What advice do you have for others who would like to pursue this career?

Find personal interests within the field and explore them. Design for yourself first and establish a reputation as an innovator. Try to get published in professional conferences and network as much as possible.

Fashion: Fashion Designer

Job Description: Fashion designers help create the billions of clothing articles, shoes, and accessories purchased every year by consumers. Designers study fashion trends, sketch designs of clothing and accessories, select colors and fabrics and oversee the final production of their designs.

Fashion merchandising is a related career. Merchandisers buy and sell textiles, apparel and accessories at both the wholesale and retail levels. They advise designers on market trends, collect specifications from buyers, get samples approved and negotiate prices.

Training and Educational Qualifications: Fashion designers usually have a 2- or 4-year degree and are knowledgeable about textiles, fabrics, ornamentation, and fashion trends. Designers must have an eye for color, detail, balance and proportion, plus excellent communication and problem-solving skills. Despite the advancement of computer-aided design, sketching ability remains an important skill in fashion design. A good portfolio often is the deciding factor in getting a job.

Job Outlook: Slower than average growth is projected. Competition is expected be keen, while relatively few job openings will arise because of low job turnover and a small number of new openings created annually. The best opportunities will be in design firms that create mass-market clothing sold in department stores and retail chain stores. Few jobs are expected in design firms catering to high-end stores as demand for expensive, high-fashion design declines.

Salary: Median annual earnings for fashion designers are $62,610. The middle 50 percent earn between $42,140 and $87,510. The lowest 10 percent earn less than $30,000, and the highest 10 percent earn more than $117,120.

Significant Facts:

- In 2006, the highest concentration of fashion designers were employed in either New York or California.

- Almost one-fourth of fashion designers are self-employed.

- Fashion designers usually have a 2- or 4-year degrees.

INDUSTRY RESOURCES:

Fashion Group International
8 West 40th Street, 7th Floor
New York, NY 10018
Email: info@fgi.org
Internet: www.fgi.org

American Apparel & Footwear Association
1601 N. Kent Street, Suite 1200
Arlington, VA 22209
Email: mrust@apparelandfootwear.org
Internet: www.apparelandfootwear.org

International Textile and Apparel Association, Inc.
P.O. Box 136
Monument, CO 80132
Phone: (719) 488-3716
Email: info@itaaonline.org
Internet: www.itaaonline.org

Profile: Fashion Designer

Name: Erin
Age: 26
Title: Designer/Merchandiser

Employer: D2 Brands, a division of Delta Galil Ltd.
Education: BFA Fashion
Years in Industry: 5

CAREER LADDER:

Freelance CAD artist, assistant designer, designer, designer/merchandiser

Did you have an internship in this field prior to starting your job?

I interned in the design department of Tommy Hilfiger women's sportswear; I was the assistant for cut-and-sew knit clothing. It was a paid internship where I put together mood boards, sourced fabric and prints, completed flat garment sketching, and finished up loose ends for the designer. Most importantly, it introduced me to a lot of people working in fashion who were able to put me in touch with the right people to find the non-corporate design job I wanted after graduating.

Which companies have the best internships in this field and are known to help launch successful careers?

Most large companies in this field have internship programs, but the paid internships are best because the companies are more prone to actually utilize your skill sets if they have to pay you anyway. Internships are invaluable because you are forced to lose the fantasy world of just creating pretty art that school often encourages, and you realize fashion is first and foremost a business.

Where are the best cities to live to find jobs like yours?

New York.

What is your typical day like?

The morning is devoted to answering emails with overseas factories. Because of the many differences in time zones, the morning hours are the only time we're both in the office at the same time. Increasing consumer demand for cost-effective products is shifting almost all production overseas, and it's very hard to communicate design concepts to factories where English is not their first language. It's a little insane how much detail you literally have to spell out to make even a simple shirt, and that is also very time consuming when the process involves a large international team.

In the afternoon I usually review prototype submits sent from the factories for approval; when we finally reach the stage of approved samples, I present them to our sales team. In fashion you are in a constant search for new, better, cooler, hotter things; so whenever I can find time, I run around the city looking for new aesthetic inspiration, be it from store windows, movies, people watching, trim and fabric shopping, or wherever. I also try to read as much as I can about the business side of fashion and

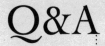

Profile: Fashion Designer

Q&A

retailing from periodicals to give me an inside edge on designing things I have logical reason to believe will sell well.

What are your job responsibilities?

Concept/trend research, design, basic technical instructions to create design, fabric and trim sourcing and development, proto and sample approval, overseas factory communication, presenting trends and samples to sales and buyers, merchandising collections.

What is your favorite part of your job?

Combining right and left brain habits! It's easy to make things which are just "pretty," but making things that are pretty with valid reasons for existing is so satisfying when you get great sales results back from stores!!

What do you dislike about your job?

There's no crystal ball to tell you aesthetic instincts are right or wrong, so I'm always a little plagued by self doubt. But I think if I didn't have this, I wouldn't put as much thought into design.

How did you know you wanted to pursue this career?

I've always been obsessed with fashion, but not in a let's-max-out-the-credit-cards kind of way. Instead, I love the personal expression fashion allows, and I enjoy manipulating visual images to play with different personalities and stereotypes. If life really is just a stage—men and women merely players—then it's our costumes which first define who we want to be.

Describe how you got into this industry and how you got your most recent job.

Hard work, humility, and about 3,000 responses to ads I found in WWD.

If you weren't doing this job, what similar careers might you consider?

Writing about fashion or curating fashion exhibits. But I'd always be a frustrated designer on the inside!

What publications do you read?

Women's Wear Daily (WWD), W, Worth Global Style Network (WGSN), Retailing Today, Wall Street Journal Weekend Edition.

What advice do you have for others who would like to pursue this career?

Learn how to master the computer! Everything nowadays is computer-based. Also try to get at least a basic working knowledge of marketing. If you're not tied into commercial appeal, no one will want to hire you.

Profile: Fashion Merchandiser

Name: Roshella	**Employer: Gap, Inc.**
Age: 28	**Education: BA Fashion**
Title: Merchandiser	**Merchandising**
	Years in Industry: 6

CAREER LADDER:

Assistant Product Manager, babyGap (newborn)
Product Manager, babyGapnewborn (infant and accessories)
Merchandiser, Forth & Towne

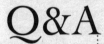

Did you have an internship in this field prior to starting your job?
I interned at S&K Menswear where I assisted the VP of Men's Suits (allocation, story boards, etc.) and I did product development and design at GAP Kids.

Do you know of which companies have the best internships in this field that are known to help launch a successful career?
I can think of three:

1. Gap Corp, San Francisco: RMP, retail management program which is a four-phase program for college grads. If you graduate from the program successfully, you are placed within that organization.

2. Gap, NYPD: NY product development and design intern during your junior/senior year in college. Not as guaranteed as the RMP, but you get great experience and networking. This is how I got my job.

3. Ralph Lauren also has internships.

Where are the best cities to live to find jobs like yours?
New York, Los Angeles, Miami, Atlanta.

What is your typical day like?
Read the business from the week prior. Make decisions on how to react to the business trends in-season and for future seasons. Work on open issues from seasons in development (i.e., fabric issues, pre-booking for fabrics). Attend fittings.

What are your job responsibilities?
I communicate business to a cross-functional team, including weekly, midseason and postseason. I also create the line plan and strategy for the future season to guide the design team, partnering with design, planning and production to hit seasonal plans and margin targets for the season. I partner with planning to buy a line by identifying key drivers and positioning proper inventory levels and I shop competition to

Profile: Fashion Merchandiser

Q&A

develop retail strategy. I am always on the look-out for potential business opportunities as well.

What is your favorite part of your job?

Assorting the line, identifying key outfits.

What do you dislike about your job?

The huge amount of time working with planning.

Have you had any turning-point or "light bulb" moments in your career that have helped you get to where you are today?

Most recently I was at a plateau in my kids' product development career and decided to head back to my roots and try merchandising. I knew that getting this type of experience under my belt would reap rewards in the future. I'm lucky enough that I work for a company that promotes internal placement. Not only was I able to get experience in a new job function, but I got experience in a new business (women's).

How did you know you wanted to pursue this career?

During high school, I worked in a mall and completely enjoyed merchandising in the store and window display. I took a fashion marketing class my junior year in high school and knew it was my calling.

Describe how you got into this industry and how you got your most recent job.

I got a work study job at Gap in college and was able to work my way up the ladder. I always knew I wanted to work in corporate, so I became a merchandising manager in the store and pursued other opportunities in the corporation.

What do you consider your greatest professional accomplishment?

The fact that when interviewing for my current job, I had referrals with such high praise on my work ethic and contributions I've made to the teams in the past. That's what ultimately landed me the job.

If you weren't doing this job, what similar careers might you consider?

Event planning, fashion shows, parties. Marketing in the fashion industry.

What professional publications and Web sites do you read?

Women's Wear Daily, Retailing Today, Earnshaws, WGSN.com.

What advice do you have for others who would like to pursue this career?

Internship, internship, internship!

Profile: Fashion Merchandising Manager

Name: Heather	**Employer:** Levenger
Age: 29	**Education:** BFA, Fashion Design
Title: Product/Merchandising Manager	**Years in Industry:** 5

CAREER LADDER:

Intern, Gap, Inc.
Assistant Production Manager, Gap, Inc.
Product Development Manager (Private Label), Evelyn & Arthur (10 store small boutique)
Product Development Manager, Levenger (Leather Bags/Briefs, Small Leathers, and Folios)

Did you have an internship in this field prior to starting your job?

I interned at Gap, Inc. in San Francisco during the summer before my senior year in college. It was an amazing experience that I will never forget. I was able to learn so much in a short two-month internship and also gained one of the five job offers that were given out of the 65 intern class. I got to learn first hand how fast-paced and ever-changing the retail industry is and I found out I loved every minute of it.

Which companies have the best internships in this field and are known to help launch successful careers?

Because I experienced my internship with the Gap, it holds a high rank on my list. Gap also has programs for college graduates that take them on a several-month rotation through the departments at Gap. This provides the graduates with an opportunity to find their perfect match and know what they would like to pursue.

Where are the best cities to live to find jobs like yours?

These days there are companies in the fashion industry popping up everywhere. New York is the obvious place for fashion, but you can also find Target in Minneapolis.

What is your typical day like?

Busy! I spend a lot of time communicating with our Asian associates since that is the primary location where our product is developed. We email for follow-up on development of product, cost negotiations, and on-time deliveries. There are a lot of meetings within my day, from everything dealing with planning our seasons to looking at sales. I manage a big area of the business so at times the day can be very stressful, but that is just retail—you really have to love it.

What are your job responsibilities?

I manage Men's Leather Bag's/Brief's, Small Leathers (wallets, etc.), and Folios and Journals. Within these areas I do the product development, costing, exposure plan of products, colors for the season, and I communicate daily with the Far East, as well as so much more.

Profile: Fashion Merchandising Manager

Q&A

What is your favorite part of your job?

The product development part—coming up with that new idea and new product and putting my mark on the product while hoping that the customer responds the way I want them to.

What do you dislike about your job?

There are times when a problem with a product can take the best of you. You are pressured to have a product here and the factory informs you of a problem or a delay which then sends you in a tail spin trying to fix things. I remember something my boss at the Gap said to me one time during such a stressful event: "Heather, at the end of the day it's just a t-shirt; don't let it get the best of you." That simple comment has carried me through my stressful times dealing with the day-to-day stresses of retail/fashion.

Have you had any turning point or "light bulb" moments in your career that have helped you get to where you are today?

I'm a perfectionist and I have always been determined to climb the ladder. I was a workaholic at one point, but one day I realized I could not do that to myself or I was going to get burnt out very quickly. I have learned to take time for myself and it has helped me a lot in my everyday work. I am more creative and refreshed.

How did you know you wanted to pursue this career?

I started college as a graphic design major. Then after a summer internship, I realized it wasn't something I could do for the rest of my life. So I dug deep and realized I loved fashion and loved design and drawing. That led me to change my major to fashion design. After my internship at the Gap, I realized I had made the right choice. Fashion is always changing and fast paced and that is what I need. It keeps me on my toes. I come into work every day and I never know what to expect.

Describe how you got into this industry and how you got your most recent job.

I started in the industry with an internship at the Gap Headquarters in San Francisco. Then I went on to work in SF after graduating from college. At the end of two years, I transferred to the Miami office because I wanted to be closer to my family in Atlanta. I worked at the Gap office in Miami for a little over a year and then had to move to South Florida because I got married and my husband's job was in Delray Beach. I commuted for awhile from Miami to Delray and after spending more than three hours a day in the car commuting, I made the tough decision to leave Gap. I went on to work for a 10-store retail boutique and worked in their main office as the product development manager for the Private Label line which was 75 percent of their product. After a year, I was approached by Levenger and decided it was a good move

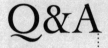

Q&A

to make. This job brought me into a new area of product that I wasn't familiar with, so I decided to take the challenge and broaden my knowledge of product.

If you weren't doing this job, what similar careers might you consider?

I would love to one day open my own boutique in Charleston, South Carolina.

What professional magazines publications do you read?

I'm always looking at *Women's Wear Daily* to see the trends and to check out what is happening in the industry.

What advice do you have for others who would like to pursue this career?

I am a strong promoter of internships because they provide the opportunity to find out if this career field is something you can find passion in. You really have to love fashion to be in this industry because it is tough at times.

Profile: Fashion Executive

Name: Jaz	**Employer:** Paul Davril-licenced
Age: 38	Apparel of Kenneth Cole and
Title: Vice President of Design	Ecko Red
and Merchandising	**Education:** BFA in Fashion Design
	Years in Industry: 15

CAREER LADDER:

Designer; Design Director; Vice President of Design and Merchandising; Vice President of Merchandising; Vice President of Design and Merchandising

Where are the best cities to live to find jobs like yours?

New York is it. Next would be Los Angeles, but there are fewer opportunities there. After Los Angeles, Miami. There are random placements for people in other places; for example, the Limited and Walmart have opportunities in the Midwest. Others out of New York City are companies like LL Bean, Lands End and Chico's.

What is your typical day like?

A lot of follow up, production issues or clear ups. Attend fittings. Review approvals on strike offs or knit downs. Update the line plan for changes. Review sketches.

What are your job responsibilities?

Create the line—the overall look, theme and color. Distribute specific categories to the designers. Create and distribute a calendar. Review all designs. Pass off reviewed art and tech packs. Review all approvals and fits. Correspond between the various overseas offices. Create line plans.

What is your favorite part of your job?

Actual designing, seeing the finished product walking down the street, having great sell-throughs.

What do you dislike about your job?

The calendar.

Have you had any turning-point or "light bulb" moments in your career that have helped you get to where you are today?

Yes, just being loyal. My first boss said I would have to be more cutthroat if I were going to last in this industry. She was my least favorite boss and taught me everything about what I did not want to be.

How did you know you wanted to pursue this career?

I saw the movie *Mahogany* when I was seven and wanted to be Diana Ross.

Q&A

Describe how you got into this industry and how you got your most recent job.

I knew that I wanted to go to school for design, so I took sewing in high school to determine if I was even decent at it. Then I applied to design-oriented schools. After graduating, I moved to New York to get a job—it was all part of the plan for me. I found my current position through a headhunter (actually while searching for another position). I was not interested in the position they had available, but they had another one that they told me might become available in the near future. I came back and took that one.

What do you consider your greatest professional accomplishment?

The line that I created at PDI for Kenneth Cole Women's. I created the product from scratch as though it were a start-up.

What magazines do you read?

WWD, Vogue, Harper's Bazaar, Collezoni, Vanity Fair, Town & Country, InStyle.

What advice do you have for others who would like to pursue this career?

Just believe in yourself. If you don't, you can't expect others to believe in your vision. Be humble and loyal. Never burn bridges—it is a very small fashion world.

Fashion Editor/Stylist

Job Description: Editors review, rewrite, and edit the work of writers. An editor's responsibilities vary with the employer and type and level of editorial position held. At fashion magazines, editors also decide what material will appeal to readers, review and edit articles, offer comments to improve the work and suggest possible titles. In some instances, fashion editors are also stylists at the magazine where they are employed, in which capacity they view the latest collections by all the designers to help decide what should be featured in the magazine. They often write about fashion for the magazine as well.

Training and Educational Qualifications: A college degree generally is required for a position as a writer or editor. Although some employers look for a broad liberal arts background, most prefer to hire people with degrees in communications, journalism, or English. For those whose training involved specializing in a particular area—such as fashion, business, or law—additional background in the chosen field may be expected. A background or dedicated interest in fashion is advantageous for working as a fashion editor.

Job Outlook: Employment of salaried writers and editors is expected to grow as fast as the average for all occupations. Magazines and other periodicals increasingly are developing market niches, appealing to readers with special interests. Businesses and organizations are developing newsletters and Web sites, and more companies are experimenting with publishing materials directly on the Internet. Online publications and services are growing in number and sophistication, spurring the demand for writers and editors, especially those with Internet experience. Advertising and public relations agencies, which also are growing, should be another source of new jobs.

Salary: Median annual earnings for salaried editors are $48,640. The middle 50 percent earn between $34,850 and $67,820. The lowest 10 percent earn less than $25,430, and the highest 10 percent earn more than $97,700. Median annual earnings for those working for newspaper, periodical, book, and directory publishers are $50,650.

Significant Facts:

- Most jobs in this occupation require a college degree in communications, journalism, or English, although a degree, interest or background in fashion might be particularly useful in pursuing a job as a fashion editor.

- The outlook for most writing and editing jobs is expected to be competitive because many people are attracted to the occupation. This is especially true for fashion magazines.

- Online publications and services are growing in number and sophistication, spurring the demand for writers and editors, especially those with Internet experience, which may provide more opportunities for people putting fashion content normally seen in print into an online format.

INDUSTRY RESOURCES:

American Society of Magazine Editors/ Magazine Publishers of America
810 Seventh Avenue, 24th Floor
New York, NY 10019
Phone: (212) 872-3700
Internet: www.magazine.org

Profile: Fashion Editor/Stylist

Name: Seth

Age: 25

**Title: Market Editor/Freelance
  Fashion Stylist**

Employer: *OUT* magazine

Education: BFA Fashion

Years in Industry: 3

CAREER LADDER:

Intern, Nylon *magazine; fashion assistant,* Men's Vogue; *fashion stylist, represented by Timothy Priano of ARTISTS; market editor,* OUT

Did you have an internship in this field prior to starting your job?

Yes, I was an intern for Nylon magazine where I assisted Fashion Director, Kusum Lynn (now at JANE magazine).

Which companies have the best internships in this field and are known to help launch successful careers?

I did several internships in different areas of fashion until I found something that I love in the fashion editorial industry. Some people prefer to work at *Vogue* or for other large publications that are very corporate. The name definitely says a lot on a resume and the contacts you could meet are priceless. However, smaller magazines usually need things from an intern and your day-to-day duties are much more interesting and educational. As long as people know and respect the publication, you can't go wrong.

Where are the best cities to live to find jobs like yours?

It is basically limited to large cities for most work (New York, Los Angeles, Miami, Chicago, Dallas). But every region has a magazine and it basically depends on where you prefer to live and if there are any jobs available in that market. In New York, it is a bit easier to find opportunities for employment because the number of jobs available is much greater than other areas. But it is also the most competitive market.

What is your typical day like?

Being the market editor, I have to go out into the city on appointments to view the latest collections by all the designers. This includes fashion week and private appointments for smaller labels that do not have fashion shows in the tents. I also style for the magazine. So on any given day, I can be in different places looking at a collection, on location doing a shoot (either in New York or out of town or overseas) or I could be sitting in my office doing credits for photo shoots and requesting garments for a shoot. I also have to attend certain events with PR representatives.

What are your job responsibilities?

I make sure certain advertisers are featured in our fashion pages while also creating interesting visuals for the pages—something to keep readers interested in what we are showing them. I also write for the fashion advice

Q&A

column of our Web site (www.out.com). And I attend editorial meetings that keep everyone up to date on the progress of any pertinent issues.

What is your favorite part of your job?

Traveling, going to fashion week (New York and Europe), parties, free stuff. I love my job in general. It's a great environment.

What do you dislike about your job?

It's editorial, so I don't get paid enough.

Have you had any turning point or "light bulb" moments in your career that have helped you get to where you are today?

Absolutely. I had a relatively unfortunate experience with a previous job, but it was totally my fault for being inexperienced and immature. I really realized that I had to grow up and become a professional.

How did you know you wanted to pursue this career?

I started with the internship at *NYLON* and it felt right. I felt comfortable and confident that I could do what was expected of me.

Describe how you got into this industry and how you got your most recent job.

In fashion, it's 40 percent education/experience and 60 percent who you know and if they like you. I started with the internship at *NYLON*. Someone there helped me get the job at *Men's Vogue*. From there, I started styling with an agency. Then I applied for an open position at *OUT* magazine. I had a letter of recommendation from Timothy Priano and a personal reference who knew the newly appointed editor-in-chief of *OUT*, as well as my experience, education and portfolio.

If you weren't doing this job, what similar careers might you consider?

I would most likely stick to doing freelance styling with artists.

What professional magazines/newspapers/journals/Web sites do you read?

I read most of the magazines on newsstands today, especially men's fashion books. Since that is where I am, I like to know what other publications are doing and if I'm actively competing with larger publications.

What advice do you have for others who would like to pursue this career?

Do internships! Unless your last name is Hearst or Fairchild, you need to start making your connections as soon as possible. Intern all throughout school (I did three internships during winter breaks). Don't wait until you graduate. If you intern early, you can start working soon after graduating and start getting paid.

Jeweler

Job Description: Jewelers and precious stone and metal workers use a variety of common and specialized hand tools and equipment to design and manufacture new pieces of jewelry; cut, set, and polish gem stones; repair or adjust rings, necklaces, bracelets, earrings, and other jewelry; and appraise jewelry, precious metals, and gems.

Training and Educational Qualifications: Jewelers usually learn their trade in vocational or technical schools, through distance-learning centers, or on the job. Colleges and art and design schools offer programs that can lead to the degrees of bachelor or master of fine arts in jewelry design. Formal training in the basic skills of the trade enhances one's employment and advancement opportunities. Many employers prefer jewelers with design, repair, and sales skills.

Job Outlook: Employment of jewelers and precious stone and metal workers is expected to experience little or no change. Many employers have difficulty finding and retaining jewelers with the right skills and the necessary knowledge. Some technological advances have made jewelry making more efficient; however, many tasks cannot be fully automated.

Salary: Median annual earnings for jewelers and precious stone and metal workers are $29,750. The middle 50 percent earn between $22,390 and $40,160. The lowest 10 percent earn less than $17,760, and the highest 10 percent earn more than $54,940.

Significant Facts:

- About half of all jewelers are self-employed.

- Jewelers usually learn their trade in vocational or technical schools, through distance-learning centers, or on the job. Jewelry designers usually have degrees in design and in particular, jewelry design.

- Prospects for new jewelers should be excellent; many employers have difficulty finding and retaining workers with the right skills to replace those who retire or who leave the occupation for other reasons.

INDUSTRY RESOURCES:
Gemological Institute of America
5345 Armada Drive
Carlsbad, CA 92008
Phone: (800) 421-7250
Internet: www.gia.edu

Jewelers of America
52 Vanderbilt Avenue, 19th Floor
New York, NY 10017
Phone: (800) 223-0673 or (646) 658-0246
Email: info@jewelers.org
Internet: www.jewelers.org

Profile: Jewelry Designer

Name: Mia
Age: 28
Title: Jewelry Designer

Employer: Liz Claiborne
Education: BFA, Metals and Jewelry
Years in Industry: 6

CAREER LADDER:

Customer Service Representative at a jewelry company
Junior Designer at Jacmel Jewelry
Designer and Senior Designer, Liz Claiborne.

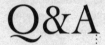

Which companies have the best internships in this field and are known to help launch successful careers?
Tiffany, Liz Claiborne, and small local businesses.

Where are the best cities to live to find jobs like yours?
New York is the place for corporate jobs, but smaller more art-related jewelry jobs can be found in various parts of California, Massachusetts, Washington State and also abroad in Germany, London and Paris.

What is your typical day like?
I have several meetings throughout the day and lots of projects, deadlines, and waiting for approvals due to a very long list of chain of command. I work late often—sometimes until 10:00 or 11:00 p.m. or even midnight.

What are your job responsibilities?
Trend and color development. We work to create a "market message" and interpretation of current fashion trends appropriate for our brand. Doing that includes other aspects of my job such as sketching, research and development trips to China. I also manage freelancers and junior designers and communicate daily with the vice president, looping her into what's going on and getting approvals. I initiate designs, finding the hot items and making sure we register them in our lines.

What is your favorite part of your job?
Color palette development, designing actual groups and attending design presentations.

What do you dislike about your job?
Chains of command and pointless meetings. Lack of trust from higher levels to empower people to make the right decisions.

How did you know you wanted to pursue this career?
I sort of fell into it when I was 14 years old and started the design school back in Croatia. All my friends wanted to be in the popular

Q&A

departments, such as painting and graphic design. I figured I should try something different.

Describe how you got into this industry and how you got your most recent job.

I moved to New York five days before September 11, 2001. I did not have a job or anything lined up, but I answered a few ads after that horrible day and started in a customer service position at a fine jewelry company. I found my most recent job through a posting on stylecareer. com, a Web site that is geared towards fashion positions. I applied and went on six interviews. Then I had to do a design project. After that, I was hired.

If you weren't doing this job, what similar careers might you consider?

Architecture or shoe design.

To what professional associations do you belong and what professional publications do you read?

I attend Jewelry Design Professional Network (JDPN) presentations and I read *Ganoskin*, which is all about jewelry design

What advice do you have for others who would like to pursue this career?

There are many aspects of this career. I never thought that I would be working a corporate job, but I readily fell into it. You must be ready to try things and continue to challenge yourself. Always be open to trying/learning something new. It will keep you fresh and it will keep your views changing. Even when you must take the convoluted way to get to a point, embrace the process; the end result is that much more enjoyable.

Museum: Conservator

Job Description: Conservators manage, care for, preserve, treat, and document works of art, artifacts, and specimens—tasks that may require substantial historical, scientific, and archaeological research. They use x-rays, chemical testing, microscopes, special lights, and other laboratory equipment and techniques to examine objects and determine their condition, their need for treatment or restoration, and the appropriate method for preserving them.

Training and Educational Qualifications: When hiring conservators, employers look for a master's degree in conservation or closely related field, together with substantial experience. There are only a few graduate programs in museum conservation techniques in the United States. Competition for entry to these programs is keen; to qualify, a student must have a background in chemistry, archaeology or studio art, and art history as well as work experience.

Job Outlook: Faster than average employment growth is expected through 2016. Keen competition is expected for most jobs because qualified applicants generally outnumber job openings. Conservation program graduates with knowledge of a foreign language and a willingness to relocate will have an advantage over less qualified candidates.

Salary: Median annual earnings of museum technicians and conservators are $34,340. The middle 50 percent earn between $26,360 and $46,120. The lowest 10 percent earn less than $20,600, and the highest 10 percent earn more than $61,270.

Significant Facts:

- Conservators usually specialize in a particular material or group of objects, such as documents and books, paintings, decorative arts, textiles, metals, or architectural material.

- Most conservators work in museums, at historical sites, and in similar institutions; educational institutions; or in federal, state, or local government.

- Prospective employers look for a master's degree in conservation or closely related fields.

INDUSTRY RESOURCES:

The American Institute for Conservation of Historic and Artistic Works (AIC)
1717 K Street NW, Suite 200
Washington, DC 20036-5346
Phone: (202) 452-9545
Email: info@aic-faic.org
Internet: aic.stanford.edu

Profile: Conservator

Name: Jayne	**Employer: Self-employed**
Age: 45	**Education: BA Art History, MS**
Title: Paper Conservator	**Art Conservation**
	Years in Industry: 25

CAREER LADDER:

Art Conservation Volunteer

Art Conservation Technician

Internships, Paper Conservation

Paper Conservator, Smithsonian

Paper Conservator (private practice)

Did you have an internship in this field prior to starting your job?

I had several internships. I began my career with volunteer positions and art conservator technician positions—two unpaid internships in the paper conservation labs at the Smithsonian's Freer Gallery of Art and the Walters Art Gallery in Washington, DC—before entering my graduate program in art conservation. These programs were quite difficult to get into (with only about four programs in North America that accept approximately 10 students out of 100 applicants). I was accepted to graduate school after those internships, which I believe were crucial to my acceptance. I then had two summer internships as well as an 11-month internship in my third year of graduate school. I spent my summers interning at the Baltimore Museum of Art, the Hagley Museum in Winterthur and the Canadian Centre for Architecture in Montreal. My third-year internship was at the National Archives in Washington, DC.

Do you know of which companies have the best internships in this field that are known to help launch a successful career?

The most important thing for an internship is that the conservator you work for be respected and in good standing in the field. It doesn't matter whether he or she is in private practice or working in a museum, but it is good to get experience with both.

Where are the best cities to live to find jobs like yours?

Conservators (and conservation opportunities) seem to be clustered in three locations in the U.S.: New York, LA and Washington, DC. Outside these areas, we tend to be more spread out. In terms of actual numbers, these three areas are the easiest to find opportunities. However, if you plan to go into private practice, you may find that you can be a big fish in a small pond in other areas of the country.

What is your typical day like?

I work two and a half days per week and my days vary. I might put a print in a humidity chamber to prepare it for bathing in the afternoon. While that is humidifying, I might make a batch of wheat starch paste and mend another drawing or print. When the first print is ready, I

Q&A

spend an afternoon bathing it, allowing time in between washings by working on other objects. Or I might have some photography to do. I take color slides of all my objects before and after treatment for documentation. Because I don't have a permanent setup for photography, I tend to do it in large batches so it takes most of the day. I also see clients by appointment. Most of my clients come to me and I set aside time to look at their objects and discuss the treatment with them.

What are your job responsibilities?

As a private conservator working alone, I do everything—administrative and treatment.

What is your favorite part of your job?

I actually enjoy most of it but the treatment part is the most satisfying. I love starting treatments but have a hard time declaring them finished; I just don't want to let go and declare it done.

What do you dislike about your job?

I miss having colleagues. I'm pretty sociable and used to enjoy having a cup of coffee in the mornings with co-workers. My dream would be to have a studio outside my home with one or two other conservators.

Have you had any turning-point or "light bulb" moments in your career that have helped you get to where you are today?

The original "light bulb" came at the end of my freshman year when a co-worker at my part-time job told me she wanted to be an art conservator. I'd never heard of such a job and it really fired my imagination. My second "light bulb" was probably when I got back from Europe and realized I wanted to get myself on track toward pursuing a future in art conservation. And finally, there was the moment when I realized that I wanted to go to grad school rather than take the much longer apprenticeship route into the field.

How did you know you wanted to pursue this career?

My original decision to pursue this career was actually pretty flaky in retrospect. I heard about the field and just decided it was for me. What I've often told people since then is that I like this field because it allows me to use both my hands and my brain. I like the satisfaction of actually seeing something improved and made better. And history and art are both valuable to me.

What do you consider your greatest professional accomplishment?

Just getting into and through the program was an accomplishment. My favorite accomplishment was the "Chinese Paper Project." I took a collection of ethnographic paper objects, most of which had never been touched—some of these objects were still in the original mailing

Q&A

containers from when they were collected in the field—and got the whole thing in much better shape. I started by surveying the collection (their existing database was not terribly useful; it was inaccurate and incomplete) and determined which objects needed to be re-housed and which needed treatment. Then I carried out all the re-housing and most of the treatment. That collection was in *such* better shape after I was through with it—what a great feeling! There have been other individual treatments that have given me great satisfaction because I loved the object or it was an interesting or challenging treatment.

If you weren't doing this job, what similar careers might you consider?

Actually, I went through a period a couple years ago when I thought about leaving the field. I briefly considered whether I wanted to go into something food related. I love baking and cooking.

To what professional associations do you belong and what professional publications do you read?

I belong to the American Institute for Conservation (our national organization), the Washington Conservation Guild (regional affiliate), and The Institute of Conservation (a European organization based in the UK), International Institute for Conservation (AIC's parent organization) and the International Council of Museums. Several Internet sites I visit are Conservation Online (palimpsest.stanford.edu) and the Ink Corrosion Web site (knaw.nl/ecpa/ink/).

What advice do you have for others who would like to pursue this career?

Don't take your application to the programs lightly. Assume that you may apply more than once before getting in. Understand that you are giving three years of your life to the program when you do get in—you cannot do this part-time and they don't want you to have a life outside of school: Some of my classmates were separated from their families during this time and got no sympathy from their professors for this. It was rough.

Getting as much experience with different conservators as possible is very, very important. For one thing, this will tell you whether you really want to be in this field. This is a career that does not pay well—you do it because you love it. And finally, be flexible. You never know which experiences will be truly valuable.

Museum Curator/Museum Director

Job Description: Curators administer the affairs of museums, zoos, aquariums, botanical gardens, nature centers, and historic sites. (The head curator of the museum is usually called the museum director.) Curators direct the acquisition, storage, and exhibition of collections, including negotiating and authorizing the purchase, sale, exchange or loan of collections. They are also responsible for authenticating, evaluating, and categorizing the specimens in a collection.

Training and Educational Qualifications: For employment as a curator, most museums require a master's degree in an appropriate discipline of the museum's specialty—art, history, or archaeology—or in museum studies. Many employers prefer a doctoral degree, particularly for curators in natural history or science museums. Earning two graduate degrees—in museum studies (museology) and a specialized subject—gives a candidate a distinct advantage in this competitive job market.

Job Outlook: Curator jobs are attractive to many people, and many applicants have the necessary training and knowledge, but there are only a few openings. Consequently, candidates may have to work part time, as an intern, or even as a volunteer assistant curator or research associate after completing their formal education. Substantial work experience in collection management, research, exhibit design, or restoration, as well as database management skills, will be necessary for permanent status. Another related career in museums is a museum preparator, who performs skilled preparatory work for museum collections.

Salary: Median annual earnings for curators are $46,300. The middle 50 percent earn between $34,410 and $61,740. The lowest 10 percent earn less than $26,320, and the highest 10 percent earn more than $80,030.

Significant Facts:

- Curatorial positions often require knowledge in a number of fields. For historic and artistic conservation, courses in chemistry, physics and art are desirable.

- Because curators—particularly those in small museums—may have administrative and managerial responsibilities, courses in business administration, public relations, marketing and fundraising also are recommended.

- Most curators specialize in a particular field, such as botany, art, paleontology or history. In small institutions with only one or a few curators, one curator may be responsible for a number of tasks, from maintaining collections to directing the affairs of the museum.

INDUSTRY RESOURCES:

Association of Art Museum Curators
174 East 80th Street
New York, NY 10021
Phone: (212) 879-5701
Internet: www.artcurators.org

American Association of Museums
1575 Eye Street NW, Suite 400
Washington DC 20005
Phone: (202) 289-1818
Internet: www.aam-us.org

Profile: Museum Curator

Name: Linda
Age: 48
Title: Curator
Employer: Powhatan Plantation

Education: BFA, Commercial Arts, Pursuing an MBA and a Museum Management Certificate

Years in Industry: As a curator, 3 years; freelance and other art specific jobs, 20 years

CAREER LADDER:

Curator
High School Teacher/Director
Freelance Muralist, Painter, Illustrator,
    Architect Tech, Instructor
Creative Consultant for High School
Set Designer

Artist/Director Busch Gardens
Art Instructor
Craft Director
Garment Artist
Porcelain Artist

Where are the best cities to live to find jobs like yours?

In the field of historical preservation and curator-ship, the Colonial Williamsburg area is ideal. However, for arts in general, the area is extremely lacking.

What is your typical day like?

No two days are really the same. Typically, I check house conditions and make adjustments, oversee the grounds and housekeeping, contact other curators, schedule maintenance, write for grant money, schedule art classes and art exhibitions, schedule cultural art events, perform managerial duties, teach some art classes, act as a docent and schedule tours.

What are your job responsibilities?

The preservation of a 1735 historical home which is both on the national and state registration logs as a significant historic landmark.

What is your favorite part of your job?

I deal with thousands of people from all over the world in a year's time, which is interesting. I also like interacting with others who work in museums.

What do you dislike about your job?

My salary is quite low. I imagine larger institutions in larger metropolitan areas pay more.

Describe how you got into this industry and how you got your most recent job.

I was first hired as an activities director. Within a week, they realized my background and began to shift me to my current position.

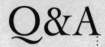

Profile: Museum Curator

Q&A

What do you consider your greatest professional accomplishment?

The murals I did inside and out on the Busch Gardens, Pompeii Ride (took 9 months to complete).

If you weren't doing this job, what similar careers might you consider?

Museum management.

To what professional associations do you belong?

Virginia Museum Association.

What advice do you have for others who would like to pursue this career?

Be tough and remember you are doing it for the love of the arts.

Profile: Museum Preparator

Name: Keith	**Employer: Princeton University**
Age: 32	**Education: BFA and MFA Painting**
Title: Museum Preparator	**Years in Industry: 5**

CAREER LADDER:

Art Services, Philadelphia, PA, Packing
Self-employed Freelance Preparator
Elementary Art Teacher, Phil-Mont Christian Academy
Museum Preparator, Princeton University Art Museum

Did you have an internship in this field prior to starting your job?

Coordinator for the Mural Team through Service Opportunities for Students. I managed student-executed mural projects and worked at facilitating requests from local non-profit agencies within the greater Savannah area.

Which companies have the best internships in this field and are known to help launch successful careers?

Small museums are great places to get experience with the care and handling of art because you are more likely to be assigned many roles and duties.

Where are the best cities to live to find jobs like yours?

New York. There are over 20 shipping and packing companies in New York, and these are some of the best places to gain experience in problem-solving and best practices.

What is your typical day like and job responsibilities?

My job involves installation, gallery maintenance, lighting, fabrication of exhibition furniture, mat and frame works on paper, and packing and shipping of art and artifacts. My daily activities include responding to requests from curators and registrars to unpack or pack objects, install work or perform routine gallery maintenance. When there is a large exhibition, several weeks will be devoted to the rough preparation (carpentry, painting) to installation of the work, then labeling and lighting.

What is your favorite part of your job?

Installation of Asian galleries, especially Chinese works on paper.

What do you dislike about your job?

Unsuccessfully searching for things in storage.

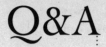

Profile: Museum Preparator

Q&A

How did you know you wanted to pursue this career?

The constant direct access to world-class art is addictive. There are constantly discoveries of clever tricks that artists and their assistants use to efficiently install and transport their work.

Describe how you got into this industry and how you got your most recent job.

I worked as a freelance contractor for Princeton University Art Museum and responded to an application.

If you weren't doing this job, what similar careers might you consider?

Teaching.

What professional publications do you read?

Art in America, Modern Painters, Artforum, Fine Woodworking, Art Papers, New American Paintings.

What advice do you have for others who would like to pursue this career?

Try to find work in a shipping/storage/installation company.

Museum Educator

Job Description: Museum educators design and lead educational programs and services in a museum. They often create and distribute educational materials and publications for museum visitors and may be responsible for conducting staff training sessions.

Training and Educational Qualifications: Museum educators usually have a bachelor's degree in an art-related field such as art education or art history.

Salary: Museum educators (museum education specialists) earn an annual salary between $32,627 and $59,103.

Significant Facts:

- Museum educators usually have a bachelor's degree in an art-related field such as art education or art history.

- Museum educators design and lead educational programs and services in a museum.

- Museum educators often create and distribute educational materials and publications for museum visitors.

INDUSTRY RESOURCES:

Museum Education Roundtable
P.O. Box 15727
Washington, DC 20003
Phone: (202) 547-8378
Email: info@mer-online.org
Internet: www.mer-online.org

American Association of Museums
1575 Eye Street NW, Suite 400
Washington, DC 20005
Phone: (202) 289-1818
Internet: www.aam-us.org

National Art Education Association
1916 Association Drive
Reston, VA 20191-1590
Phone: (703) 860-8000
Email: jfleming@naea-reston.org
Internet: www.naea-reston.org

Description, Training and Salary Source: Salary.com Salary Wizard® September 4, 2008. Used with permission.

Profile: Museum Educator

Name: Tanya Brown Merriman
Age: 34
Title: Associate Director of Teacher Programs, Museum Education Department; Visiting Instructor, Art Education Department

Employer: Art Institute of Chicago
Education: BA English. MAT English, EdD Curriculum Studies
Years in Industry: Education, 10; Museum Education, 1

CAREER LADDER:

Education Director/Assistant Principal, Small Public Arts Integrated High School
Curriculum Coordinator/Assistant Principal, Catholic Elementary School
English Teacher/Department Chair, Catholic High School

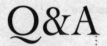

Do you know of which companies have the best internships in this field that are known to help launch a successful career?

Any large museums in large cities with education departments usually offer internships.

Where are the best cities to live to find jobs like yours?

Large cities like Chicago, New York and Los Angeles.

What is your typical day like?

A typical day for me includes a great deal of communication with my colleagues, collaborative organizations or schools and my students. I spend one to four hours a day in meetings, on the phone or answering email. The rest of the time is spent planning for the future, working to support my staff, researching particular pieces of art, and actually in the galleries of the museum. I attend programs that have been created by my peers so that I can learn more about the collection and more importantly, remain inspired so that I can share that inspiration with our visitors.

What are your job responsibilities?

Managing a staff of four; establishing and maintaining relationships with schools and other arts organizations; overseeing the creation of resources for the Teacher Resource Center; overseeing and conducting educational resources for teachers.

What is your favorite part of your job?

My favorite part of my job—and the part that is the most important to me—is being able to live out my own critical and social justice orientation through the work I am doing at the museum. This means looking at pieces of work and not only seeing the beauty and the aesthetic worth but also seeing the potential for teaching teachers—and through them, students—about ourselves, about social context, about dominant culture, about humanity and about the restorative qualities of art.

Profile: Museum Educator

Q&A

What do you dislike about your job?

I don't like that there is never enough time in the day to do all the things I want or need to do.

Have you had any turning-point or "light bulb" moments in your career that have helped you get to where you are today?

I have them all of the time, probably because I work directly with art, so the art inspires this. My most recent turning point was realizing that we need to create resources for teachers that are skills-based. In other words, we need to focus on literacy or critical thinking skills rather than resources that are collection-based. This would help teachers see the role of art in fostering these skills, as well as promote the universal qualities of collections, since people tend to gravitate towards what they like.

How did you know you wanted to pursue this career?

The museum has always been one of my favorite places on earth. As I developed my career as an educator, I always wanted to explore museum education but wasn't really even sure how I would go about doing that. I became involved in opening an arts integrated high school and after that experience was even more convinced of the potential for the arts to have a truly profound impact on cognition and learning. I was very fortunate to be hired by the museum, and I am so glad that they recognized the importance of bringing someone with an education background into this position.

Describe how you got into this industry and how you got your most recent job.

The school that I helped open developed an extensive partnership with the School of the Art Institute. Through that partnership, I was able to establish a number of professional connections with the school and the museum. When my position was eliminated due to budget cuts, I was extraordinarily lucky that I qualified for this position, and I got hired!

What do you consider your greatest professional accomplishment?

Right now I feel so happy to be at this place where my education and my work are really culminating. I am being challenged every day, and I really like feeling smart. Knowing that I am a part of a process that interrupts the potential for schools to be damaging places for children of color, but also working to make art such an integral part of helping children of color succeed and flourish, is incredible. Also, seeing my daughter at the museum and knowing that she will be raised among the art and all of the important things happening here is just amazing to me every day.

Profile: Museum Educator

Q&A

If you weren't doing this job, what similar careers might you consider?

If I weren't here at the museum, I would be thinking seriously about teaching at the college level. I might also want to investigate creating and publishing educational resources for children.

What professional publications do you read?

Art News, Art Daily, Rethinking Schools.

What advice do you have for others who would like to pursue this career?

Go into the galleries and spend time with the art. Becoming inspired and really thinking about and responding to the art requires a different kind of mind space that is slower, more deliberate and meditative than the place that we are when we are answering the phone and pushing paper. Don't feel guilty about going into that place. Exploit it.

Chapter 3

Careers for Dancers

Dancers often begin their training in childhood, usually by age eight for girls and by the teenage years for boys. Dance careers generally begin in the late teenage years or in early adulthood. Because of dancing's strenuous physical demands, professional dancers usually retire by their thirties and often pursue second careers. Some remain in the field by teaching dance or becoming choreographers. Others change careers entirely.

In the world of professional dance, dancers may work in several different settings, including ballet companies, modern dance companies, musical theater productions on and off-Broadway, opera companies, and in commercials, television shows and motion pictures. Each type of dance requires expert training in that particular style. In general, ballet dancers have the shortest careers among all types of dancers.

Employment for professional dancers is often seasonal and many work in other jobs to supplement their income. Off-season jobs include teaching dance or performing as a guest artist with another dance company. In recent years, many dancers have become certified to teach Pilates, the now-popular fitness technique. Dancers have been aware of Pilates for decades; since it has become mainstream, many have used the skills that they have acquired as dancers to transition into teaching Pilates. This is sometimes a stream of part-time income (or can become a full-time second career).

There are several career paths related to dance that may interest dancers once they stop performing or if they decide not to become performers. These somewhat different vocational paths can include choreography, dance education, dance therapy, physical therapy specializing in treating dancers, teaching Pilates, or working in arts administration for a dance organization or company, which is described in the last chapter of this book.

Choreographer

Job Description: Dancers work with choreographers who create new dances and develop new interpretations of existing ones. Because dance routines are original to choreographers, they instruct performers at rehearsals and teach the dance moves that will achieve the desired effect. In addition, choreographers are often involved in auditioning performers.

Training and Educational Qualifications: Choreographers typically are experienced dancers with years of practice working on stage. Through their performances as dancers, they develop reputations that often lead to opportunities to choreograph productions.

Job Outlook: Choreographers face intense competition for jobs. Only the most talented find regular employment. The public's continued interest in dance will sustain larger dance companies, but funding from public and private organizations is not expected to keep pace with rising production costs. For many small and midsize organizations, the result will be fewer performances and more limited employment opportunities.

Salary: Median annual earnings of salaried choreographers are $34,660. The middle 50 percent earn between $21,910 and $49,810. The lowest 10 percent earn less than $15,710, and the highest 10 percent earn more than $64,040.

Significant Facts:

- Choreographers create original dances and develop new interpretations of existing dances.

- Dancers and choreographers face intense competition; only the most talented find regular work.

- Choreographers typically are experienced dancers with years of practice working on stage.

INDUSTRY RESOURCES:

Society of Stage Directors and Choreographers
1501 Broadway, Suite 1701
New York, NY 10036-5653
Phone: (800) 541-5204 or (212) 391-1070
Email: info@ssdc.org
Internet: www.ssdc.org

Profile: Choreographer

Name: Amy	**Employer:** Amy Marshall Dance Company
Age: 36	
Title: Choreographer and Artistic Director	**Education:** BA Dance and Theater
	Years in Industry: 14 years

CAREER LADDER:

Dancer with H.T., Chen, Parsons Dance Company, Cortez and Co., and Taylor 2; Founder/ Choreographer/Artistic Director/Dancer with Amy Marshall Dance Company

Q&A

Did you have an internship in this field prior to starting your job?

In 1991 I had an internship at a dance company that is no longer in existence (CoDanceCo). It was a small company with only two staff members, so they needed assistance with office administrative work. I also helped them with their gala opening night performance reception.

Do you know which companies have the best internships in this field that are known to help launch a successful career?

None really help to launch a career; it's the audition that counts. I recommend interning with a company that you may have interest in—a company in which you would like to be a member—and use it as a net-working tool. You will still have to audition, but at least they will know who you are.

Where are the best cities to live to find jobs like yours?

One can be a choreographer in any city, but some have found that New York City has the most opportunities to show their work. Many dancers choose location depending on companies, i.e., which ones they feel will do their work justice.

What is your typical day like?

Every day is different, but I will usually have the following activities: personal training a client, morning or evening at his or her home, rehearsal with the company from 12:00 p.m. to 3:00 or 4:00 p.m. And somewhere in between all that, I make phone calls to presenters in an effort to get bookings. I also invite the press, book agents and donors to attend showcases and performances. I organize upcoming self-presented shows, take a ballet class and go to the gym before my day is done.

What are your job responsibilities?

I do personal training, teach at Hofstra University and choreograph for the company.

What is your favorite part of your job?

Putting on a show and having the dancers and audience members alike feel as if they have experienced something they've never experienced before—a sense of revelation and elation.

Profile: Choreographer

Q&A

What do you dislike about your job?

Not enough money to pay for a full-time administrative staff and not enough to pay the dancers full-time.

Have you had any turning-point or "light bulb" moments in your career that have helped you get to where you are today?

No, it has always been a drive within me. I knew from my first show that I had a mission as a choreographer and as a leader. Every time I stray from it, I have been pulled back by a deep force and connection. It has never been one thing, but an underlying feeling that I have to listen to; otherwise I am not being true to myself.

How did you know you wanted to pursue this career?

I have known that I wanted to dance since I was 14 years old, but it took a while for me to actually consider choreography as a career. I left Taylor 2 in 1999 and received a call from the dance department chair of my alma mater. She asked me to choreograph a full evening-length show at the Goucher Summer Arts Camp. I gathered some dancers together and did the show. At the moment it was over, I realized that I was supposed to be doing this as a career.

How did you get into this industry?

I was drawn to this industry when I was in high school studying theater and dance, and I continued my studies in college. I went to New York City the day I graduated and started auditioning. That's how I started dancing professionally. And I got my most recent job by creating it for myself!

What do you consider your greatest professional accomplishment?

Choreographing and producing performances of great talent and true art, and especially having the dancers and audiences really enjoy it. I feel I have accomplished my goal when I see it all come together and everyone is left with a feeling of inspiration.

If you weren't doing this job, what similar careers might you consider?

Team building and team coaching for corporations.

To what professional associations do you belong and what professional publications do you read?

My company belongs to the Association for Performing Arts Presenters (APAP) and we have also been a part of South Carolina Dance Association (SCDA). I read *Dance Magazine* and *Dance Spirit*.

Profile: Choreographer

Q&A

What advice do you have for others who would like to pursue this career?

Be ready to get a strong business head together and don't get overwhelmed by wearing so many hats in the beginning. After you've put on one show, each one thereafter gets easier. Don't forget to have a sense of humor and try not to take things too personally. Meet each challenge and move on without getting a chip on your shoulder. The rewards will come, but they take time. You must build integrity before you get praise. And that comes through sticking it out—longevity has a lot to say for your worth.

Dancer

Job Description: Dancers work in a variety of settings and may perform ballet, modern, folk, ethnic, tap, jazz, and other popular kinds of dance. They also work in opera, musical theater, television, movies, music videos, and commercials in which they also may sing and act. Dancers most often perform as part of a group, although a few top artists perform solo.

Training and Educational Qualifications: Because of the strenuous and time-consuming training required, some dancers view formal education as secondary to actual dance instruction. Many dancers and dance teachers believe that dancers should have a foundation in classical dance before selecting a particular dance style. Ballet training for women usually begins at 5 to 8 years of age. Men often begin their ballet training between the ages of 10 and 15.

Job Outlook: Dancers face intense competition for jobs. Only the most talented find regular employment. Continued public interest in dance will sustain larger dance companies, but funding from public and private organizations is not expected to keep pace with rising production costs. Many small and midsize organizations will stage fewer performances and offer fewer employment opportunities.

Salary: Earnings from dancing are usually low because employment is part of the year and irregular. Median hourly earnings of dancers are $9.55. The middle 50 percent earn between $7.31 an hour and $17.50 an hour. The lowest 10 percent earn less than $6.62; the highest 10 percent earn more than $25.75 an hour.

Significant Facts:

- Many dancers stop performing by their late thirties, but some remain in the field as choreographers, dance teachers, or artistic directors.

- Most dancers begin formal training at an early age—between 5 and 15—and many have their first professional audition by age 17 or 18.

- Dancers and choreographers face intense competition; only the most talented find regular work.

INDUSTRY RESOURCES:

Dancers in the major opera ballet, classical ballet, and modern dance corps belong to the American Guild of Musical Artists; those who appear on television belong to the American Federation of Television and Radio Artists; those who perform in films belong to the Screen Actors Guild; and those in musical theater are members of the Actors' Equity Association.

American Guild of Musical Artists
1430 Broadway, 14th Floor
New York, NY 10018
Phone: (212) 265-3687
Internet: www.musicalartists.org

American Federation of Television and Radio Artists
260 Madison Avenue
New York, NY 10016-2401
Phone: (212) 532-0800
Internet: www.aftra.org

Screen Actors Guild
5757 Wilshire Boulevard
Los Angeles, CA 90036-3600
Phone: (323) 954-1600
Internet: www.sag.org

Actor's Equity Association
165 West 26th Street
New York, NY 10036
Phone: (212) 869-8530
Internet: www.actorsequity.org

Profile: Dancer

Name: John Michael
Age: 25
Title: Dancer
Employer: Alonzo King Lines Ballet

Education: North Carolina School of the Arts (4 years) and summer sessions at School of American Ballet, Pacific Northwest Ballet and American Ballet Theater (ABT)
Years in Industry: 7

CAREER LADDER:

American Ballet Theater Studio Company
American Ballet Theater – Corps de Ballet
Cedar Lake Ensemble
Lar Lubovitch Dance Company

The Washington Ballet – Principal Guest Artist
Trey McIntyre Project – Principal Dancer and
   General Manager
Alonzo King Lines Ballet

Did you have an internship in this field prior to starting your job?
Yes, I was a member of the ABT Studio Company. It was little pay but a huge responsibility right out of school. It provided me with a training ground to learn valuable skills essential to being in a professional company that are not taught in schools (i.e., artistic understanding, scheduling of time and energy, responsibility without an overseer).

Do you know which companies have the best internships in this field that are known to help launch a successful career?
Most major ballet companies have second companies that resemble an internship. Find the company/choreographer that you want to work with and see if they have a second company.

Where are the best cities to live to find jobs like yours?
It depends on the art that the individual wants to pursue. Most say that New York is the center of the dance world, but the craft of the art is deteriorating in that declining empire. The best cities in which to live and get a job are the cities that house the company/choreographer you most want to dance with.

What is your typical day like?
Morning ballet class from 11:30 a.m. to 1:00 p.m. and then rehearsals of current repertoire and creation of new choreographic works from 1:00 p.m. to 5:00 p.m.

What are your job responsibilities?
Creating. Dancing. Being "present," focused, and receptive so that art can be created.

What is your favorite part of your job?
Making art.

Profile: Dancer

Q&A

What do you dislike about your job?
Touring.

Have you had any turning-point or "light bulb" moments in your career that have helped you get to where you are today?
I knew that being in a large company such as ABT was counterproductive to the type of art and dancing I was longing to do. Large companies are warehouses of talent with little new growth or cultivation. For me, there came the moment when I realized I could not consider myself a dancer as long as I continued there, and I knew—no matter what the hardships might be financially—that I had to go out and find true inspiration, not just the status of being in ABT.

How did you know you wanted to pursue this career?
Creativity has many outlets. When you find the one that helps express your true essence, it is your duty to pursue it.

How did you get into this industry?
I attended the ABT summer intensive in New York, which led to a job in the ABT Studio Company out of high school and a position in the first company after six months in the second. After leaving ABT, I danced with Lar Lubovitch Dance Company (I had worked with Lar at ABT). I also guested with The Washington Ballet, performing works by Trey McIntyre. Trey McIntyre and I went on to form Trey McIntyre Project, now in its third year of touring.

I met Alonzo King (Alonzo King Lines Ballet) when he choreographed a piece on me while briefly dancing at the newly formed Cedar Lake Ensemble. In Alonzo I found everything I had been seeking in the art of dance: creative genius, but more importantly, a way of working that directly links to the soul and the truly important aspects of dancing.

What do you consider your greatest professional accomplishment?
The ability to continue growing deeper and deeper with my work.

If you weren't doing this job, what similar careers might you consider?
Arts management.

What professional publications do you read?
I read *Pointe* and *Dance Magazine* to check up on friends and current events, *Danceview* online for reviews, and Dance/USA's quarterly reports for management development.

Q&A

What advice do you have for others who would like to pursue this career?

Find what it is that excites you about this art—the reason dance first enticed you—and always be true to that. Never get sidetracked by quantifiable goals such as technique, money, status, fame or power.

Dance Therapist

Job Description: As defined by the American Dance Therapy Association, "Dance/Movement Therapy is the psychotherapeutic use of movement as a process which furthers the emotional, social, cognitive, and physical integration of the individual." Dance therapists work with individuals who have social, emotional, cognitive and/or physical problems. They work with persons of all ages in both groups and individually, acting as consultants and engaging in research. Because dance therapy is considered a part of the medical field, therapists usually receive insurance reimbursement for their services.

Training and Educational Qualifications: Many dance therapists have an undergraduate background or interest in dance. Those inclined toward the field must pursue a master's degree in dance/movement therapy, which is the minimal educational requirement to becoming a dance therapist. The American Dance Therapy Association grants the designation of "Dance Therapists Registered (DTR)" to entry-level dance/movement therapists who have a master's degree and have completed 700 hours of a supervised clinical internship. The designation, "Academy of Dance Therapists (ADTR)", is reserved for experienced dance therapists and is awarded only after DTRs have completed 3,640 hours of supervised clinical work in an agency, institution or special school, with additional supervision from an ADTR.

Job Outlook: Because dance therapy is a newer profession, current information on a job outlook is difficult to ascertain. As the profession continues to grow, jobs are likely to continue to be available.

Salary: Salaries vary according to geographic regions.

Significant Facts:

- Dance therapy is practiced in numerous settings, including mental health rehabilitation, medical, educational, nursing homes, day care, forensics, disease prevention, and health promotion programs and in private practice.

- A master's degree in dance/movement therapy is required to enter the profession.

- Dance therapists usually receive insurance reimbursement.

INDUSTRY RESOURCES:

American Dance Therapy Association
2000 Century Plaza, Suite 108
10632 Little Patuxent Parkway
Columbia, MD 21044
Phone: (410) 997-4040
Email: info@adta.org
Internet: www.adta.org

Profile: Dance Therapist

Name: Susan Kierr
Age: 65
Title: Dance/Movement Therapist
Employer: Tulane University Hospital

Education: BA Psychology, MA Expressive Therapy
Years in Industry: 35

CAREER LADDER:

Creative dance instructor, dance/movement therapist, activity director, team manager, dance/movement therapy supervisor, dance/movement therapy consultant.

Do you know which companies have the best internships in this field that are known to help launch a successful career?

The universities that offer graduate dance therapy programs require—and usually help arrange—internships for their students.

Where are the best cities to live to find jobs like yours?

It was easier to find my kind of work when I lived in Boston than later when I moved to New Orleans years ago, but that is changing.

What is your typical day like?

On any given day, it is likely that I have spent four to six hours moving and dancing or meeting with other professionals who are involved with the same cases. I also document in hospital records in connection to the cases I see.

What are your job responsibilities?

With hospital work, I do dance groups and document the individual cases in their charts.

What is your favorite part of your job?

Dancing with people and watching them "light up."

What do you dislike about your job?

Dancing with people and seeing their injuries or illnesses take over, so the joy never happens.

Have you had any turning-point or "light bulb" moments in your career that have helped you get to where you are today?

Yes, when I was teaching dance and I saw that many people seemed to gain a sense of well-being while in dance class. I realized this was more important to me than if they became more accomplished in the technology of dance. It seemed like therapy and then I learned that dance therapy existed as a form of psychotherapy, so I began to go in that direction.

Profile: Dance Therapist

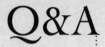

How did you know you wanted to pursue this career?

I always felt better when I danced and I wanted a career that allowed me to help other people feel better.

How did you get into this industry?

I met a doctor who listened to my story about dance and invited me to work with his patients. That was the beginning. Today, I live in a part of the country that has suffered a natural disaster; I live in Louisiana, post-Hurricane Katrina. I have been working with children whose parents asked me to help the kids manage anxiety as the next hurricane season came and went.

What do you consider your greatest professional accomplishment?

I have published articles and I've served on the board of the American Dance Therapy Association. I also introduced the concept of dance/movement therapy to several hospitals where it had never been done; that made me feel like a pioneer in my field.

If you weren't doing this job, what similar careers might you consider?

Probably social work.

To what professional associations do you belong what professional publications do you read?

American Dance Therapy Association. I read their journal and their Web site.

What advice do you have for others who would like to pursue this career?

It is not likely that this career will lead to the earning of high salaries but it is extremely rewarding.

Pilates Instructor

Job Description: The Pilates method is a physical movement program designed to stretch, strengthen and balance the body through postural symmetry, breath control, and muscular flexibility. There are two basic forms of Pilates: one is through group or "mat" classes and the other is through individual or group instruction on various pieces of equipment, often referred as "apparatus" work.

Training and Educational Qualifications: The most important characteristic that an employer looks for in a new group fitness instructor is the ability to plan and lead a class that is motivating and safe. Most organizations encourage their group instructors to become certified, and many require it. As recently as 1995, The Pilates Method Alliance created the first nationally recognized legal certification for the Pilates method. Prior to the creation of the Pilates Method Alliance, only former students of Josef Pilates himself, the creator of the Pilates technique, taught and trained Pilates instructors in the Pilates Studio in New York City. (Nationally recognized personal trainer and group exercise instructor certifications do not qualify instructors to teach the Pilates method.)

Job Outlook: Employment of fitness workers is expected to increase much faster than the average for all occupations through 2016 as an increasing number of people spend more time and money on fitness. Businesses are likewise recognizing the benefits of health, fitness, and wellness programs for their employees.

Salary: Median annual earnings of personal trainers and group exercise instructors are $25,910. The middle 50 percent earn between $18,010 and $41,040. The bottom 10 percent earn less than $14,880 while the top 10 percent earn $56,750 or more.

Significant Facts:

- Many group fitness and personal training jobs are part time, but workers can increase their hours by working at several different facilities or in clients' homes.

- Night and weekend working hours are common.

- Most fitness workers need to be certified.

- Employment prospects are expected to be good because of rapid growth in the fitness industry.

INDUSTRY RESOURCES:

The Pilates Method Alliance
P.O. Box 370906
Miami, FL 33137-0906
Phone: (305) 573-4946
Internet: www.pilatesmethodalliance.org
Email: info@pilatesmethodalliance.org

Profile: Pilates Instructor

Name: Karen
Title: Pilates Instructor and Founder of Studio Body Logic

Education: BFA Dance, graduate work in dance
Years in Industry: 12

CAREER LADDER:

Dancer, Dallas Ballet, Fort Worth Ballet and Washington Ballet
Corp Member, Milwaukee Ballet
Pilates instructor and studio owner

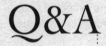

Did you have an internship in this field prior to starting your job?

I completed the Pilates Studio certification program with Romana Kryzanowska, the world-renowned protégé of Joseph Pilates of New York. This training is an equivalent to an internship. The entire program was held in New York City. At that time I was able to go to New York on long weekends and most of a summer to complete the program. In total, it ended up being about 800 hours of training.

Do you know which companies have the best internships in this field that are known to help launch a successful career?

To get certified in the Pilates technique, you will enter a comprehensive training program. But first, you must have prerequisite hours of Pilates instruction, a certain amount of time spent on mat work and apparatus work. Plus, you have to have the work in your body, an understanding of the exercises, and the history behind the work. The actual number of hours of the training program is estimated to be between 600 and 700, but it easily works out to be over 800 hours. There are many new training programs that have opened in the past five years; in fact, there is no one certifying center or program, and this makes it hard to find a good instructor. It was easier to know you were getting the right training years ago when I did it. In my opinion, training at The Pilates Studio was the best. Apprentices teach, observe, and practice at studios during their training program.

Where are the best cities to live to find jobs like yours?

I have always believed that if you are a good teacher, students will come. In fact, people will seek out good instruction, regardless of factors such as other studios or how small the town is. The Pilates boom happened about five years ago, and many people these days are interested in Pilates.

What is your typical day like?

I spend a couple of days a week mainly doing office work. Three days a week, I teach at one of the two studio locations. I manage a staff of 22 faculty and four office personnel; six are full-time and the others are part-time employees.

Profile: Pilates Instructor

Q&A

What are your job responsibilities?

There are 20 million things you have to do as a part of running a small business. Basically, there are three parts of my job: teaching, working with the apprentices, and the business aspects of the studio. When you have your own small business, you do a little of everything, even things like sweeping the floors and empting the trash—a lot of little things go into your day that are not always glamorous. People always think having your own store-front business is fun and lucrative. What they don't see is the overhead of running a storefront and that you are totally responsible for the business 24-7. There are no vacations when you have your own business. Regardless of how great your staff may be, you are the one leading it. When things go wrong financially or otherwise, it will be the owner not drawing a salary or working a 70-hour week. I had no idea regarding the overhead and constant responsibility a small service business requires when I started my studio.

What is your favorite part of your job?

Teaching.

What do you dislike about your job?

When I have to have a conversation with faculty or staff members about a situation or problem that they need to address. It can be a weekly occurrence with a large staff and it is the hardest part of my job.

Have you had any turning-point or "light bulb" moments in your career that have helped you get to where you are today?

I had a turning point, but it wasn't a sudden moment. I went to NYC and took Pilates classes at two studios as a part of recovering from a dance injury. I wanted to meet people in the certification program. I met people at The Pilates Studio, which is what it was called then. I was a union dancer and I was given a scholarship through Career Transitions for Dancers to pay for my Pilates certification. And it just felt right.

How did you know you wanted to pursue this career?

My decision to become a Pilates instructor was influenced by circumstances—one day I was dancing, then I was injured, and my career was over the next day. It was a tough time in my life because I lost a wonderful career, the fulfillment of a life long dream. It broke my heart. Then I found Pilates. To have something else that is very fulfilling, that I am passionate about, and that I can use to help people is really incredible.

How did you get into this industry?

I was a ballet dancer with the Dallas Ballet, Fort Worth Ballet, Milwaukee Ballet and Washington Ballet. I sustained an injury to my knee and even after a couple of years of physical therapy, I could not dance

Q&A

again. In fact, I walked with a cane or crutches for most of the two years.

Pilates helped me. I started with mat work and slowly started doing apparatus work that helped my injury. So I decided to get certified. I was in a graduate dance program and was planning to teach dance. I never planned to open a studio, but I started teaching a few students and things just grew on their own.

What do you consider your greatest professional accomplishment?

Being a dancer—it was a hard road to get to there.

If you weren't doing this job, what similar careers might you consider?

I'd still be a dancer or teach dance.

To what professional associations do you belong and what publications do you read?

I belong to Power Pilates and the Pilates Method Alliance. I read *Pilates Style*.

What advice do you have for others who would like to pursue this career?

Find a really good training program, preferably a training program that is national or internationally based. A large program gives you an expanded network of people to be involved with. Try to study with someone who worked with Joseph Pilates himself—they are scattered in different parts of the country so if you search thoroughly, you just might find one and that is best training there is.

Physical Therapist for Dancers

Job Description: Physical therapists provide services that help restore function, improve mobility, relieve pain, and prevent or limit permanent physical disabilities from injuries or disease. Therapists examine patients' medical histories and then test and measure their strength, range of motion, balance, coordination, posture, muscle performance, respiration, and motor function. Based on their findings for each client, physical therapists develop plans describing a treatment strategy, its purpose, and the anticipated outcome.

Training and Educational Qualifications: All states require physical therapists to graduate from an accredited physical therapist educational program and then pass a licensure examination before they can practice. Physical therapist programs seeking accreditation are required to offer degrees at the master's degree level and above, in accordance with the Commission on Accreditation in Physical Therapy Education. Besides classroom and laboratory instruction, students receive supervised clinical experience.

Job Outlook: Employment of physical therapists is expected to grow much faster than the average for all occupations through 2016. The impact of proposed federal legislation imposing limits on reimbursement for therapy services may adversely affect the short-term job outlook for physical therapists. However, the demand for physical therapists should continue to rise as growth in the number of individuals with disabilities or limited function spurs demand for therapy services.

Salary: Median annual earnings of physical therapists are $66,200. The middle 50 percent earn between $55,030 and $78,080. The lowest 10 percent earn less than $46,510, and the highest 10 percent earn more than $94,810.

Significant Facts:

- Employment is expected to increase much faster than the average for other occupations, as growth in the number of individuals with disabilities or limited functioning will continue to impact the demand for therapy services.

- Job opportunities should be particularly good in acute hospital, rehabilitation, and orthopedic settings.

- Nearly 6 out of 10 physical therapists work in hospitals or in physical therapy offices.

INDUSTRY RESOURCES:

American Physical Therapy Association
1111 North Fairfax Street
Alexandria, VA 22314-1488
Phone: (703) 684-2782 or (800) 999-2782
Internet: www.apta.org

International Association for Dance Medicine and Science
Department of Dance
1214 University of Oregon
Eugene, OR 97403-1214
Phone: (541) 465-1763
Internet: www.iadms.org

Profile: Physical Therapist for Dancers

Name: Vanessa	**Education:**
Age: 32	**BA Sociology**
Title: Senior Physical Therapist	**MS Physical Therapy**
Employer: PT Plus (private practice) and Harkness Center for Dance Injuries (non-profit)	**DPT (Doctorate of Physical Therapy)**
	Years in Industry: 5

CAREER LADDER:

Staff physical therapist and certified Pilates instructor

Did you have an internship in this field prior to starting your job?

Most internships in this field are a part of physical therapy school. My last one was at The Harkness Center for Dance Injuries. I also volunteered with the organization for several months prior to starting graduate school. Upon completion of the program, I began working at the Hospital for Joint Diseases, the organization through which Harkness functions. I started a dance mentorship/fellowship there; this was a paid internship in which we learned advanced manual therapy skills, backstage/triage protocols, taping, research, etc.

Do you know which companies have the best internships in this field that are known to help launch a successful career?

Harkness definitely has the best mentorship program that I know of. So much time, attention, and detail was put into the most specific aspects of dance medicine. I know of no other organization that has this commitment to training. They make sure the therapists all have a cohesive body of knowledge.

Where are the best cities to live to find jobs like yours?

Any place where there is a concentration in the arts. All performing artists have occupational hazards that must be addressed, preferably by a therapist trained in dance medicine. New York City is the mecca for performing artists, but I would also think other large progressive cities might have a need for these kinds of services, especially any city with a major ballet company.

What is your typical day like?

I work 7:30 a.m. to 4:00 p.m. I take a client every 30 minutes and work with him or her one-one-one, hands on. After that, the patient can start prescribed exercises that continually change and advance as I begin working with the next client. I take a one-hour lunch but much of this is used for medical chart documentation, progress notes to doctors and keeping up with insurance authorizations.

Profile: Physical Therapist for Dancers

Q&A

What are your job responsibilities?

- Full evaluation and assessment of musculoskeletal disorders.

- Create plan of care to address the dysfunction.

- Follow up with MD regarding prognosis and plan of care.

- Keep up with insurance authorization with the help of our office manager, write progress notes to obtain more visits from insurance company.

- Return client to sport/activity/performance with enhanced sense of well being and better understanding of anatomy and prevention of future injury.

What is your favorite part of your job?

I love how every new patient is completely different. I feel a little like a detective because I listen and look for all the clues and then try to put the big picture together. I love creating an individualized plan of care and watching that plan take shape as the patient begins to feel better.

What do you dislike about your job?

I dislike all the paperwork. Insurance companies have made it very difficult for us. We spend more and more time sitting and documenting when the time could be better used with one-on-one patient interaction. Multi-tasking sometimes is overwhelming. Often there are four people that I am watching at once, and keeping track of what each one of them is doing sometimes feels daunting and exhausting.

How did you know you wanted to pursue this career?

I wanted to pursue a career that involved motion and movement and I knew that I did not want to sit at a desk all day long. I was dancing in New York City and was getting a little tired of not knowing when the next paycheck was coming. Actually, I never meant to end my dance career; I just wanted to have a backup plan. But now I am so happy with my career choice.

How did you get into this field?

I started volunteering at Harkness Center, then had an affiliation, and then got my first job there. Basically I just kept up good connections. When I volunteered, I tried to always be available for any sort of extra work. Remember, the people with whom you volunteer will be the ones you ask to write your recommendation to get into school.

Profile: Physical Therapist for Dancers

Q&A

What do you consider your greatest professional accomplishment?

Completing the doctorate of physical therapy and completing the Harkness Dance Fellowship. Both were grueling because they were on top of a full-time job.

If you weren't doing this job, what similar careers might you consider?

Pilates instructor, massage therapist, personal trainer, medical doctor, osteopath, nutritionist, yoga instructor.

To what professional associations do you belong?

American Physical Therapy Association (APTA), International Association of Dance Medicine and Science (IADMS), and Pilates Method Alliance (PMA).

What advice do you have for others who would like to pursue this career?

Pursue volunteer work in a number of types of physical therapy. There are many different specialties that it's important to check them all out. In fact, during my training, I was worried at one point that I had picked the wrong field. I had an affiliation at a nursing home and we did the same thing day after day with each and every single patient. But then I learned there were jobs like the one I now have, which involves creating individualized plans of care for many different clients.

What I like about the field of orthopedic manual therapy and physical therapy in general is the amount of creativity it affords the therapist. Nothing is set in stone. It is up to the practitioner to design a plan of care that will best reach the patient's goals. This could never be the same for each and every person because we are all individuals.

Also, don't lose hope if you have a sub-par experience when you are out in the field. You can make your practice your own by respecting your own sense of creativity and movement sense. A less than exciting affiliation is all part of the learning experience.

Don't worry if you are not a science nerd. The serious science courses in graduate school all relate to the human body, and as a dancer or future physical therapist, this is extremely interesting information. Don't let a lack of love for the hard sciences deter you from pursuing a more scientific profession like physical therapy as opposed to massage, yoga, or Pilates.

Dance Education: Dance Teacher (K-12)

Job Description: Dance teachers work in private schools with dance departments or in public school systems in states that offer dance teacher positions and dance teacher certification. They teach various forms of dance to students of all ages, choreograph dance pieces for performance, direct rehearsals, and organize performances for the community.

Dance teachers can also become dance studio owners or they can own/manage privately run schools of dance. They are responsible for hiring staff and faculty, maintaining studio space and producing recitals. Studio owners are typically dancers themselves, as well as trained dance instructors.

Training and Educational Qualifications: Requirements for regular licenses to teach kindergarten through grade 12 vary by state. Most states with dance teacher certification require dance teachers to have a bachelor's degree in dance and to have completed an approved teacher training program with a prescribed number of subject and education credits, as well as supervised practice teaching. A number of states require that teachers obtain a master's degree in education within a specified period after they begin teaching. The National Dance Education Organization maintains a list of states that offer dance teacher certification in public schools. The list also shows where jobs in public school systems can be found. There is no specific education requirement for dance studio owners.

Job Outlook: Through 2016, overall student enrollment in elementary, middle, and secondary schools—a key factor in the demand for teachers—is expected to rise more slowly than in the past as children of the baby boom generation leave the school system. However, employment should continue to grow as fast as the average for teachers from kindergarten through the secondary grades. Projected enrollments will vary by region.

Salary: Median annual earnings of kindergarten, elementary, middle, and secondary school teachers range from $43,580 to $48,690; the lowest 10 percent earn $28,590 to $33,070; the top 10 percent earn $67,490 to $76,100.

According to the American Federation of Teachers, beginning teachers with a bachelor's degree earned an average of $31,753 in the 2004–05 school year. The estimated average salary of all public elementary and secondary school teachers in the 2004–05 school year was $47,602. Private school teachers generally earn less than public school teachers, but they may be given other benefits such as free or subsidized housing.

Significant Facts:

- In addition to conducting classroom activities, teachers oversee study halls and homerooms, supervise extracurricular activities and accompany students on field trips.

- Public school teachers must have at least a bachelor's degree in dance, complete an approved teacher education program and be licensed.

- Dance teachers may open their own private dance studios; dance studio owners have no educational requirement.

INDUSTRY RESOURCES:

American Federation of Teachers
555 New Jersey Avenue NW
Washington, DC 20001
Phone: (202) 879-4400
Internet: www.aft.org

National Education Association
1201 16th Street, NW
Washington, DC 20036-3290
Phone: (202) 833-4000
Internet: www.new.org

Dance Educators of America
P.O. Box 607
Pelham, New York 10803
Phone: (800) 229-3868
Internet: www.DEAdance.com

National Dance Education Organization
4948 St. Elmo Avenue, Suite 301
Bethesda, Maryland 20814
Phone: (301) 657-2880
Internet: www.ndeo.org

Profile: Dance Teacher

Name: Gary
Age: 56
Title: Teacher/Resident Choreographer
Employer: Montgomery Public Schools, Montgomery, Alabama

Education: BS Management of Human Resources, MEd Dance Anthropology and Performance

I was also a full scholarship student to the School of American Ballet and The Harkness Ballet.

Years in Industry: 50 (including all dance training)

CAREER LADDER:

Teacher/Resident Choreographer, Public Relations Manager, Scenic and Costume Designer, Booker T. Washington Magnet High School and Carver Creative and Performing Arts Center

Original faculty (Dance) and public relations, Alabama Governor's School for the Arts and Technology

Technical Advisor to the Tim Burton film Big Fish

Teacher, Resident Choreographer, Colorado Springs Ballet Academy and Company

Counselor, Teacher, Business Manager, Institutional Chef, Teen Challenge of the Rocky Mountains, Woodland Park and Crestone

Counselor, 700 Club, Dallas

Artistic Director, The Montgomery Ballet Company

Director, School of the Montgomery Ballet, Company

Artistic Director, The Fountain Dance Theater

Lead Dancer/Show Captain/Dancer, Le Folies Bergere, Tropicana Hotel, Las Vegas

Soloist/Principal Dancer, San Francisco Ballet

Dancer, Ballet Classico de Bellas Artes, Mexico City, Mexico

Dancer, Pennsylvania Ballet, Philadelphia

Dancer, Harkness Youth Dancers

Dancer, Virginia Ballet Company

 **Q&A**

Did you have an internship in this field prior to starting your job?
In public education, no. As a professional dancer, yes, with the Harkness Ballet of New York.

Do you know which companies have the best internships in this field that are known to help launch a successful career?
It depends on what you want to do (dancer vs. teacher/choreographer). If you want to dance professionally, nearly all companies have an apprentice program/company.

Where are the best cities to live to find jobs like yours?
One would think major cities, but that is not always the case. Frequently, the smaller cities and towns outshine the major metropolitan areas when it comes to dance and arts education.

What is your typical day like?
I get to school at 6:00 a.m. and do all my paperwork for the day; classes start at 8:15 a.m. I teach three 96-minute classes and have a 96-

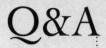
Profile: Dance Teacher

Q&A

minute planning period. Class time also includes choreography. Additionally, there are after-school rehearsals and performances.

What are your job responsibilities?

I teach ballet, jazz, tap, choreography, design, computer design, and commercial art.

What is your favorite part of your job?

Creative work and choreography.

What do you dislike about your job?

The unending bureaucratic difficulties that go along with public education. A litigation mad society preys upon paranoid school systems.

Have you had any turning-point or "light bulb" moments in your career that have helped you get to where you are today?

My first principal asked me to write an essay that explained how a full-length ballet touched upon other areas of society, from the historical and anthropological aspects, to the theological and artistic. It was a life-changing moment and opened the door for all the awards that followed (Disney American Teacher Award honoree, Toyota International Teacher, and USA Today Team Teacher, to name a few).

How did you know you wanted to pursue this career?

I didn't. I was in a place where my back was against the wall and, quite literally, God stepped in and said that this was where I would go.

How did you get into this industry?

I've danced since I was six. Unlike most people who don't have a clue what they want to do, I knew at six that I was a dancer, and it is to that end that I've lived my life. A dancer is not just someone who performs but someone who teaches and creates as well. Real dancers are tour guides—they are capable of taking *anyone* anywhere because dance is the universal language!

What do you consider your greatest professional accomplishment?

My original choreographic, across-the-curriculum interdisciplinary works based on the lives of the Impressionists, including Toulouse Lautrec, Monet, and Degas.

If you weren't doing this job, what similar careers might you consider?

Ski bum! I'd make a great tour guide for a slope in Summit County, Colorado – or even at Disney World.

Profile: Dance Teacher

Q&A

To what professional associations do you belong?

Alabama Education Association; Alabama Dance Council; Alabama State Council on the Arts; International Dance Council, United Nations, International Network of Performing and Visual Arts Schools; Kappa Delta Pi, an International Honor Society in Education; National Education Association; National Dance Educators Association; Magnet Schools of America; and Phi Delta Kappa: The Professional Association in Education.

What advice do you have for others who would like to pursue this career?

If you are not an artist, then you are not a teacher! You *must* work creatively—otherwise you're nothing more than a mechanic.

Profile: Dance Teacher/Dance Studio Owner

Name: Jennifer

Age: 37

Title: Owner/Director, Dance Express LLC

Education: AS Early Childhood Education, BFA Dance

Years in Industry: Dancing 33 years, Teaching 20 years

CAREER LADDER:

Dance teacher assistant, dance supply store clerk, dance teacher, day care teacher, after-school dance program director, founder of dance studio/dance teacher

Did you have an internship in this field prior to starting your job?

At the time that I was going to school, they didn't call it an internship. I did, however, teach dance at a studio as an "intern."

Where are the best cities to live to find jobs like yours?

There are dance studios everywhere!

What is your typical day like?

My day starts with the administrative work that is a part of the business: make necessary phone calls; type up newsletters and attendance sheets; type choreography and class notes; do the business accounting; cut music; work on costumes; work on fundraising. Later in the day, I head to the studio, teach classes and then clean the studio from top to bottom.

What are your job responsibilities?

Everything: I am the owner, the director, a teacher, a choreographer, an accountant, the cleaning crew, office worker, seamstress, and the list goes on.

What is your favorite part of your job?

Teaching and choreographing.

What do you dislike about your job?

The grunt work like office paperwork and cleaning.

Have you had any turning-point or "light bulb" moments in your career that have helped you get to where you are today?

Yes, prior to college, I thought I wanted to be a professional dancer. But during college, I realized that I wanted to be a dance teacher at the local level. I wanted to be the first teacher to see the passion for dance develop in a student.

How did you know you wanted to pursue this career?

I have always known I would do something with dance.

Profile: Dance Teacher/Dance Studio Owner

Q&A

How did you get into this industry?

The story begins with my mother taking me to see the *Nutcracker* when I was two years old and my saying, "I want to dance, Mommy!" I have been dancing since then. About two years ago, an opportunity presented itself and my father helped me open my dance studio.

What do you consider your greatest professional accomplishment?

I hope it is still yet to come, but I have had quite a few students graduate from high school and pursue dance in college as I did. Some of them have gone on to have professional careers in ballet companies and performing in Las Vegas shows.

If you weren't doing this job, what similar careers might you consider?

If I weren't doing anything with dance at all, I would be working with youth in some capacity—most likely as a teacher.

To what professional associations do you belong and what professional publications do you read?

I belong to the Professional Dance Teachers Association (PDTA) and the International Tap Association (ITA). I read *Dance Teacher Magazine*, *Dance Spirit* magazine, and *Pointe* magazine.

What advice do you have for others who would like to pursue this career?

You have to really love it! There is not a lot of money in this profession.

Dance Professor (Postsecondary)

Job Description: Dance professors teach various levels of dance technique (ballet, modern, jazz, ethnic dance) and related courses which may include dance composition, dance history, dance education and dance kinesiology. Professors may also teach Labanotation, which is a written form of preserving choreography in community colleges, arts conservatories, colleges and universities.

Training and Educational Qualifications: Colleges and universities usually consider holders of the master's of fine arts (MFA) in dance for full-time, tenure-track positions, and it is usually expected that prospective dance professors also have professional performing and choreography experience. Sometimes positions are filled by dancers with esteemed careers but without formal degrees; in many cases, these positions are part-time but not always. There are very few vacancies for dance professors who focus on teaching dance history; those in this specialty usually have PhD degrees in either performance studies or dance history rather than the MFA in dance.

Job Outlook: Overall, employment of postsecondary teachers is expected to grow much faster than the average for all occupations through 2016. A significant proportion of these new jobs will be part-time positions. Job opportunities are generally expected to be very good—although they will vary somewhat from field to field—as numerous openings for all types of postsecondary teachers will result from retirements of current postsecondary teachers and continued increases in student enrollment. Many colleges and universities do not have dance departments so there are fewer dance professor opportunities available. However, compared to other academic disciplines, there may be fewer qualified applicants for available dance professorships. Most college dance departments focus on modern dance and as a result, there are often more jobs for those who can teach various levels of modern dance.

Salary: Earnings for college faculty vary according to rank and type of institution, geographic area, and field. According to a 2006-07 survey by the American Association of University Professors, salaries for full-time faculty averaged $73,207. By rank, the average was $98,974 for professors, $69,911 for associate professors, $58,662 for assistant professors, $42,609 for instructors, and $48,289 for lecturers.

Significant Facts:

- Opportunities for postsecondary teaching jobs are expected to be good, but many new openings will be for part-time or non-tenure track positions.

- Educational qualifications for postsecondary dance teacher jobs can be very specific (a teacher of modern, a teacher of ballet, or a teacher of dance education or dance history) depending on the subject being taught and the type of educational institution.

- An MFA plus professional performance and choreography experience is generally required.

INDUSTRY RESOURCES:

Office of the Society of Dance History Scholars
3416 Primm Lane
Birmingham, AL 35216
Phone: (205) 978-1404
Internet: www.sdhs.org

Profile: Dance Professor

Name: Jennifer
Age: 45
Title: Assistant Professor of Dance
Employer: University of Washington

Education: BFA Dance, MFA Dance
Years in Industry: 10 years as a professor, 12 years as a dance teacher, 27 years as a dancer and choreographer

CAREER LADDER:

Assistant Professor at University of Washington
Assistant Professor at University of South Florida
Teacher, Harrison Arts Center, Performing Arts High School
Professional Dancer and Choreographer

Did you have an internship in this field prior to starting your job?
I did not have a formal internship. However, I was given a teaching associateship as a part of the MFA program in which I participated.

Where are the best cities to live to find jobs like yours?
There isn't a specific best place to be a professor. It has more to do with the institution and when jobs are available.

What is your typical day like?
There is no typical day. That is what I love. Generally, we juggle teaching, research (both scholarly and creative) and service *every* day.

What are your job responsibilities?
I teach all levels of modern dance, teaching methods for undergraduates and graduate students, dance history, composition, improvisation, creative process. Choreographing for concerts is also part of my job. Additionally, I choreograph and/or perform on a national and international level, conduct research in my area, and I sit on committees from department, college, university, community and national organizations. Of course I meet with students regularly, and I serve as a graduate advisor and recruiter.

What is your favorite part of your job?
Teaching and contact with my students, but also, having the freedom to do the research I want to do.

What do you dislike about your job?
We have to teach too much, sit on too many committees, and run our program on no money. This is a problem all over the country.

Have you had any turning-point or "light bulb" moments in your career that have helped you get to where you are today?

There are too many to count. But I will say that when I lived in NYC and was running a dance company and dancing for many wonderful people, I was tired of the struggle of surviving there and thought about quitting. My father said, "You cannot see the path you are on. You need to trust it is the right one." I didn't quit. Now I have a job that is perfect for me, and I'm where I want to live. It is a gift.

How did you know you wanted to pursue this career?

I had no other choice. The career chose me.

How did you get into this field?

I began dancing in college in 1979 at UCLA when they had a dance program. The summer after my sophomore year, I went to New York City on a scholarship with a dance company and fell in love with NYC. I dropped out of school and lived there for seven years. That made me very marketable when I went back to school to finish my BFA and obtain my MFA. I received a full, $55,000 fellowship from OSU based on my professional experience. I chose to be willing to move "anywhere" for a job in my field and nearly died at a performing arts high school in the middle of nowhere, but that led to my first university job at a fantastic dance program at the University of South Florida in Tampa. That job led to my job here. I would not be here had I not paid "my dues" at the other jobs.

What do you consider your greatest professional accomplishment?

My students.

To what professional associations do you belong?

International Association for Dance Medicine and Science and National Dance Education Organization.

What professional publications do you read?

Journal of Dance Education and *Journal of Dance Medicine and Science.*

What advice do you have for others who would like to pursue this career?

With regard to teaching in higher education, a professor at OSU wisely said to his students, "You can work in this field two ways. You can move anywhere for a job and that will hopefully lead you to the job you want. Or you can move to a community where you want to live, invest in that community and work your way to a higher education institution."

Chapter 4

Careers for Musicians

Musicians usually have a passion for music at an early age, and performance can begin in early young adulthood. Some especially gifted young people start their music careers as children or teenagers. Individuals who wish to pursue a vocation in music can attend music conservatories that offer a performance degree in music known as a bachelor's of music (BM). Graduate study is pursued by many students to enable them to teach music in higher education settings. Degrees granted in music performance at this level are the master's in music (MM) and the doctorate of music (DMA).

Something unique to professional music is the tendency of many musicians to combine multiple talents in their careers. In many cases, there is no one set career path that they might have. A professional musician might be a composer *and* a performer or a teacher *and* an arranger. As a result, while some musicians do choose one career to make a living, many other musicians blend their talents in several areas. Also, many musicians offer private lessons to supplement their incomes while performing or teaching in pubic or private schools or at the college or university level.

In today's competitive entertainment environment, musicians must also be business savvy in terms of promotion of their music. It is important that they have at least a basic understanding of music production and recording contracts if they wish to have their music heard not only live, but also via recordings. For this reason, musicians interested in recording often seek representation from an agent or manager who might also assist them in business matters. However, the fast pace of technology (for example, the growing usage of downloading music) is quickly changing the music industry and today, many musicians are involved in producing music themselves. Oftentimes, today's artists are just as savvy—if not more so in some cases—than many agents or managers. Therefore, when such a musician does seek representation, he or she will be sure to choose someone who is knowledgeable about the latest trends in the industry.

Arranger

Job Description: Arrangers transcribe and adapt musical compositions to a particular style for orchestras, bands, choral groups, or individuals. They often write the parts for all the instruments that will play the composition as well as the score for any vocals. Components of music—including tempo, volume, and the mix of instruments needed—are arranged to express the composer's message. While some arrangers write directly onto staff paper, others use computer software.

Training and Educational Qualifications: Musicians need extensive and prolonged training and practice to acquire the necessary skills, knowledge, and ability to interpret music at a professional level. Formal training may be obtained through private study with an accomplished musician, in a college or university music program, or in a music conservatory. Courses typically include music theory, music interpretation, composition, conducting, and performance in a particular instrument or in voice. Music directors, composers, conductors, and arrangers need considerable related work experience or advanced training in these subjects.

Job Outlook: Overall employment of musicians, singers, and related workers is expected to grow about as fast as the average for all occupations through 2016. Most new wage and salary jobs for musicians will be in religious organizations. Slower-than-average growth is expected for self-employed musicians, who generally perform in nightclubs, concert halls, and other venues. Growth in demand for musicians will generate a number of job opportunities, and many openings also will arise from the need to replace those who leave the field each year because they are unable to make a living solely as musicians.

Salary: The median hourly earnings rate of musicians and singers is $19.73. The middle 50 percent earn between $10.81 and $36.55 an hour. The lowest 10 percent earn less than $7.08, and the highest 10 percent earn more than $57.37. Median hourly earnings are $23.37 in performing arts companies and $13.57 in religious organizations.

Significant Facts:

- Some arrangers write directly into a musical composition, while others use computer software.

- Arrangers need advanced training in music theory, music interpretation, composition and performance.

- Musicians need extensive and prolonged training and practice to acquire the necessary skills, knowledge, and ability to interpret music at a professional level.

INDUSTRY RESOURCES:

American Society of Music Composers and Arrangers
P.O. Box 17840
Encino, CA 91416
Phone: (818) 994-4661
Internet: www.asmac.org

Profile: Arranger

Name: David
Age: 32
Title: Self-Employed Orchestral Arranger

Education: BA Music, MA Composition
Years in Industry: 7

CAREER LADDER:

After graduating from college, I started as a music copyist—someone who prepares the sheet music players read. This is literally a case of taking the score and copying it by hand or nowadays, preparing the music electronically. It's steady, well-paid work but it's boring, stressful and creatively bereft. Luckily, it wasn't long before I got my first orchestration gig. Initially, I assisted other orchestrators and then gradually began to take on my own clients. Roughly 80 percent of my work is in the film and television industry and 20 percent is for classical-crossover and pop artists. What I do as an orchestral arranger varies immensely from client to client. For example, some composers produce very detailed electronic demos where it is a case of transcribing the music note for note, adding dynamics, articulations and phrasing, ironing out basic problems in the voice leading and tweaking timbral color. More typically though, a composer will provide you with something that requires a bit more work; you, as the arranger, are required to add (or subtract) harmonic, melodic and rhythmic elements as you see fit. As my business has grown, I have earned more clients by word of mouth and personal recommendation.

Q&A

Where are the best cities to live to find jobs like yours?

The hub of the film and television industry is Los Angeles. In the United Kingdom, London is the best city to live. However, once established, an arranger could live pretty much anywhere so long as he or she has access to an Internet connection since the basic material we work with is sent and received via email/ftp.

What is your typical day like?

It varies. I work from my home studio. Deadlines in film and television/commercial music can be very tight. There are long days. If there is a last minute rush, I can work 14 to 16 hours a day for weeks on end. But there are also periods when I have no work at all.

What are your job responsibilities?

Principally, to produce an orchestral score that reflects the composer's intentions. Insuring that the finished score is error-free is also extremely important so that the recording session can run smoothly.

What is your favorite part of your job?

Hearing the scores performed once they are finished. I spend months in a basement working with the music in my head. The culmination of all my effort is the recording session, working with world-class musicians, and hearing the music performed.

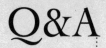

Q&A

What do you dislike about your job?

The hours are very tough. And it's hard work sometimes. It impacts on family and social time. I think an arranger has to be mentally tough to deal with the often rigorous schedule.

Have you had any turning-point or "light bulb" moments in your career that have helped you get to where you are today?

I haven't had any moments like that. It's been a gradual process. The depth of knowledge you're expected to have as an arranger is so vast that you can't do anything but continuously improve. If you get a phone call from a new client about an exciting project, it's a good feeling.

How did you know you wanted to pursue this career?

I didn't make a conscious decision to become an arranger. I was helping out other composers and realized I was good at it. I work in a niche market. In the United Kingdom, there are only a small number of arrangers who work at a consistently high level. I am one of the younger generation and although I've done well so far, I'm still working my way up.

What do you consider your greatest professional accomplishment?

My latest accomplishment that I am most proud of is working with Andy Price on the BBC's new production of *Robin Hood*.

If you weren't doing this job, what similar careers might you consider?

I might have gone into music therapy.

To what professional associations do you belong?

I am a member of the Musician's Union, British Writers' Music Council and the MCPS-PRS Alliance.

What professional publications do you read?

Film Score Monthly.

What advice do you have for others who would like to pursue this career?

Listen. Listen. Listen. Get out and hear orchestral performances. Play in orchestras yourself so you can experience how they work, how they read, how they interact with both good and bad music. Get scores out. Read relevant books such as *Instrumentation and Orchestration* and *The Study of Orchestration*. These books can be dry reading but if you use them in the right context, they can be very helpful. It's also expected

Profile: Arranger

Q&A

that you will have a decent knowledge of the relevant software programs. To generate work as an arranger, contact composers directly but be prepared to have a thick skin—some composers won't mind being contacted and others will. Also, do your own composing and arranging and try to get someone to perform it.

Composer

Job Description: Composers create original music such as symphonies, operas, sonatas, radio and television jingles, film scores, and popular songs. They transcribe ideas into musical notation, using harmony, rhythm, melody, and tonal structure. Although most composers and songwriters practice their craft on instruments and transcribe the notes with pen and paper, some use computer software to compose and edit their music.

Training and Educational Qualifications: Musicians need extensive and prolonged training and practice to acquire the necessary skills, knowledge, and ability to interpret music at a professional level. Formal training may be obtained through private study with an accomplished musician, in a college or university music program, or in a music conservatory. Courses typically include music theory, music interpretation, composition, conducting, and performance in a particular instrument or in voice. Music directors, composers, conductors, and arrangers benefit from considerable related work experience or advanced training in these subjects.

Job Outlook: Overall employment of musicians, singers, and related workers is expected to grow about as fast as the average for all occupations through 2016. Most new wage and salary jobs for musicians will arise in religious organizations. Slower-than-average growth is expected for self-employed musicians, who generally perform in nightclubs, concert halls, and other venues. Growth in demand for musicians will generate a number of job opportunities, and many openings will arise from the need to replace those who leave the field each year because they are unable to make a living solely as musicians.

Salary: Median annual earnings of salaried music directors and composers are $39,750. The middle 50 percent earn between $23,660 and $60,350. The lowest 10 percent earn less than $15,210, and the highest 10 percent earn more than $110,850.

Significant Facts:

- Some composers use computer software to compose and edit their music.

- Composers study music theory, music interpretation, composition, conducting and performance.

- Most new wage and salary jobs for musicians will arise in religious organizations.

INDUSTRY RESOURCES:

American Composers Forum
332 Minnesota Street, Suite East 145
St. Paul, MN 55101-1300
Phone: (651) 228-1407
Internet: www.composersforum.org

American Society of Composers, Authors and Publishers
One Lincoln Plaza
New York, NY 10023
Phone: (212) 621-6000
Internet: www.ascap.com

American Society of Music Composers and Arrangers
P.O. Box 17840
Encino, CA 91416
Phone: (818) 994-4661
Internet: www.asmac.org

Profile: Composer ~ TV/Film

Name: Wendell Hanes	**Employer: Volition, Inc.**
Age: 34	**Education: BA Modern Culture and Media**
Title: TV/Film Music Composer	**Years in Industry: 10 years**

CAREER LADDER:

After college, I became a freelance writer for YSB and SPIN magazine, chair stacker for Spike Lee lectures at LI University, cashier for Service Merchandise, production assistant for Blackside documentary film company, apprentice editor for 40 Acres and A Mule, apprentice editor for Vito Desario Editing, dialogue replacement editor, sound designer and music composer.

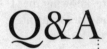

Did you have an internship in this field prior to starting your job?

I was hands-on and had to learn on the job. My boss told me I had to sink or swim. He was an editor and he gave me commercials that he was editing and asked me to create music for them. I had scored some of my own short films while I was in college, so I brought that intuition into the job and just created music based on pure instinct. I learned hints on music arrangement and structure from looking at other composers' reels and listening to advice from editors.

Do you know of which companies have the best internships in this field that are known to help launch a successful career?

Yes, basically any of the top music houses in the business. Amber music, Elias Arts, Sacred Noise, Volition, Inc., Duotone, JSM Music, Human Worldwide are some of the best.

Where are the best cities to live to find jobs like yours?

New York and LA are the two best places for composers who are interested in film work because those are areas where most productions take place. But I believe you can make your career happen everywhere if you are willing to travel and use the phone or Internet vigorously.

What is your typical day like?

If I have a commercial to do, I watch the commercial about ten times in a row and determine which instruments I'm going to need. If there are any instruments that I don't play, I have to call a musician in, for example, a xylophone player, singer or an upright bass player. Once I figure out what I need to make the commercial, I play the piano part, the bass part, the trumpet part and the drum part. If there is singing involved, I record the singers. Then I mix the music so it sounds great.

When I'm not scoring a commercial, I am on the phone networking, finding new contacts or writing press releases for commercials that I win. I am always thinking of creative ways to collaborate on future projects with clients. I believe in creating my own projects to score instead

Profile: Composer - TV/Film

Q&A

of waiting to be hired by someone else. I have written a children's feature animation and a movie script that I am currently shopping.

What are your job responsibilities?

Making as much music of top quality as possible and strengthening and creating new contacts.

What is your favorite part of your job?

Playing that first note that paints a full canvas of music—I really enjoy the process as much as the end result. I love creating something out of nothing, adding sound to silence, and creating a new musical space to live in where I'm surrounded by the melodies and harmonies of beautiful, colorful, inspirational and motivational textures of sound. I love getting into that zone with a piece of music I create, knowing that I have the power to take the music in any direction I want, just as a painter can do with one stroke of his or her brush. That's a great feeling.

What do you dislike about your job?

Deadlines that are ridiculously close like a few hours or overnight. People who hire composers can often give you a very short turn around time, but you have to abide by their rules if you want to keep up. In my business, you have to rush your inspiration. There's no time to wait for that falling star to jumpstart your creativity. The Mary J Blige's and Jay Z's of the world have the luxury of waiting until they are in the mood to write a song. They can take a week if they really want to. *Not in my business.* Clients have come up to me and said, "Can you write a hit song for our commercial campaign by tomorrow?" I have to say "yes" or they will move to the next person. So I rush to the studio and write music and lyrics, record the vocals with a singer, and mix it down basically in *half* a day because half the day has passed by the time they ask you to do it. Oh yeah, and it has to be a hit!!!

Have you had any turning-point or "light bulb" moments in your career that have helped you get to where you are today?

Yes, a car accident changed my television broadcasting career into a music career. I was house bound for an entire summer and my dad bought me a keyboard. I learned how to produce my own music that summer and discovered that music was my passion.

How did you know you wanted to pursue this career?

I kept winning commercials with music I created and I enjoyed the process as well. Success will make a believer out of you fast.

Describe how you got into this industry and how you got your most recent job.

I took a casual tip from a friend to meet a commercial director and after about 30 minutes, she recommended me. I interviewed with the

Q&A

company and they hired me as an apprentice editor and a "sound guy" because at that time there was no sound equipment—they just knew they wanted to fill a void in their company. Eventually, the boss bought me the equipment I needed to make music. I worked as a staff composer for about eight years and then formed my own company.

What do you consider your greatest professional accomplishment?

Being able to support my wife and daughter. Winning a Cannes Lion at the Cannes film festival—it's like the equivalent of winning a Grammy in the music industry.

If you weren't doing this job, what similar careers might you consider?

I'd be a script writer for television and film.

To what professional associations do you belong?

I belong to the American Federation of Musicians (AFM), the American Federation of Television and Radio Artists (AFTRA), the Association of Independent Commercial Producers (AICP), the Association of Music Producers (AMP), the American Society of Composers, Authors, and Publishers (ASCAP), and the Screen Actors Guild (SAG). Many of these associations are necessary in order to get paid.

What professional magazines/newspapers/journals/Web sites do you read?

I read *Hollywood Reporter, Adweek, Shoot Magazine, VIBE, Rolling Stone, Inked,* and *Billboard.*

What advice do you have for others who would like to pursue this career?

Take any job at a music house in your area that is offered to you—just get your foot in the door. You can be a receptionist and have your music heard by co-workers on a daily basis just because you're in the environment. Chances are that someone is going to like something you do if you're good. Then maybe that "someone" will give you a shot. And all you need is one shot to get noticed. That's what happened to me. It can happen to you. Also, know who your competition is, but don't be intimidated by them. Motivation and confidence breed success. Always create as if you have something to prove, even if it is only to yourself. Don't be scared. After all, it's just life. *Live it! Enjoy it! Create it!*

Conductor/Music Director

Job Description: Conductors lead instrumental music groups, such as symphony orchestras, dance bands, show bands, and various popular ensembles in performance. They audition and select musicians, choose the music most appropriate for their talents and abilities, and direct rehearsals and performances. Choral directors lead choirs and glee clubs, sometimes working with a band or an orchestra conductor. Directors audition and select singers and lead them at rehearsals and performances with the goal of achieving harmony, rhythm, tempo, shading and other desired musical effects.

Training and Educational Qualifications: Musicians need extensive and prolonged training and practice to acquire the necessary skills, knowledge, and ability to interpret music at a professional level. Formal training may be obtained through private study with an accomplished musician, in a college or university music program, or in a music conservatory. Courses typically include music theory, music interpretation, composition, conducting, and performance in a particular instrument or in voice. Music directors, composers, conductors, and arrangers need considerable related work experience or advanced training in these subjects.

Job Outlook: Overall employment of musicians, singers, and related workers is expected to grow about as fast as the average for all occupations through 2016. Most new wage and salary jobs for musicians will arise in religious organizations. Slower-than-average growth is expected for self-employed musicians, who generally perform in nightclubs, concert halls, and other venues. Growth in demand for musicians will generate a number of job opportunities, and many openings also will arise from the need to replace those who leave the field each year because they are unable to make a living solely as musicians.

Salary: Median annual earnings of salaried music directors and composers are $39,750. The middle 50 percent earn between $23,660 and $60,350. The lowest 10 percent earn less than $15,210, and the highest 10 percent earn more than $110,850.

Significant Facts:

- Music directors and conductors need considerable related work experience or advanced training in music theory, music interpretation, composition, conducting and performance.

- National Association of Schools of Music accredits more than 600 college-level programs in music.

- Most new wage and salary jobs for musicians will arise in religious organizations.

INDUSTRY RESOURCES:

Conductors Guild
5300 Glenside Drive, Suite 2207
Richmond, VA 23228
Phone: (804) 553-1378
Internet: www.conductorsguild.org

American Federation of Musicians
New York Headquarters
1501 Broadway, Suite 600
New York, NY 10036
Phone: (212) 869-1330
Internet: www.afm.org

American Orchestra Symphony League (ASOL)
33 West 60th Street, 5th Floor
New York, NY 10023-7905
Phone: (212) 262-5161
Internet: www.symphony.org

Profile: Conductor

Name: Jonathan McPhee

Title: Conductor

Employers:

Boston Ballet, Music Director/ Principal Conductor

Symphony by the Sea, Music Director

Lexington Symphony, Artistic Advisor and Principal Conductor

Longwood Symphony Orchestra, Music Director

Education: BM Juilliard, MM Juilliard, Licentiate of the Royal Academy of Music (LRAM), Royal Academy of Music, London

Years in Industry: 26

CAREER LADDER:

Aside from my current positions, I have been a guest conductor for dance companies, opera companies and symphony orchestras.

Dance Companies: *New York City Ballet, The Royal Ballet (England), Martha Graham Dance Company, Joffrey Ballet, National Ballet of Canada, The Australian Ballet, American Ballet Theater, Dance Theater of Harlem, Houston Ballet, and the Norwegian Ballet.*

Opera Companies: *Opera Boston, the American Opera Center in New York, and Boston University Opera.*

Orchestras: *BBC Scottish Symphony, Buffalo Philharmonic, The Hague Philharmonic, Rochester Philharmonic, San Francisco Symphony, Orchestre Colonne (Paris), the National Philharmonic Orchestra in London, the Danish Radio Symphony Orchestra, and the Bergen Philharmonic in Norway. As a Pops conductor, I have conducted the Boston Pops, the Colorado Symphony "Pops," and Radio City Music Hall's Grand Night for the Irish.*

Where are the best cities to live to find jobs like yours?

You have to be willing to travel and to be transitory as a conductor. Many conductors have relationships with several orchestras at once. Since it can typically take several guest spots over a period of 3 to 5 years to find the right fit between orchestra and conductor for a "permanent" position, the reality is that you need several positions to make sure that in transition you still keep an international or national presence. Early in my career, I had two apartments—one in Boston and one in New York—and I commuted between the two cities. You should not expect to live in one spot.

How many conductors are in the United States?

It depends on the level. There are really only about ten jobs in conducting at the top level in the United States, but only three or four of them are held by Americans. There are only four top jobs in conducting for ballet companies in the United States: New York City Ballet, American Ballet Theater, Boston and San Francisco Ballet. Basically, there aren't a lot of *top* jobs. However, there are more jobs in regional orchestras.

Q&A

What is your typical day like?

Every single day is different. I start the day by checking emails. But later I may have a morning orchestra rehearsal, an afternoon dance rehearsal, or I may have a finance committee meeting or another meeting because I am considered senior management with the Boston Ballet. You have to be quick on your feet because what you think you'll be doing in a day doesn't actually happen—there could be some kind of last-minute crisis like an orchestra committee problem. Just finding a couple hours of peace to study is a rare treat.

What are your job responsibilities?

I manage the music budget for the Boston Ballet, and I work with dancers in rehearsals to shape musical performances as they learn their parts so that when they get to the stage they are working in unison with me and the orchestra. I also manage the orchestra, deal with union issues that come up, and do auditions for orchestra vacancies and the substitution list. Additionally, I work with the board of directors and do fundraising. For the symphonic groups I work with, I do more budgets and fundraising, and I work with the Board of Directors on strategies for the organization. Of course there is programming, development of educational outreach programs, and the selection of soloists for performances. I also work with the marketing staff to identify the "hook" to pitch to reporters and to get media coverage to entice people to attend performances. All this is in addition to rehearsing and performing with the orchestra.

What is your favorite part of your job?

Rehearsing and performing.

What do you dislike about your job?

There are a lot of meetings that can be time-consuming and not always efficient.

How did you know you wanted to pursue this career?

I was about six years old and a college orchestra came to our school to perform a holiday concert. I remember looking at the person in front of the orchestra and surmising, "He's thinking the music and they are playing the music he is thinking," and I thought it was the coolest thing in the world. I came home and told my parents that I was going to be a conductor. I never let go of that dream. And at a young age, I determined what I thought I needed to learn to become a conductor. A first step was to be able to play an instrument as well as the people I would be conducting, so I made up my own program of study expectations. In addition to playing the piano, I started flute. After a while, I realized that the flute was the wrong instrument for me, and I switched to oboe. It turned out that I had a natural aptitude for the oboe. My family moved to England when I was twelve. I needed an oboe teacher so I walked into

Q&A

a music store and they gave me a list of names of people to call from the union book. I ended up getting the principal oboe of the BBC Orchestra as my teacher.

How did you get into this career path?

I finished high school early, which meant waiting a year before starting at Eastman School of Music where I had been accepted. Rather than wait the year, my teacher encouraged me to go to London and audition for the Royal Academy of Music. I was accepted.

Determined to make the most of my education, I double- or triple-majored all through my education. I started at the Royal Academy of Music in London studying oboe and conducting. At Juilliard I studied conducting, oboe and English horn. When I came out of Juilliard, I continued to pursue conducting, but I also took several major symphonic auditions on oboe and English horn. That resulted in my becoming the principal oboe of the New Jersey Symphony Orchestra. But I only stayed for one season. I had to prove to myself that I could hold a position and play in a major orchestra. But I really wanted to continue the pursuit of a conducting career. It was at that point that I had to make a choice between playing and conducting.

No one travels the same path to become a conductor. It's a combination of preparation and opportunity—preparing in the hopes that you will get a break and be ready at that point to make the most of it, and just taking every opportunity that arises while making your own way, then seeing in what unexpected directions you might be led. It was this combination that shaped the beginning of my career. I was working with the Royal Philharmonic Orchestra and freelancing in my last year at the Royal Academy of London when I was told I would either have to change my citizenship or go back to the United States after graduation. I was well on my way in England career-wise and the thought of having to leave was like having the rug pulled out from under me. I did decide to come back to America, which meant starting all over again since I knew no one in music in the United States. It seemed apparent to me that I had to get to Juilliard but it was too late to apply to programs that year. I spent the time waiting to be accepted into Juilliard obtaining college credits for basic required courses to transfer to Juilliard, assuming I would be accepted. I successfully got into Juilliard the next year. The two internationally recognized professional programs for conductors were only the Royal Academy and Juilliard at that time. My logic was that if I wanted to work as a conductor, I had to go where the people who were working in the field were teaching.

Have you had any turning-point or "light bulb" moments in your career that have helped you get to where you are today?

I have actually had several turning points in my career. The first was when I had to leave England and come home to the United States to start

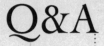

Q&A

my career over again from scratch. The second was getting sidetracked into the ballet world right after graduating from Juilliard, which was a total accident. My last concert at Juilliard was just before I graduated. I was the assistant conductor for the Juilliard Orchestra (assistant conductors typically rehearsed this orchestra but never actually conducted the orchestra in concert). The conductor who was engaged from Europe to conduct this concert was ill and had cancelled, and I was asked to fill in. When I finished the concert, a card was sent backstage that said, "Loved the performance. Please call me. Martha Graham." I thought it was a joke; I didn't think Martha Graham would come see a student concert. But I called and it was indeed Martha Graham! They were leaving on a State Department tour of Europe in a few months and she invited me to come with her company as the second conductor, which meant I would be preparing the orchestra before the company showed up in each city; and then when the company arrived, I'd go to the next city. Halfway through the tour, she switched conductors. After the tour, we headed back to New York and did six weeks at the Metropolitan Opera House in Lincoln Center. That's when George Balanchine, Director of the New York City Ballet saw me conduct and asked if I would like to conduct *Nutcracker* with NYCB. So that one concert at Juilliard changed the whole direction of my career—I was back on track to being a conductor again, this time in the United States.

What do you consider your greatest professional accomplishment?

There are many achievements I am very proud of, so it's hard to pinpoint one. The Boston Ballet Orchestra has recorded five CDs on its own label. Defying the odds, it actually earns money for the company. My favorite recording we have done together is *Romeo and Juliet*—I think it is the best out there.

If I have to choose one best accomplishment as music director, it's keeping live music as an integral part of Boston Ballet. Our culture does not fully comprehend the importance of the arts and support them as it should. Boston Ballet is the second largest musical organization in Boston, and there have been times when its future has been kind of dicey. We've always managed to pull it through one way or another.

If you weren't doing this job, what similar careers might you consider?

I can't think of anything else. I asked a mentor once, "Do I have what it takes to have a career in music?"

He gave me the best advice! He said, "If you can do anything else and be happy, do it. And if you can't do anything else and be happy, you have no choice, you have to pursue it (music)."

Q&A

I had a couple of different choices in my past. At one point, when I first came back the United States to re-launch my career before attending Julliard, I was taking acting classes and I got a lead in *Kiss Me Kate*. I could have got an equity card. I could have become an actor or gone to Julliard to pursue music—I could not do both. I decided to go to Julliard. I had too much invested in music. It was really the only choice for me.

To what professional associations do you belong?

American Society of Composers and Publishers (ASCAP), American Federation of Musicians (AFM), American Symphony Orchestra League (ASOL).

What professional publications and Web sites do you read?

Publications from the organizations I belong to as well as those from the National Association of Schools of Music.

What advice do you have for others who would like to pursue this career?

It's not going to come to *you*. You have to always learn as much as you possibly can about every facet of the arts world. Get your hands on anything that will allow you to grow as a communicator. Some conductors have this mistaken idea that it is all about them, but it's not. As a conductor, it's about the people in front of you and the people behind you—you are just moving the thoughts between the two groups. It really requires being aware that there is always more to learn and that your communication skills are what you need to work on. No one is going to come and find you. At the end of a conducting program, there may not be a manager standing outside your door. You have to keep working. You have to make your own opportunities.

Music Therapist

Job Description: Music therapy is an established healthcare profession that uses music to address physical, emotional, cognitive and social needs of individuals of all ages. While music therapy can meet the needs of children and adults with disabilities or illnesses, it can also improve the quality of life for persons who are well. Music therapy interventions can be designed to promote wellness, manage stress, alleviate pain, express feelings, enhance memory, improve communication and promote physical rehabilitation.

Training and Educational Qualifications: Students may begin their study on the undergraduate or graduate level. The entry-level curriculum includes clinical coursework and extended internship requirements in an approved mental health, special education, or healthcare facility. Upon successfully completing academic and clinical training, and subsequently passing the national examination administered by the independent Certification Board for Music Therapists, the graduate acquires the credential, Music Therapist-Board Certified (MT-BC).

Job Outlook: In 2005, seventy-nine new music therapy jobs were created, according to the American Music Therapy Association. A job outlook projecting into the future was not provided.

Salary: The 2006 Membership Survey of the American Music Therapy Association concludes that the overall average salaries of music therapists is $43,997 and the overall median salary is $40,000. Salaries increase with years of experience. For example, a music therapist with 1-5 years of experience falls into the average salary bracket of $34,977 but with more than 25 years of experience, music therapists' average salary is $60,493; however, salaries vary greatly and can be as high as $150,000.

Significant Facts:

- According to the American Music Therapy Association, the top four settings for music therapy work are in schools, geriatric and children's facilities, and in private practice.

- There is a concentration of music therapists in five states: New York, California, Pennsylvania, Texas and Ohio.

- A music therapy student must participate in a clinical internship program and take a comprehensive exam prior to becoming a certified music therapist.

- Music therapists must be skilled musicians as well as trained therapists.

INDUSTRY RESOURCES:

American Music Therapy Association, Inc.
8455 Colesville Road, Suite 1000
Silver Spring, MD 20910
Phone: (301) 589-3300
Email: info@musictherapy.org
Internet: www.musictherapy.org

Sources: American Music Therapy Association, Inc. Web site: www.musictherapy.org.

Salary data obtained and used with permission from the American Music Therapy Association.

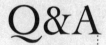

Profile: Music Therapist

Name: Tom Benson, MT-BC

Age: 46

Title: Music Therapist and Music Therapy Internship Director, Rehabilitation Services, Psychiatric Adult In-Patient Unit

Employer: Langley Porter Psychiatric Institute and Clinics, affiliated with the

University of California, San Francisco Medical Center

Education: BA Music Therapy, Board Certification, Professional Certificate in Guided Imagery and Music (GIM)

Years in Industry: 20+

CAREER LADDER:

Music therapist and music therapy internship director, music therapist, music therapy intern, psychiatric nurses aide

Q&A

Did you have an internship in this field prior to starting your job?

In 1986, I interned where I now am employed. In general, internships are accepted as a part of becoming a music therapist. Most internships are full-time for six months after degree requirements are completed. Seventy-three college and university music therapy programs follow the internship requirements set by the American Music Therapy Association.

Where are the best cities to live to find jobs like yours?

There are hotbeds that have a high concentration of jobs in music therapy. Since the concept of music therapy started in Kansas, the profession is recognized there and in the surrounding states in the Great Lakes region. New York, Pennsylvania, Texas, California, and Florida also have many jobs. But there are opportunities spread throughout the country. In some states, such as California, the state mandates that every hospital setting must have someone who does rehabilitation services (it can be dance/movement therapy, art therapy, occupational therapy, recreation therapy, or music therapy) and each hospital's culture makes that decision. As a result, there are plenty of jobs in rehabilitation therapy, including expressive therapies like music.

What is your typical day like?

I work normal hours, about 8:00 a.m. to 5:00 p.m. In the morning, I find out who the new patients are and determine to which rehabilitation programs they should be assigned. Then I have a meeting with other members of the hospital staff—nurses, social workers, and doctors (psychiatrists)—to talk about patients' treatment needs. Afterward, I lead a community meeting with all of the patients to welcome new patients and talk about plans for the day.

I do most of my work in group therapy. At 11:00 a.m. I have my group therapy session that deals with symptom awareness, coping skills,

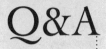

Q&A

and ways of managing the symptoms. In the afternoon, I have another group but it varies on which type it is—it could be another music therapy session, or a movement session incorporating Tai Chi or some other movement. I do a fair amount of talking therapy, music therapy, and bringing in other expressive art media with music, such as movement with music. Every day I also do written assessments of the patients' progress. That takes about one-third of my day.

What are your job responsibilities?

My primary responsibility is clinical: to provide individual and group therapy using expressive arts and music therapy. I also provide skill training for managing patients' illnesses. I'm a member of a multidisciplinary hospital team whose members strategize with other hospital staff to create rehabilitation plans for patients. I am responsible for the documentation of patients' treatment progress in their medical records. And in my particular job, I also manage the hospital's music therapy internship program.

What is your favorite part of your job?

The clinical working with patients and seeing them get better.

What do you dislike about your job?

I'm quite happy in the work that I do. I have a good position within my facility. My work is well understood by others because it is an intensive and supportive treatment environment. Because of the types of patients in our care—some of whom have severe illnesses—we see rapid progress and we get many "thank yous" from them and appreciation from others for our work when they see that progress has been made.

How did you get into this industry?

I was involved in music as a child; I played the piano and the guitar. In high school, I noticed I had an interest in human behavior without thinking of it as a career. I grew up in Berlin, Germany, and I have dual citizenship. I had planned to stay in Germany but I had an opportunity to go to college in the United States for one year. I wanted to do it just for the experience, even though I had no intention of staying for more than a year. I had to declare a major, and in my mind, it didn't matter what it was because I was only going to stay for one year. So I checked the "music therapy" box on the form. After the first year, I liked music therapy and I had enough funding to stay another year. By that point, I was halfway through the music therapy program. I returned to Germany to work as a nurse's aid for a year and then came back to the United States to complete my music therapy degree. When I met my wife, also a music therapy student, I decided to stay. I did my internship where I currently work. After that, I worked five years at a private psychiatric hospital. Then I was invited to come back and work at the site of my internship. And I am still here today.

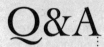
Profile: Music Therapist

Q&A

What do you consider your greatest professional accomplishment?

I have two things I would consider to be my greatest accomplishments: (1) My hospital is considered to have one of the best psychiatric settings in which music therapy interns can study—I am proud that we are held in such high esteem—and (2) the quality of the clinical work here. The joy and excitement that allow people to think and behave in a healthy way is part of the freedom I have to bring in the expressive arts in what I do.

If you weren't doing this job, what similar careers might you consider?

The ministry—it is related to expressive arts and mental health in that spirituality is embedded in therapy practice.

To what professional associations do you belong and what professional publications do you read?

I belong to the American Music Therapy Association. I read the *Journal of Music Therapy* and *Music Therapy Perspectives*.

What advice do you have for others who would like to pursue this career?

You have to be an excellent musician first before becoming a music therapist. You must have a love for music and excellent skills. In fact, you can't be a therapist first—you must be a musician first. The foundation has to be the expressive art. Then you learn therapy. If you don't have quality music in music therapy, then the experience of therapy through music will not happen.

Musician

Job Description: Musicians play musical instruments as soloists or as part of a group. Many musicians entertain live audiences in nightclubs, concert halls, and theaters featuring opera, musical theater, or dance; others perform exclusively for recording or production studios. A great many musicians are employed by religious institutions.

Training and Educational Qualifications: Aspiring musicians begin studying an instrument at an early age. Musicians need extensive and prolonged training and practice to acquire the necessary skills, knowledge, and ability to interpret music at a professional level. Formal training may be obtained through private study with an accomplished musician, in a college or university music program, or in a music conservatory. For university or conservatory study, an audition generally is necessary.

Job Outlook: Overall employment of musicians is expected to grow about as fast as the average for all occupations through 2016. Most new wage and salary jobs for musicians will arise in religious organizations. Slower-than-average growth is expected for self-employed musicians.

Salary: Median hourly earnings of musicians and singers are $19.73. The middle 50 percent earn between $10.81 and $36.55. The lowest 10 percent earn less than $7.08, and the highest 10 percent earn more than $57.37. The median hourly rate in performing arts companies is $23.37 and in religious organizations, $13.57.

According to the American Federation of Musicians, weekly minimum salaries in major orchestras ranged from about $700 to $2,080 during the 2004–05 performing season. Each orchestra works out a separate contract with its local union, but individual musicians may negotiate higher salaries. Top orchestras have a season ranging from 24 to 52 weeks, with 18 orchestras reporting 52-week contracts. In regional orchestras, minimum salaries are often less because fewer performances are scheduled. Regional orchestra musicians are paid for their services, without any guarantee of future employment. Community orchestras often have even more limited levels of funding and offer salaries that are much lower for seasons of shorter duration.

Significant Facts:

- Musicians, singers, and related workers held about 264,000 jobs in 2006. Around 35 percent worked part time; almost half were self-employed.

- Musicians, singers, and related workers are employed in a variety of settings. Of those who earn a wage or salary, almost two-thirds were employed by religious organizations.

- Competition for jobs is keen; those who can play several instruments and perform a wide range of musical styles should enjoy the best job prospects.

INDUSTRY RESOURCES:

American Federation of Musicians
New York Headquarters
1501 Broadway, Suite 600
New York, NY 10036
Phone: (212) 869-1330
Internet: www.afm.org

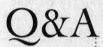

Profile: Musician

Name: John	**Employer: Madrid State Orchestra**
Age: 40	**and Chorus (Spain)**
Title: Principal Cello	**Education: BM Cello**
	Years in Industry: 19 years

CAREER LADDER:

Assistant Principal Cellist Windsor Symphony Orchestra, Ontario, Canada
Principal Cellist Windsor Symphony Orchestra, Ontario, Canada
Co-Principal Cellist Tenerife Symphony Orchestra, Canary Islands, Spain
Principal Cellist (ORCAM) Madrid State Symphony Orchestra, Spain

Q&A

Did you have an internship in this field prior to starting your job?

In the orchestra world, we gain work experience through freelance work: small contracts playing in smaller orchestras, filling in bigger orchestras on a sub list or just freelance gigs playing in pick-up groups. Internships are either rare on non-existent. We have auditions to fill in positions for a few months or up to a year.

I was in the Orchestral Training Program (OTP) at the Royal Conservatory of Toronto—it's the closest program to an internship that exists. We gave concerts every two weeks with professional directors so it's as close as you can come to working in an orchestra without already having a job. This program has since joined another artist program there and is called the Glenn Gould Professional School. It is really amazing due to the formation it gives (even business and Web skills).

Do you know which companies have the best internships in this field that are known to help launch a successful career?

There are a few orchestras that have internships or even schools for young players who can work in their orchestras. For example, in Madrid, Spain there is the OSM, Madrid Symphony Orchestra. They have a school that allows young players get experience playing in their orchestra.

There are two factors to getting a job in general. First is how well you play, which is relatively objective, and second is the factor of whom you know or who knows you. It definitely helps to win a job if you have lived in that city all your life or a significant amount of time, studied there, and have studied with the same musicians who are in the orchestras. You have made contacts and that networking can pay off. This might not get you a job, but it can help. And of course, a lot depends on the level of professionalism of the orchestra and who serves on the audition jury.

Where are the best cities to live to find jobs like yours?

Large cities in the United States like New York, Philadelphia, Chicago, Boston, San Francisco, Washington, DC, etc. Of course, in

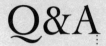

Q&A

Europe there are many more orchestras in comparison to the general population and Germany has an opera orchestra in just about every tiny village.

The problem—especially in the United States—is low turnover. For example, there are many cellists being pumped out of conservatories/universities every year and maybe a total of 200 orchestral cello jobs (a wild guess) that you can actually win to make a living. Musicians audition and audition until they get a job (or quit the instrument) and usually stay there until they retire. That means a particular position or job can be filled, and then remain filled, during a period of up to 35 years. That's why you get 200 players at an audition for one job. Europe is better in this sense because it's funded by the government. For example, in Madrid there are four full-time orchestras. Even Berlin and Vienna don't have that many anymore. Cultural programs are paid for by the government in Spain, and there is a conservatory system that hires many instrumentalists to teach throughout the country.

What is your typical day like?

I have rehearsal from 10:30 a.m. to 2:00 p.m. Then in the afternoon, I either have time off or a rehearsal. Or I might have a concert or we may play in the pit in the National Theater for Zarzuela. Even though we might not work as much as a big German, French or English orchestras (and they get paid a lot more as well), we do work a lot. But the hours are never regular so you can't know what you will do with total certainty in the months to come. I don't have a set day off. The big plus of my job is that I can ask for almost whatever time I want off, (without pay) and get it. That gives me the freedom to do other concerts, such as a program with my quartet, without a conflict.

What are your job responsibilities?

I'm head of the cello section. Besides administrative tasks, I also organize rotations (who gets a concert off or gets to work because there is a reduction in the amount of cellists needed). Basically all problems related to the section go through me. Besides this, I must have the repertoire for any given concert prepared at the first rehearsal with all solos assigned. It's also my job to have all the bowing put in (organizational markings we put in the part to play and phrase together within the cello section and with the other string sections) in agreement with the concertmaster. I lead the section—which implies that they follow me—while I have an eye on the conductor, the other on the concertmaster and the third eye on the rest of the principal strings.

What is your favorite part of your job?

The opportunities that have arrived through my job. I have played as guest soloist on a few occasions with my orchestra. Since my orchestra organizes chamber music concerts and contemporary chamber music

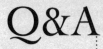

Q&A

through certain foundations, my string quartet, Cuarteto Breton, has played on these series a number of times. Imagine, I got paid to play Olivier Messiaen's *Quartet for the End of Time*, one of the most important chamber works of the first half of the 20th century. I couldn't get these kinds of opportunities in any other place.

What do you dislike about your job?

In my job, few musicians are dedicated or interested in trying to change things for the better (i.e. to raise the artistic level or even try to improve working conditions). They just want to receive their paycheck, go home and not have problems. Besides that, I would say that the hours are a dislike, since they are always changing or never set. I can't tell you what day of the week I have off because we have no official day off. You can work ten days straight, then have your time off; it's hard to organize your life or other activities.

Have you had any turning-point or "light bulb" moments in your career that have helped you get to where you are today?

Yes, a great turning point for me was getting to be an artist-in-residence at the Banff Center in Alberta, Canada. I was there for eight months with the sole purpose of studying cello in my studio in the mountains and learning from the special guests who came. One was Lluis Claret, a cellist who lives outside of Barcelona. I loved how he played—he has a very organic, relaxed manner of playing. So even though I had a job, I sold all my belongings and I moved to Barcelona to study with him. But it was worth it. From there, I won jobs that allowed me to stay.

How did you know you wanted to pursue this career?

We always had classical music playing at home. But it wasn't until after I first saw a live orchestral concert that I knew I wanted to play an instrument. At 11, I asked my Dad what I had to do to become a cellist, so my parents bought a cello and I started private lessons.

How did you get into this industry?

I knew that by age 17, if you weren't a soloist (as in a concert soloist who tours and plays concertos in different orchestras) already winning competitions, it wasn't likely that you would become one. I determined that playing in an orchestra was what was best for me and I wanted to be a principal cello. Before I became a professional, I was principal cello in many small semi-professional groups working freelance and in youth orchestras.

When I finished the Orchestra Training Program in Toronto, I landed a job as Assistant Principal Cello in Windsor Ontario, Canada. Since there was no Principal, I quickly started to play as Principal. This lasted until I went to be in Residence at Banff. There, as I mentioned before, I met Lluis Claret, decided to study with him and moved to

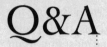

Q&A

Barcelona. I heard of a job for co-principal cellist in Tenerife which I auditioned for and won. Then I did a few auditions until I won the Principal job here in Madrid.

I've lived in Madrid for nine years. I doubt that I will ever leave because there isn't any other place in the world that I find more possibilities than here, at least for me. My opportunities for work come from Spain's resources: four full-time orchestras, many foundations who put on chamber music series, contemporary music, recording sessions and movie soundtracks.

What do you consider your greatest professional accomplishment?

I'm not sure that I have one accomplishment that is clearly above the rest. In general terms I would say that it is being able to have the opportunity to be invited as a soloist, to have a stable string quartet or to be featured in a film like "Iberia" de Carlos Saura.

If you weren't doing this job, what similar careers might you consider?

I would wish to only play chamber music and if I could choose specifically, string quartet repertoire. If we are talking about a profession outside playing the cello, I'd like to be a music director because playing under them for 28 years, I have an idea of what works and what doesn't.

What advice do you have for others who would like to pursue this career?

Be honest with yourself regarding your abilities and possibilities. Be sure you understand the realities of the profession and what you might have to do to get there: personal sacrifice, moving, practicing, not being able to have stable income, buy a house, etc. Know that it might take you years to get a job. Face the hard reality that you might not get a job and find yourself stuck with having to start all over again in a new career because there are not that many fields or jobs closely related to being a professional orchestra musician. If you are lucky, you might be able to find various other jobs, some outside music, to be able to make ends meet. I personally have been very lucky in my career.

Music Executive

Job Description: Music executives work in recording companies or own their own companies. They find and mold talent, arrange recording "deals," schedule concerts for their artists, write press releases, prepare radio and other artist promotion packages and manage all the ins and outs of the business that supports their talent.

Training and Educational Qualifications: No formal training is required for starting a business; however, entrepreneurs starting businesses in the music industry usually have training in music or a bachelor's degree in music. Individuals seeking employment in the recording companies usually have a similar background and sometimes have done internships in the music industry.

Job Outlook: Keen competition is expected for top executive positions because the prestige and high pay attract a large number of qualified applicants. Employment of top executives—including chief executives and general and operations managers—is expected to have little or no change through 2016.

Salary: Top executives are among the highest paid workers in the U.S. economy. However, salary levels vary substantially depending on the level of managerial responsibility, length of service, and type, size, and location of the firm. For example, a top manager in a very large corporation can earn significantly more than a counterpart in a smaller firm.

Median annual earnings of general and operations managers are $85,230. The middle 50 percent earn between $58,230 and $128,580. Because the specific responsibilities of general and operations managers vary significantly within industries, earnings also tend to vary considerably. Median annual earnings of chief executives are greater than $145,600 although chief executives in some industries earned considerably more.

Significant Facts:

- Many jobs in the music industry are in cities in which entertainment and recording activities are concentrated; these include New York, Los Angeles, Las Vegas, Chicago and Nashville.

INDUSTRY RESOURCES:

National Association of Record Industry Professionals
P.O. Box 2446
Toluca Lake, CA 91610-2446
Phone: (818) 769-7007
Email: info@narip.com
Internet: www.narip.com

Profile: Music Executive

Name: Tony Scafide

Age: 43

**Title: President/Founder,
Generation Media Inc.**

Education: BM Music Composition

Years in Industry: 18 years

CAREER LADDER:

Music copyist, advertising sales, music director, media specialist, marketing associate, public relations manager, recording company founder/president

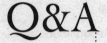

Do you know which companies have the best internships in this field that are known to help launch a successful career?
SONY, EMI, IMG, Universal.

Where are the best cities to live to find jobs like yours?
New York, Los Angeles.

What is your typical day like?
I get into the office at 10:00 a.m. and read through about 75 emails that all need action. Then I meet with my employees and get an update of the progress of our projects. I make calls from 11:00 a.m. until 2:00 p.m. and then take a break for lunch. Coming back to the office means making more calls. I usually answer inquiries about our clients until 7:00 p.m. Then there is always a concert or music event to attend for one of our clients or another new artist we are considering working with. It's not uncommon for me to stay out until 1:00 a.m. and then get up the next morning and do it all again.

What are your job responsibilities?
In any business there must be attention given to day-to-day management. I am responsible for three employees who are actively soliciting new business; writing press releases; preparing radio promotion charts for record label clients; answering to clients on the daily, weekly and monthly progress of their public relations accounts; putting out fires both literally and figuratively.

What is your favorite part of your job?
Getting press and radio spots for a new client that is very talented and has never worked with a professional PR house before.

What do you dislike about your job?
Trying to promote music or careers of artists who are not very talented but who will make it because we do our job extremely well. There is always a little guilt with this type of account.

Profile: Music Executive

Q&A

Have you had any turning-point or "light bulb" moments in your career that have helped you get to where you are today?

The light bulb came when I had a meeting with my first client. He offered me more money to work for him than he offered my employer at the time. And he only wanted me to do consulting work for him. I knew right then and there that if I could strike the deal with him, I would leave my job with two weeks notice and never look back.

How did you know you wanted to pursue this career?

It combined the two things I love the most in life—classical and jazz music and the ability to verbally communicate enthusiasm and excitement to others when discussing music. I also had a great advantage coming from a large company in the music business that opened the doors to all the music writers in the United States and all the music directors at over 500 radio stations.

How did you get into this industry?

I was a musician who found my way to music composition. I continued my education in that field and even worked other jobs to support my music composition. Eventually my background in music became a key component when being hired to work for media companies. When I had my own not-for-profit performing arts group, I did all the publicity work for them and began to learn the craft of public relations. I eventually was hired by a large company that gave me the education and experience I needed to start my own company.

What do you consider your greatest professional accomplishment?

Hiring my first employee and creating a sustainable business.

To what professional associations do you belong?

American Society of Composers, Authors and Publishers.

What advice do you have for others who would like to pursue this career?

I think you must be able to work with people who are very passionate about their careers and who will expect results for the money they pay you. If you do not have good writing and verbal skills, a publicity and promotion career is not for you. You have to be able to discuss the finer points of classical music and jazz with some very smart writers, editors, and clients as you progress in this profession. If you are unable to pick up a phone and call someone you never have spoken with before, you will not be able to do public relations. Email alone will not make it happen. If you can't do this, you will not be able to represent these artists competently.

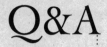

Profile: Music Executive

Q&A

You should also have a passion to discover new ideas and trends and be very computer literate. And most of all, you must be able to "bill" for your time with confidence. Being a natural sales personality is a great asset. You must possess the ability to sell—especially "intangibles" (e.g., your concepts and ideas)—to writers, editors, and the media, as well as clients. Otherwise, you will not survive and certainly cannot thrive.

Recording/Audio Engineer

Job Description: Recording engineers operate and maintain video and sound recording equipment. They may also operate equipment designed to produce special effects.

In film, recording engineers perform one of the final jobs in postproduction—adding prerecorded and live sound effects and background music by manipulating music, dialogue, and background sound to fit the picture. Their work is becoming increasingly computer driven as electronic equipment replaces tape-recording devices. The best way to gain experience in sound editing is through work in radio stations, with music groups, in music videos or by adding audio to Internet sites.

Managers in the field may oversee audio and video technicians who set up and operate audio and video equipment. Sound engineering technicians operate equipment to record, synchronize, mix, or reproduce music, voices, or sound effects in recording studios, sporting arenas, theater productions, or movie and video productions.

Other titles in this general field include sound mixers or re-recording mixers who produce soundtracks for movies or television programs. After filming or recording is complete, these workers may use a process called "dubbing" to insert sounds.

Training and Educational Qualifications: The best way to prepare for a broadcast and sound engineering technician job is to obtain technical school, community college, or college training in broadcast technology, electronics, or computer networking. In the motion picture industry, people are hired as apprentice editorial assistants and work their way up to more skilled jobs.

Job Outlook: Job growth in this field will be limited by consolidation of ownership of radio and television stations and by labor-saving technical advances. Employment of broadcast and sound engineering technicians in cable and pay television is expected to grow.

The area promised the most growth for recording and audio engineers is the motion picture industry. Data supports an expectation of *rapid* growth. However, job prospects are expected to remain competitive because of the large number of people who are attracted by the glamour of working in motion pictures.

Salary: Median annual earnings of sound engineering technicians are $43,010. The middle 50 percent earn between $29,270 and $65,590. The lowest 10 percent earn less than $21,050, and the highest 10 percent earn more than $90,770.

Significant Facts:

- About 30 percent of recording engineers work in broadcasting, mainly for radio and television stations; and 17 percent work in the motion picture, video, and sound recording industries.

- Evening, weekend, and holiday work is common.

INDUSTRY RESOURCES:

Audio Engineering Society, Inc.
International Headquarters
60 East 42nd Street, Room 2520
New York, NY 10165-2520
Internet: www.aes.org

Cinema Audio Society
859 Hollywood Way #632
Burbank, CA 91505
Email: casoffice@cinemaaudiosociety.org
Internet: www.cinemaaudiosociety.org

Society of Broadcast Engineers, Inc.
9102 North Meridian Street, Suite 150
Indianapolis, IN 46260
Internet: www.sbe.org

Profile: Audio Engineering – Management

Name: Lisa Nigris
Age: 41
Title: Director of Audio/Visual Services

Employer: New England Conservatory
Education: BM, Music Production and Engineering
Years in Industry: 19

CAREER LADDER:

Internships, staff recording engineer, assistant director, director

Did you have an internship in this field prior to starting your job?

Yes, I had two. In one internship, my responsibility was to assist different engineers at one recording studio. In the other position, I assisted one engineer at many different recording studios. In many ways, it was the best of both worlds.

Do you know of which companies have the best internships in this field that are known to help launch a successful career?

Though I have not dealt with internships for quite a while, I would imagine that either getting your foot in the door at a studio or "attaching yourself" to an engineer would still work. Be creative—check out your local radio stations or TV station, in addition to traditional recording studios. I have not heard of a *paid* internship in this field in my area.

Where are the best cities to live to find jobs like yours?

New York, Los Angeles, Nashville. Also, there are jobs in television and radio, as well as college campuses, across the country. Sound for video games may also be a way to go. Many of these jobs seem to be in New York or California.

What is your typical day like?

I was a recording engineer earlier in my career for almost 15 years. My mornings would include orchestral rehearsal recording; in the afternoons, it was recording studio sessions. Evenings and weekends were concert recording. Most concert recording engineers worked evenings and weekends for performances.

I segued into a more administrative position in my field after I started a family and today I do a lot of event planning, scheduling, and sometimes recording during the day. My typical day turned from the responsibilities that go with a recording engineering job to those that are a part of an administrative career *overseeing* recording.

What are your job responsibilities?

I am responsible for all the audio visual needs of New England Conservatory. I supervise a professional staff of four and a student staff of sixteen. We provide services for roughly 600 events a year—it's a lot to

Q&A

keep track of. A "slow week" consists of about fifteen events so there are a lot of little details to track and manage.

What is your favorite part of your job?

Overseeing an event to the point that it goes off without a hitch.

What do you dislike about your job?

Dealing with hostility from someone making a less that reasonable request for services on very short notice. In a creative environment, people sometimes get last minute ideas and want to include them as part of their event. While often I can make these requests happen, occasionally I can't; and it's difficult to deal with the "you're my best friend when you give me what I want, but the devil when you can't" attitude.

How did you know you wanted to pursue this career?

I knew at an early age that I wanted to be in music. When I was a freshman in high school, I got a Yamaha DX-7 and discovered that I enjoyed manipulating the sounds more than I liked playing the keyboard. That is probably the first time I was acquainted with some facet of audio engineering.

How did you get into this industry?

I graduated with honors and was invited to apply for my first position; this is rare. I applied and ultimately got it. Most of my classmates never found engineering jobs. It's not an easy road. It's no easier than being a successful musician. Engineering is an art form and people have to appreciate the talent that goes with it, the complete proficiency on all of the gear and software.

Have you had any turning-point or "light bulb" moments in your career that have helped you get to where you are today?

My turning point was bittersweet. When I went from being an engineer to being an administrator, I was almost lost at first. My identity was being an engineer. It was difficult to have to transition from people viewing me as an engineer to viewing me as an administrator, but I realized that I had gone as far as I was going to go with engineering. I wanted to start a family.   For me, working nights and weekends was not my desire once I had a child, so I made the personal decision to become an administrator. My job is still creative but in a different way than it was when I was an audio engineer.

What do you consider your greatest professional accomplishment?

Achieving an isolated audio ground in New England Conservatory's Jordan Hall. In 1995 Jordan hall was restored. During this process, audio and video recording, PA system, and isolated electrical lines were installed in the hall running to the equipment room, control rooms,

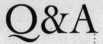

Profile: Audio Engineering - Management

Q&A

electric room, etc. It was an enormous project and quite rushed in the end despite many 100-hour weeks. During the grand opening, the balcony speakers blew because of a ground discharge and that was when we realized that there were literally hundreds of ground loops in the system. I and the director at the time had done all of the wiring outside of the hall itself, but union electricians did all of the wiring inside the hall. They were used to welding—not soldering—delicate wires, so almost every connector inside the hall needed to be cleaned up or replaced. At some point during this process, the director resigned and I was promoted. Four months later, and after a lot more 100-hour weeks, we found the last ground loop. When that ground was finally isolated, it was a great feeling—almost euphoric. I have great affection for this hall which was wrought with technical problems. To see it in top shape now gives me great pride.

To what professional associations do you belong?

Audio Engineering Society.

What publications do you read?

Every audio magazine out there.

What advice do you have for others who would like to pursue this career?

From an engineering perspective, my advice is to get the most experience possible. Familiarize yourself with all styles of music and all types of equipment so you're ready for any gig offered to you. Also, hone your customer relations skills; if you are difficult to work with, no one will work with you.

From a managerial standpoint, I would say to be detail-oriented. With event management, nothing can fall through the cracks. If someone doesn't have the people or equipment he or she needs, it can be disastrous. You have to be incredibly organized and able to resolve problems creatively and quickly. No one can keep everything straight in his or her head, so find a system of organization. Not every system works for everyone, so figure out what works best for you, a PDA, Outlook reminders, a notebook—whatever—and stick to it. In this business people who cannot be trusted to keep information straight generally find themselves out of work.

Profile: Sound Designer/Film Editor

Name: Sandy
Age: 55
Title: Sound designer/film editor/ graphic artist/musician. I also teach "Sound Design for Directors" to thesis students at UCLA.

Employer: Self-employed
Education: BFA Film
Years in Industry: 30

CAREER LADDER:

After I graduated from college, I worked on a few commercials in New York, recording sound and cutting. I also worked as a musician (keyboards, alto and baritone sax) on tour with Bruce Springsteen, Hall & Oates, Chuck Berry, Jr., Walker & the Allstars, and Dwayne Eddy. I've recorded with James Brown and Weird Al Yankovic. I'm currently finishing a wonderful little independent called "Quid Pro Quo" and I've been commissioned to do the cover art on a lost recording of Janis Joplin.

Do you know which companies have the best internships in this field that are known to help launch a successful career?
Soundelux/Todd-AO

Where are the best cities to live to find jobs like yours?
Los Angeles and New York.

What is your typical day like?
Crisis management with an occasional dab at the actual creative work at hand.

What are your job responsibilities?
On a feature film, I'm responsible for everything that you hear (except the music).

What is your favorite part of your job?
The final mix—when everything comes to life.

What do you dislike about your job?
The fact, in most cases, that I'm not the final arbiter of my own work.

Have you had any turning-point or "light bulb" moments in your career that have helped you get to where you are today?
When I was asked to do sound design on *Jaws*.

How did you know you wanted to pursue this career?
I was able to synthesize all of my experiences as an artist into one area. Film is a very sculptural format (length/width/time). When editing picture, it's like forming marble—you chip away until you find the

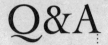

Profile: Sound Designer/Film Editor

Q&A

form. When you design sound, it's like working in clay—you start with the armature and continually add to it until you find the form. Graphic work is self evident.

How did you get into this industry?

It started as a "stop-gap" and here I am!

What do you consider your greatest professional accomplishment?

I received the British Academy Award for my work on *JFK* and an award for *Aladdin*.

If you weren't doing this job, what similar careers might you consider?

Directing, composing.

To what professional associations do you belong and what professional publications do you read?

I'm on the executive board of the Academy of Motion Picture Arts and Sciences and past president of the Motion Picture Sound Editors; I am a voting member of the Grammy Awards, The Motion Picture Editor's Guild, American Federation of Musicians, and AFTRA. I subscribe to *Variety*.

What advice do you have for others who would like to pursue this career?

Keep an open mind—technology is in a state of constant flux but the essence of the work remains personal. An internship is always a good idea.

Singer

Job Description: Singers interpret music and text, using their knowledge of voice production, melody, and harmony to produce a vocal product. They sing character parts or perform in their own individual style. Singers are often classified according to their voice range—soprano, contralto, tenor, baritone, or bass—or by the type of music they sing, such as opera, rock, popular, folk, rap or country.

Training and Educational Qualifications: Musicians need extensive and prolonged training and practice. Formal training may be obtained through private study with an accomplished musician, in a college or university music program, or in a music conservatory. Young persons considering careers in music should have musical talent, versatility, creativity, poise and a good stage presence. Because quality performance requires constant study and practice, self-discipline is vital.

Job Outlook: Competition for jobs for musicians, singers, and related workers is expected to be keen. The vast number of persons with the desire to perform will continue to greatly exceed the number of openings. Talent alone is no guarantee of success. Most new wage and salary jobs for musicians will arise in religious organizations. Slower-than-average growth is expected for self-employed musicians.

Salary: The median figure for hourly earnings of musicians and singers is $19.73 in May 2006. The middle 50 percent earn between $10.81 and $36.55 an hour. The lowest 10 percent earn less than $7.08, and the highest 10 percent earn more than $57.37. The median for hourly wages in performing arts companies is $23.37 and $13.57 in religious organizations.

Significant Facts:

- Aspiring musicians begin studying an instrument or training their voices at an early age.

- Part-time schedules and intermittent unemployment are common; many musicians supplement their income with earnings from other sources.

- Competition for jobs is keen; those who can perform a wide range of musical styles should enjoy the best job prospects.

INDUSTRY RESOURCES:

American Federation of Musicians
New York Headquarters
1501 Broadway, Suite 600
New York, NY 10036
Phone: (212) 869-1330
Internet: www.afm.org

Society of Singers
15456 Ventura Boulevard, Suite 304
Sherman Oaks, CA 91403
Phone: (818) 995-7100
Internet: www.singers.org

Profile: Singer/Songwriter

Name: Jon Peter Lewis
Age: 27
Title: Singer/Songwriter
Employer: Self-employed

Education: High School, Some College
Years in Industry: 2

CAREER LADDER:

Band member rock/blues bands, Playmill Theater (summer stock), American Idol, *Cockaroo Entertainment*

Where are the best cities to live to find jobs like yours?
Los Angeles, New York, Nashville.

What is your typical day like?
It's always different. I make a lot of phone calls. Sometimes I'm rehearsing, and I might also be recording or performing.

What are your job responsibilities?
I write and perform songs.

What is your favorite part of your job?
Creative release.

What do you dislike about your job?
Lack of security.

Have you had any turning-point or "light bulb" moments in your career that have helped you get to where you are today?
Absolutely. The first happened while working at the Playmill Theater. My father was a musician and I grew up thinking that some day I'd do the same thing. Life happened so quickly though, and before I knew it, I was 24 and setting my sights on medical school while working in a really low-paying theater group. When I came across some video tapes of AI, I thought that might be an opportunity to give music a shot.

The second turning-point moment happened for me just after I was let go from *American Idol*. I was wondering what I'd do with myself—whether I'd go back to school or pursue music. At that same time, I started writing my first songs. I had a really overwhelming feeling that this was what I wanted to do with my life—so I stuck with it.

How did you know you wanted to pursue this career?
It makes me feel good—that is how I knew this was the career for me.

What have you done in your career so far?
I have released one full-length album, *Stories from Hollywood*, with all original songs. This album includes my double single "If I Go

Q&A

Away/Man Like Me." I also wrong a song, "It's Christmas," which was released by EMI Canada on the *Now Christmas 2* compilation CD, and I recorded "California Christmas," which was released on by Breaking Records for the Breaking Christmas compilation in 2006.

What do you consider your greatest professional accomplishment?

Writing and recording a song that reached the top 15 in Canada.

If you weren't doing this job, what similar careers might you consider?

Musical theater, acting, or voice-overs.

To what professional associations do you belong?

American Federation of Television and Radio Artists (AFTRA).

What professional magazines and Web sites do you read?

Rolling Stone, Blender, Spin, MTV.com.

What advice do you have for others who would like to pursue this career?

Every singer needs to find his or her voice. What I mean is that a singer is a dime a dozen, but there is something that is unique about each voice and that is what interests people. The only way to really make it is to pound the pavement—you gotta hustle to be heard.

Profile: Opera Singer

Name: Ruth
Age: Opera singers never reveal their ages.
Title: Singer
Employer: Self-employed

Education: BM Voice, New England Conservatory; Graduate student in opera and lieder at the Vienna Academy of Music
Years in Industry: 35

CAREER LADDER:

I've always been a freelance singer in classical music (opera and recitals) and in lighter music.

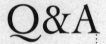

Did you have an internship in this field prior to starting your job?
Yes, I participated in Santa Fe Opera Apprentice Artist Program.

Do you know of which companies have the best internships in this field that are known to help launch a successful career?
There are many, but among the most well-known is the Metropolitan Opera.

What is your typical day like?
I spend two hours practicing, two hours on the phone making contacts, two hours administrative work (sending out materials or contracts) and one hour of exercise. On a performance day, the entire day is taken up in preparation and travel to and from the performance.

What are your job responsibilities?
Choosing repertoire for my concert programs, keeping my voice in shape, serving as my own manager and agent and overseeing publicity.

What is your favorite part of your job?
All of it!

What do you dislike about your job?
Not enough time to learn new repertoire.

Have you had any turning-point or "light bulb" moments in your career that have helped you get to where you are today?
When I was not hired by any opera house in Germany, I reassessed my career. I knew that the audience for programs of lighter music was much larger than that for classical vocal recitals. I had done these lighter programs for years and simply decided to expand in this direction.

How did you know you wanted to pursue this career?
When I began singing lessons in high school, I found that singing became a greater passion than literature.

Profile: Opera Singer

Q&A

How did you get into this industry?

When I was a student, I entered local pageants in the Miss Massachusetts Pageant program (part of the Miss America system). In the pageants, talent was always fifty percent of the points, so it was a good place to showcase my ability as a singer. I won several titles, the last being Miss Boston, had a brochure made up and mailed it out to women's organizations. The calls started coming in for programs.

What do you consider your greatest professional accomplishment?

The fact that I am still in demand, I am singing well, and continue to come up with ideas for new programs.

If you weren't doing this job, what similar careers might you consider?

Arts administration, fund raising, psychotherapist, English teacher, voice teacher.

What professional publications do you read?

Opera News Magazine.

What advice do you have for others who would like to pursue this career?

If singing is a great enough passion, you will find a way to make it happen, no matter what obstacles you encounter.

Talent Agent

Job Description: Talent agents represent performing artists to prospective employers. Agents arrange auditions and negotiate contracts on the performer's behalf. A reputable talent agent for actors will also be familiar with Screen Actors Guild (SAG), Equity and American Federation of Television and Radio Artists (AFTRA) rules and regulations, and he or she will also have established relationships with casting directors. Talent agents for musicians and dancers will be knowledgeable about union rules in those areas. Agents also may handle contract negotiations and other business matters for clients.

Training and Educational Qualifications: There is no set path to becoming a talent agent. While many agents have completed college coursework in theater, acting, writing and film, a college degree is not a prerequisite. What is required, however, is experience. It is common for those pursuing a career as an agent to intern or volunteer with a talent agency to gain experience.

Job Outlook: Employment growth for talent agents for 2006-16 is about as fast as the average for jobs in other fields.

Salary: Due to the small number of talent agents compared to other occupations, specific data for salaries in this field are not widely reported. Salaries vary depending on location, years of experience and the management company that employs agents.

Significant Facts:

- Agents usually specialize in one particular artistic field such as acting, music or dance and represent clients in those fields.

- Many agents are located in New York City or Hollywood.

- Some talent agencies, like the William Morris Agency and the United Talent Agency, have talent agent training programs.

INDUSTRY RESOURCES:

Association of Talent Agents
9255 Sunset Boulevard, Suite 930
Los Angeles, CA 90069
Phone: (310) 274-0628
Internet: www.agentassociation.com

Talent Managers Association, Inc.
4804 Laurel Canyon Boulevard #611
Valley Village, CA 91607
Phone: (310) 205-8495
Internet: www.talentmanagers.org

Profile: Talent Agent

Name: Andrea
Age: 55
Title: Vice President
Employer: Columbia Artists Management, LLC (CAMI), the leading company for classical music in the world
Education: One year of college education in London and then hands-on experience in the field
Years in Industry: 33 years

CAREER LADDER:

I began in the arts with acting and as an assistant director. Then I helped run an arts festival in Italy. In 1976, I came to the United States to set up the same festival, which is known as the Spoleto Festival; it still runs today in Charleston, South Carolina. Later, I owned a production company for off-Broadway plays and television films before having a restaurant for four years. I entered the field of talent management in 1986—a colleague I had worked with at the Spoleto Festival had entered the field and asked me to join her.

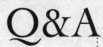

Do you know of which companies have the best internships in this field that are known to help launch a successful career?

CAMI has internships.

Where are the best cities to live to find jobs like yours?

For classical music, it's New York, London, Berlin, Vienna and Paris.

What is your typical day like?

It depends what is happening with my artists. No day is like another. There are at least one or two disasters every day. I meet with a lot of people and spend a huge amount of time on the telephone. I could be at an audition. Days start late and end late—many times not before 10:00 p.m. If you go to an evening performance and take your artist out to dinner after the show, it's much later.

What are your job responsibilities?

I used to manage many more artists than I do now. I had about 100 artists and a full staff to assist me. At that time, I used to search for new talent. Today I don't. I actually left the business in 1997 and came back in 2000 with a new strategy. I no longer have a huge roster of talent to deal with. I have my four stars and I devote my time to them.

What is your favorite part of your job?

As a manager I do everything, but interpretation of a role for a client and helping him or her make their career as successful as possible are the best parts.

What do you dislike about your job?

Contracts. Especially recording contracts.

Profile: Talent Agent

Q&A

Have you had any turning-point or "light bulb" moments in your career that have helped you get to where you are today?

A turning-point moment for me was when I left the business for awhile and decided to come back on my own terms. I didn't feel that I could do good work for 100 people but that is the nature of the business. Some artists get more attention than others. To be a good manager, you must be committed to all of your clients. I couldn't do it for everyone. But today I can do it for the few clients I manage: two opera singers and two conductors.

If you weren't doing this job, what similar careers might you consider?

I wouldn't consider doing another job within the classical music world. Outside this field, I am interested in healing work.

What professional publications do you read?

Opera News, French Opera, English Opera.

What advice do you have for others who would like to pursue this career?

A talent manager has to have a very clear sense of what can be sold and what the public will and won't buy. Someone with enormous talent can have a huge career or a career that implodes and goes nowhere. You have to have a sense of who could have a huge career. In this business, we only take on artists whom we think have the potential for a world-class career.

Also, you have to be the type of person that these people will trust and allow themselves to be managed by. But you must remember to not get sucked into their lives—you have to have some distance from them.

Be honorable. You only have your name. Once your name gets sullied, it can get very tricky. Honesty is probably the most important thing.

Music Education: Music Teacher (K-12)

Job Description: Music teachers teach music courses in their specialty (voice, band, and orchestra) to private and public school students in classes that range from kindergarten through high school. Music teachers normally have to master several instruments to teach more than one in the school setting. Music teachers are also responsible for preparing student performing groups for concerts throughout the year as well as individual students for auditions for state competitions, all-county performances, or college auditions.

Music instructors give private or group lessons in voice or another instrument and are not required to have any kind of teacher certification.

Training and Educational Qualifications: Requirements for regular licenses to teach kindergarten through grade 12 vary by state. However, all states require general education teachers to have a bachelor's degree and to have completed an approved teacher training program with a prescribed number of subject and education credits, as well as supervised practice teaching. A number of states require that teachers obtain a master's degree in education within a specified period after they begin teaching. Many college music programs offer a music education major, which is the fastest route to teaching music in the school setting; otherwise, students earn a bachelor's in music and must pursue teacher certification separately, sometimes taking more than four years to graduate.

Job Outlook: Through 2016, overall student enrollment in elementary, middle, and secondary schools—a key factor in the demand for teachers—is expected to rise more slowly than in the past as children of the baby boom generation leave the school system. This will cause employment to grow only as fast as the average for teachers from kindergarten through the secondary grades. Program enrollment may vary by region.

Salary: Median annual earnings of kindergarten, elementary, middle, and secondary school teachers range from $43,580 to $48,690; the lowest 10 percent earn $28,590 to $33,070 and the top 10 percent earn $67,490 to $76,100.

According to the American Federation of Teachers, beginning teachers with a bachelor's degree earn an average of $31,753. The estimated average salary of all public elementary and secondary school teachers is $47,602. Private school teachers generally earn less, but may be given other benefits, such as free or subsidized housing.

Significant Facts:

* In addition to conducting classroom activities, teachers oversee study halls and homerooms, supervise extracurricular activities and accompany students on field trips.

* Public school teachers must have a bachelor's degree, complete an approved teacher education program and be licensed.

* Many states offer alternative licensing programs to attract people to teaching, especially for hard-to-fill positions.

INDUSTRY RESOURCES:

American Federation of Teachers
555 New Jersey Avenue NW
Washington, DC 20001
Internet: www.aft.org

National Education Association
1201 16th Street, NW
Washington, DC 20036-3290
Internet: www.nea.org

MENC: The National Association for Music Education
1806 Robert Fulton Drive
Reston, VA 20191
Internet: www.menc.org

Profile: Music Teacher

Name: LaVada **Age: 53** **Title: Music Teacher**	**Employer: Falmouth Public Schools** **Education: MEd plus 25 credits** **Years in Industry: 28+**

CAREER LADDER:

I've always been a music teacher. An educator may consider leaving teaching to take an administrative position, but I wanted to work more closely with students. The opportunity to work on the state level and to perform professionally keeps my skills and art developing.

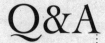

Where are the best cities to live to find jobs like yours?

Teaching jobs are available everywhere.

What is your typical day like?

My day begins at 7:35 a.m. when I have small ensembles coaching (Dixieland band, vocal jazz ensemble, chamber ensemble). Homeroom is next, followed by five classes of either small band or choral groups. My teaching day ends after tutoring individual students or directing rehearsals. A typical day might also be teaching the notes and dance moves to students participating in a school musical production. I may have meetings or rehearsals for myself into the evening such as church choir, MMEA meetings, Chorale rehearsal, etc.

What are your job responsibilities?

I teach instrumental and vocal music to seventh and eighth graders and am required to teach and assess students' achievements according to the national standards. I also direct a jazz ensemble after school, and I write curriculum. As president of the MMEA, I have a responsibility to the music educators and students of Massachusetts by leading the MMEA Board in making decisions and improvements in the health of arts in Massachusetts.

What is your favorite part of your job?

Working with young people!

What do you dislike about your job?

Not enough time to do everything I want to do with students.

Have you had any turning-point or "light bulb" moments in your career that have helped you get to where you are today?

There are always "ah ha" moments for me because every day is different. Every child is also different, so I am always working on creative ways to reach each student. I am also inspired watching a child become excited by his or her achievements.

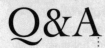

Q&A

How did you know you wanted to pursue this career?
I always enjoyed working with kids.

How did you get into this field?
I always made music myself, and I knew that I wanted to teach.

What do you consider your greatest professional accomplishment?
Helping students realize that they can do anything that they put their minds to, that they are important to every ensemble in which they participate, and that we are better *together* (working together and making each other look and sound good). It always feels great when a former student chooses to follow the same path as a music educator.

If you weren't doing this job, what similar careers might you consider?
Teaching another subject.

To what professional associations do you belong?
I belong to the American String Teachers Association (ASTA), Massachusetts Music Educators Association (MMEA), MENC: The National Association for Music Education, and the National Education Association (NEA).

What advice do you have for others who would like to pursue this career?
Teaching is an important job that gives you the opportunity to help mold the lives of young people while giving them the skills to be successful. Teaching music is important at every grade level. The rewards are seen in the students' faces and heard in the music they perform.

Music Professor (Postsecondary)

Job Description: Music professors teach their instrument of expertise (including voice) in college music programs across the country, including music conservatories, colleges and universities. Many music professors have had professional performing careers. Some adjunct while performing or they become full-time professors and sometimes continue performing while teaching.

Training and Educational Qualifications: Four-year colleges and universities usually consider PhDs for full-time, tenure-track positions, but they may hire master's degree holders or doctoral candidates for certain disciplines, such as the arts, or for part-time and temporary jobs.

In 2-year colleges, master's degree holders fill most full-time positions. However, in certain fields where there may be more applicants than available jobs, master's degree holders may be passed over in favor of candidates holding PhDs.

It is common for music professors to hold a Doctor of Musical Arts (DMA) rather than a PhD, which is a doctorate in music performance, although there are PhDs in fields like music theory or music education, among others.

Job Outlook: Overall, employment of postsecondary teachers is expected to grow much faster than the average for all occupations through 2016. A significant proportion of these new jobs will be part-time positions. Job opportunities are generally expected to be very good—although they will vary somewhat from field to field—as numerous openings for all types of postsecondary teachers result from retirements of current postsecondary teachers and continued increases in student enrollments.

Salary: Earnings for college faculty vary according to rank and type of institution, geo-graphic area and field. According to a 2006-07 survey by the American Association of University Professors, salaries for full-time faculty averaged $73,207. By rank, the average was $98,974 for professors, $69,911 for associate professors, $58,662 for assistant professors, $42,609 for instructors, and $48,289 for lecturers.

Significant Facts:

- Opportunities for postsecondary teaching jobs are expected to be good, but many new openings will be for part-time or non-tenure track positions.

- Prospects for teaching jobs will be better and earnings higher in academic fields in which many qualified teachers opt for nonacademic careers.

- Educational qualifications for postsecondary teacher jobs range from expertise in a particular field to a doctorate, depending on the subject being taught and the type of educational institution.

INDUSTRY RESOURCES:

American Association of University Professors (AAUP)
1012 Fourteenth Street, NW, Suite 500
Washington, DC 20005-3465
Phone: (202) 737-5900
Internet: www.aaup.org

The College Music Society
312 East Pine Street
Missoula, MT 59802
Phone: (406) 721-9616
Internet: www.music.org

National Association of Schools of Music (NASM)
11250 Roger Bacon Drive, Suite 21
Reston, VA 20190-5248
Phone: (703) 437-0700
Internet: http://nasm.arts-accredit.org

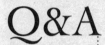

Profile: Music Professor

Name: Eric
Age: 37
Title: Music Professor, Composer, Guitarist
Employer:
Self-employed (composing/guitar performance)
The Curtis Institute of Music (teaching)

The Juilliard School Pre-College (teaching)
Education:
BM Manhattan School of Music, Diploma The Curtis Institute, DMA and MM, The Juilliard School
Years in Industry: 20

CAREER LADDER:

Composer and adjunct faculty to full-time faculty

Q&A

Did you have an internship in this field prior to starting your job?
I was a teaching assistant at Juilliard.

Where are the best cities to live to find jobs like yours?
Composers can theoretically live anywhere although major cities make contacts easier.

What is your typical day like?
My days vary. I've been at Curtis since 1999 and I teach in the musical studies department; I teach courses such as harmony, keyboard harmony and supplementary composition. Once a week, on Saturdays, I go to New York and teach in the pre-college program at Julliard. Some days I teach, sometimes I spend all day composing, and other days I have guitar performances.

What are your job responsibilities?
Writing music, teaching classroom material, guitar performance.

What is your favorite part of your job?
Creating new music.

What do you dislike about your job?
Too many teaching hours.

Have you had any turning-point or "light bulb" moments in your career that have helped you get to where you are today?
Acceptance to study at The Curtis Institute of Music with composer Ned Rorem.

How did you know you wanted to pursue this career?
Music is what I felt most passionate about in life and so I had to pursue it as a career.

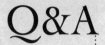

Profile: Music Professor

Q&A

How did you get into this industry?

Commissions come from personal contacts and word of mouth. I realized as a graduate student that I enjoyed teaching and that is why I pursued my doctorate in music. Teaching positions came from alumni contacts.

What do you consider your greatest professional accomplishment?

The premiere of my organ concerto at The Kimmel Center in Philadelphia's Verizon Hall in February 2007.

If you weren't doing this job, what similar careers might you consider?

Rock guitarist.

To what professional associations do you belong?

American Composers Forum, American Music Center, American Society of Composers, Authors and Publishers (ASCAP), College Music Society, and Philadelphia Musical Fund Society.

What advice do you have for others who would like to pursue this career?

Find what you love and do it.

Salaries

SALARIES FOR CAREERS IN MUSIC

Music Education
Education Early Childhood Music Educator $6–$60/hour
School Music Educator $19,000–$70,000/year
Music Supervisor, Consultant $25,000–$70,000/year
Music Professor $18,000–$150,000/year
University Music School Administrator $26,000–$182,000/year
Studio Teacher $10–$100/hour

Instrumental Performance
Performance Armed Forces Musician $21,000–$77,000/year
Orchestra Musician $300/week–$70,000/year
Small Ensemble Musician (salary varies widely)
Concert Soloist (salary varies widely)
Dance, Rock, or Jazz Band Musician $150–$355/ performance
Clinician $300–$5,000/ clinic

Vocal Performance
Dance Band or Nightclub Vocalist $150–$355/performance
Concert or Opera Chorus Member $12+/rehearsal;
$100+/performance
Concert Soloist $450+/performance
Opera Soloist $1,100+/performance

Conducting
Choir, Orchestra, or Opera Conductor $15,000–$275,000/year
Composing School Music Composer (Commissions vary)
Art Music Composer (Commissions vary)
Commercial Jingle Composer $300–$50,000/commercial
Television Show Composer $1,000–$5,000/30-minute episode
Film Score Composer $2,000–$200,000/film

Music for Worship
Organist $9,000–$57,000/year
Choir Director $5,200–$70,000/year
Cantor/Hazan $75,000–$150,000/year

Music Business
Music Dealer Sales Person $13,000–$50,000/year
Music Dealer Manager $17,000–$56,000/year
Marketing/Advertising Specialist $28,000–$116,000/year
Music, Instrument, and/or Accessories Distributor
$19,000–$75,000/year

Instrument Making and Repair
Instrument Maker $15,000–$65,000/year
Instrument Repair Technician $9–$55/hour
Piano Tuner $15–$60/hour

Salaries

Music Publishing
Publishing Sales Representative $20,000–$50,000
Copyright/Licensing Administrator $20,000–$60,000
Music Editor $20,000–$60,000
Notesetter $15,000–$50,000

Music Communications
Publisher or Editor of Music Books or Periodicals
$24,000–$100,000/year
Music Reporter $20,000–$150,000/year
Public Relations Specialist $21,000–$141,000/ year

The Recording Industry
Producer, Engineer/Mixer (NA)
Artist and Repertoire (A&R) Person (NA)
Studio Arranger (NA)
Music Copyist (NA)

The Television and Radio Industry
Radio/Television Commercial Musician $227–$1,650/13-week cycle
Copyright/Clearance Administrator (NA)
Music License Administrator (NA)
Program Director (radio) (NA)
Post Production/Scoring (NA)
Music Adviser/Researcher (NA)
Disc/Video Jockey (NA)
Music Technology Multimedia Publisher (NA)
Sound and Video Editor (NA)
Technology-based Music Instruction Designer (NA)

Music Librarianship
College, University, Conservatory, Public Library, or Orchestra
Librarian $18,000–$45,000/year

Music Therapy
Hospitals, Psychiatric Facility $20,000–$62,000/year
Special Education Facility $22,000–$42,000/year
Clinic for Disabled Children $15,000–$70,000/year
Mental Health Center $21,000–$65,000/year
Nursing Home $17,000–$65,000/year
Correctional Facility $23,000–$58,000/year
Private Practice $18,000–$77,000/year

Performing Arts Medicine
Performing Arts Medicine (MD, Physical Therapist)
$50,000–$100,000/year

This information is provided from a survey sponsored by the MENC: The National Association for Music in collaboration with other organizations. A brochure about careers in music is online at www.menc.org/careers.

Chapter 5

Careers for Writers

Perhaps more than ever before, careers that demand a high competency in writing are surfacing on the job market. Since the 1990s, a rise in Internet usage has resulted in the need for quality content to attract audiences to Web sites. Because of this, there are many opportunities for writers who are also online savvy. There is still an abundance of jobs in print as well, especially in niche environments. Business and organizations often desire to reach a particular audience and therefore, they seek to provide their audiences written content that is written just for them. Writing work in niche markets normally requires writers to specialize somewhat in their writing, or at least become aware of trends in a particular industry so that they are better able to write and create content for that audience. Some writers specialize in a certain type of writing such as grant writing, screenwriting, speechwriting, technical writing or playwriting.

In editorial work, there are numerous kinds of editors and not all jobs titles are the same across companies. One job might be considered an associate editor by one employer while it is titled senior editor at another. Most entry-level positions for prospective editors are as editorial assistants. A few different types of editors include acquisitions editors who acquire manuscripts for publication for a book publisher; copyeditors who are responsible for grammatical correctness, rewriting for clarity and creating headlines; and production editors who manage the production aspect of getting the manuscript or publication into its final published form. Roles like assistant editor, associate editor, senior editor, and managing editor are integral to the writing, as is working with other writers to create content for a particular publication or books program. All editors normally report to an editor-in-chief, an experienced editor who manages the strategic direction and general focus of the publication or books program.

Publishers of books, magazines and newspapers hire many writers and editors for positions that require quality writing and understanding of grammar. Still, almost any large organization— corporate or non-profit—hires writers and editors, as well public relations specialists, to work in corporate communications. Writing-related positions are also available in settings that may not be expected, such as associations, arts organizations, higher education institutions, hospitals, government offices, and public school systems, among others. Individuals who have a passion for the written word may also pursue careers in teaching writing, journalism, or literature at either the high school or college level.

Author/Writer

Job Description: Writers and authors develop original fiction and nonfiction for books, magazines, trade journals, online publications, company newsletters, radio and television broadcasts, motion pictures and advertisements.

Training and Educational Qualifications: A college degree generally is required for a position as a writer or editor. Although some employers look for a broad liberal arts background, most prefer to hire people with degrees in communications, journalism or English. For those who specialize in a particular area, such as fashion, business, or law, additional background in the chosen field is expected. Knowledge of a second language is helpful for some positions.

Job Outlook: Employment of salaried writers for newspapers, periodicals, book publishers and non-profit organizations is expected to increase as fast as the average. Magazines and other periodicals often develop market niches, appealing to readers with special interests. Businesses and organizations have newsletters and Web sites, and more companies are experimenting with publishing materials directly on the Internet. Online publications and services are growing, thus requiring writers with web experience.

Salary: Median annual earnings for salaried writers and authors are $48,640. The middle 50 percent earn between $34,850 and $67,820. The lowest 10 percent earn less than $25,430, and the highest 10 percent earn more than $97,700. The average for annual earnings is $50,650 in advertising and related services and $40,880 in newspaper, periodical, book and directory publishers.

Significant Facts:

- Most jobs in this occupation require a college degree in communications, journalism or English, although a degree in a technical subject may be useful for technical-writing positions.

- The outlook for most writing and editing jobs is expected to be competitive because many people are attracted to the occupation.

- Online publications and services are growing in number and sophistication, spurring the demand for writers and editors, especially those with web experience.

INDUSTRY RESOURCES:

American Society of Journalists and Authors
1501 Broadway, Suite 302
New York, NY 10036
Phone: (212) 997-0947
Internet: www.asja.org

National Writers Union
113 University Place, 6th Floor
New York, NY 10003
Phone: (212) 254-0279
Email: nwu@nwu.org
Internet: www.nwu.org

The Authors Guild
31 East 32nd Street, 7th Floor
New York, NY 10016
Phone: (212) 563-5904
Email: staff@authorsguild.org
Internet: www.authorsguild.org

Profile: Author

Name: Steve Almond

Age: 40

Title: Writer

Employer: Self-employed

Education: BA English, MFA Creative Writing

Years in Industry: I don't consider creative writing an "industry." I was a newspaper reporter for six or seven years. I still do freelance journalism, but my primary work has been creative writing for the past decade.

CAREER LADDER:

Thankfully, there isn't a career ladder in my line of work. The only way to get better is to spend time at the keyboard.

Did you have an internship in this field prior to starting your job?

I don't believe there is a way to have "an internship" in creative writing. What you can do (and I did) is to enroll in a Master's of Fine Arts (MFA) program, which is basically an academic welfare state for young writers. You get two to three years out of the rat race to learn how to write. I studied fiction.

Do you know of which companies have the best internships in this field that are known to help launch a successful career?

As I say, the best version of the internship for creative writers is the MFA program, and there are hundreds of them across the country, along with a growing number of PhD programs in creative writing.

Where are the best cities to live to find jobs like yours?

There's no geographic requirement for my line of work. You can live wherever you like. Because very few authors make enough money to survive from their books, however, most of them do some teaching. For this, it's important to be in a city with colleges or universities. And, of course, there's an argument to be made that writers are best to live in New York City where the publishing industry is based. In reality, writers should live in whatever setting is most conducive to their creative work.

What is your typical day like?

I try to write in the morning. In the afternoon, I either teach or do the sort of work that pays the bills. I also try to make time to read every day. Maybe get some exercise. I don't own a TV. TV is a giant time and energy sucker, which you can't afford if you want to do sustained creative work.

What are your job responsibilities?

My basic responsibility is to keep myself at the keyboard long enough to do some writing every day. Then I try to generate some income.

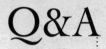

Q&A

What is your favorite part of your job?

Having the freedom to write about those things about which I feel most passionate.

What do you dislike about your job?

Writing is extremely lonely. And there's a ton of rejection to be absorbed. There's no way around either of these problems from what I've seen. You just have to learn how to withstand the isolation and disregard. Easier said than done.

Have you had any turning-point or "light bulb" moments in your career that have helped you get to where you are today?

The main thing is to realize that our culture steers people away from careers in the arts because they don't involve selling anything to anyone. This means that at crucial moments you have to make a decision that feels unpopular. For me, this was the decision to leave my job as a reporter and go back to school to study fiction. I lost my salary, health benefits, business card, and all that stuff, and I had to spend five or six years toiling in obscurity. This was the only way I was going to become serious about my creative work.

How did you know you wanted to pursue this career?

I got bored. More specifically, my heart got bored with my mind. I realized that writing newspaper articles was allowing me to be clever, and occasionally thoughtful. But I wasn't engaging my imagination or trying to say anything deeper about what it means to be human. And that just grew tiresome.

How you got into this industry?

You don't really "get into" the "writing industry." It just doesn't work like that. I decide what I want to write—a short story, a non-fiction memoir, a novel—and then set to work on it. If I work hard enough, I'm able to get a publisher to put the book into the world. Sometimes.

What do you consider your greatest professional accomplishment?

Just being able to publish a book—particularly a book of short stories—in a culture as joyously semi-literate as ours.

If you weren't doing this job, what similar careers might you consider?

Honestly, writing is about all I'm qualified to do. It would be fun to host a radio show, for instance. But it would feel like a betrayal of the sort of work I do as a writer.

Profile: Author

Q&A

What publications do you read?

The only magazine I read with any consistency is the *New Yorker*. Occasionally, I'll check out articles online. But I left journalism because I grew disenchanted with the superficiality of its coverage.

What advice do you have for others who would like to pursue this career?

The most important thing for young writers is that they honestly want to get at the truth—whether the truth comes wrapped in fiction or a straight-up non-fiction. If you want to write for any other reason (for money, or glory, say) you're not going to do too well.

Profile: Playwright

Name: Peter

Age: 30

Title: Playwright/Director/Adjunct Professor/Teaching Artist

Employer: Fordham University/LEAP

Education: BA Theater, MFA Playwriting

Years in Industry: I've been doing theater since I was 13. First high school, then in college, then after college, then in grad school, and now after grad school.

CAREER LADDER:

Since finishing graduate school, I've officially had the title of adjunct assistant professor at Fordham University. Otherwise, I've been a playwright, director and actor all along. I don't know if they qualify officially as titles, but I've consistently done all three. Lately though, my focus has been more centered on writing and directing rather than acting.

Did you have an internship in this field prior to starting your job?

Yes, I've had a few internships. I worked at New York Theater Workshop as a literary intern when I was an undergrad. I also was a general office intern at the Jean Cocteau Repertory and worked briefly as a script reader/general helper at Little Magic Films right after college and at Theater 503 in London, right after graduate school.

Do you know of which companies have the best internships in this field that are known to help launch a successful career?

I think for playwrights you should intern at theaters that have real backbones and really look for perspective from their playwrights. It isn't to say you need to always agree with the theater's choices, so much as it is to say that you should get accustomed to thinking about other people's work and begin to try and understand why people respond to that work. Also, I think a good literary internship doesn't *ever* involve getting anyone coffee because it should be more about a literary manager who is interested in your opinion. Why not New York Theater Workshop, or the Public...or even smaller theaters like The Rattlestick or the Milk Can Theater company, who are really building themselves into major companies and respond to enthusiastic and engaged interns.

Where are the best cities to live to find jobs like yours?

As a playwright, you can live anywhere, but I would say New York and Minneapolis are great places because you won't be writing in a void. Austin is great, I hear. Iowa City is a great place to be for grad school. Philadelphia seems cool too.

What is your typical day like?

I work three days a week as a volunteer coordinator for a program in Brooklyn called Vintage Pride where I match volunteers with LGBTQ seniors. At the moment, this is my bread and butter work. The other

Q&A

two days of the week are my teaching days, and on those days, I spend a few hours at A. Philip Randolph High School in Harlem teaching NYC high school kids how to write short plays. Then I hike up to the Bronx to teach my college class in the late afternoon. In the evenings, I tend to spend a lot of time seeing things, if I'm not working on my own things. Writing and rewriting and submission work fits in all around this. I recently won two awards that will allow me to leave my bread and butter work behind for a few months so that I can focus more on writing and teaching. My typical day will change. But I find that as a theater artist, my typical day changes all the time.

What are your job responsibilities?

To write plays, to teach theater, to write theater, to direct theater, to create new fans of theater.

What is your favorite part of your job?

I love the chaos of wearing a lot of hats. I love that my life is so unpredictable (even though it is utterly terrifying sometimes.) I love that I'm spending my life using my imagination to understand the world I live in…or the world someone else lives in. Oh, and theater people are the *best*. I always feel at home around them.

What do you dislike about your job?

Sometimes it's exhausting. I feel an emotional connection to my work so when something is disliked, or rejected or dismissed, it hurts. You have to clean yourself up off the floor a lot…or talk yourself down from the tree. A life in theater requires an astronomical amount of patience.

Have you had any turning-point or "light bulb" moments in your career that have helped you get to where you are today?

I'm always amazed when someone connects to my work—and when someone doesn't. Last year, I got ripped apart by the *New York Times* and it was amazing to me that despite how difficult it was to read such mean-spirited comments about something I loved, I was able to keep on doing this. But I've had amazing teachers at Iowa and Fordham who have turned the light bulb on again and again and again. My teachers at Fordham especially taught me to love *theater*, not just to love *myself in theater*. And they respected me in my growth process. When you are respected as a human being, your mind and heart are at their highest capacities for learning and deepening.

How did you get into playwriting?

I got into playwriting particularly because I just found I had a knack for it. I could do it at home with no money and I could really finally have some control over something. I got into teaching because learning to teach is something that Iowa really emphasized. They understand the practicalities of being a playwright in America.

Q&A

What do you consider your greatest professional accomplishment?

Getting a production in New York City that my friends don't have to pay for.

If you weren't doing this job, what similar careers might you consider?

Maybe screenwriting although it seems less free to me. Teaching obviously, but I prefer teaching older kids so I guess I'd have to get some scholarly experience in some other area.

To what professional associations do you belong?

Dramatist's Guild.

What professional publications and Web sites do you read?

TCG:ArtSearch and New York Foundation for the Arts Web site.

What advice do you have for others who would like to pursue this career?

Be careful about letting other writers tell you how to write and when to write and where to write and what you should write about. People often seek this advice from older playwrights, believing that this is the key to success. But I think it just makes playwrights crazy and self-conscious and frozen. Embrace your *mess* if that's your deal. Or embrace your *order* if that's your deal. There is no right or wrong way to write. Just write. If you're not writing, maybe you're not a writer. Or you're not a writer right now. That's okay too. Ultimately, comparison is destructive to the soul.

Book Publicist

Job Description: The main function of a book publicist is to get an author's writing noticed and to create "buzz" for a book prior to—and coinciding with—its release to the marketplace. Book publicists write press releases and arrange interviews. They also schedule authors' appearances, book signings and readings, and they develop relationships with media contacts to promote the authors they represent.

Training and Educational Qualifications: There are no defined standards for entry into a public relations career. A college degree combined with public relations experience, usually gained through an internship, is considered excellent preparation for public relations work; in fact, internships are becoming vital to obtaining employment. The ability to communicate effectively is essential. Many entry-level public relations specialists have a college major in public relations, journalism, advertising or communication. However, many book publicists are public relations specialists who focus on promoting authors and their books, often having backgrounds in English or another humanities field as well.

Job Outlook: Employment of public relations specialists, in general, is expected to grow faster than average for all occupations through 2016. However, the number of jobs for book publicists specifically may not grow at this same rate. Book publishing is not a growth industry compared to other types of businesses. Because of this, the prospect for landing entry-level jobs in book publishing and/or publicity is competitive due to the large number of applicants attracted to the occupation.

Salary: Average earnings for book publicists (public relation specialists) in the publishing industry are $54,310.

In general, the more revenue a publishing company earns, the higher the salaries of its publicity managers/directors. Based on company revenues, the range was on the low side, an average salary of $43,188 to a high of $89,500 for a company earning revenues of higher than $500 million.

Significant Facts:

- Most book publicity jobs are found in New York City, the nation's capital for publishing.

- Other jobs can be found in smaller presses or university presses throughout the country.

INDUSTRY RESOURCES:

Association of American Publishers (AAP)
71 Fifth Avenue, 2nd Floor
New York, NY 10003
Phone: (212) 255-0200
Internet: www.publishers.org

Profile: Book Publicist

Name: Jennifer
Age: 40
Title: Co-President

Employer: Over the River Public Relations
Education: BA English
Years in Industry: 18 years

CAREER LADDER:

Bookstore clerk, Yellow Umbrella Bookstore
Publicity Assistant, Random House
Associate Publicist, Random House
Publicist, Random House
Senior Publicist, Random House

Publicity Manager, St. Martin's Press
Publicity Director, St. Martin's Press
Associate Publicity Director, Random House
Co-President, Over the River Public Relations

Did you have an internship in this field prior to starting your job?
The closest thing I had to an internship was my summer job working at a bookstore. It was there that I learned all about the publishing business and decided I would like to pursue a career with books.

Do you know of which companies have the best internships in this field that are known to help launch a successful career?
The Radcliffe Publishing Program and the Columbia Publishing Program are both great.

Where are the best cities to live to find jobs like yours?
New York City is where all the action is for publishing.

What is your typical day like?
Days are extremely busy and require lots of multitasking. In a typical day, I'll do some press material writing, spend a lot of time making calls to the media, email authors and coordinate events.

What are your job responsibilities?
There are many aspects of my job, including writing, designing, collating, and mailing press materials, as well as researching media and keeping our publicity database up to date. I also arrange book signings, speaking engagements, lectures, readings and workshops. I make a great many calls a day; for example, I speak with TV and radio producers to arrange interviews for authors and with newspaper and magazine editors to arrange for features and reviews on behalf of our clients. Additionally, I create marketing plans for authors, submit publicity proposals and write contracts.

What is your favorite part of your job?
I love working with the authors to create unique game plans for their work. Everything else falls into place after this plan is created.

Profile: Book Publicist

Q&A

What do you dislike about your job?

The constant rejection. As in other creative fields, you have to have a thick skin. Producers and reporters are extremely busy and curt on the phone, and it takes a lot of creative maneuvering to convince them to talk to your authors.

Have you had any turning-point or "light bulb" moments in your career that have helped you get to where you are today?

It was a major change for me to start my own public relations company, and it has completely rejuvenated my career. I love being my own boss, setting my own hours and choosing which projects I would like to work on.

How did you know you wanted to pursue this career?

My aunt worked in publishing as a reader, and I always thought her life seemed so glamorous. She came home for holidays with all these manuscripts. Then she stayed up all night reading in order to meet her deadlines. I thought that was terribly exciting.

Then I worked in an independent bookstore while I was in college, and I loved meeting authors and recommending books to customers.

I had been a theater major in college before switching to English, so book publicity was especially appealing to me. There's a bit of glamour to it because you aren't stuck behind your desk all day; you get to do lots of writing, interact with all kinds of writers and celebrities and arrange posh events and parties.

Describe how you got into this industry and how you got your most recent job.

I did it the old-fashioned, straight forward way. I researched all of the top publishing companies in New York. I read up on the different career paths I could take, and I felt that publicity or sales would be the best match for me. I sent my resume to the human resources departments at the companies I admired, and then I followed up to try and schedule interviews. I went on three interviews, one in sales and two in publicity, and I ultimately took the publicity job at Random House.

I got my most recent job by taking a blind leap of faith. I quit my job with benefits at Random House and started a PR company with a fellow Random House publicist.

What do you consider your greatest professional accomplishment?

Starting my own publicity business.

Q&A

If you weren't doing this job, what similar careers might you consider?

If I weren't doing publicity, then I would probably be a handbag and jewelry designer. That's what I do in my spare time.

What professional publications and Web sites do you read?

I subscribe to *Publishers Weekly*, MediaBistro, and Publishers Lunch.

What advice do you have for others who would like to pursue this career?

You do have to be willing to work long hours and to have a thick skin, but you get to do a lot of exciting things. There's opportunity for travel and for entertainment. It's essential for you to be detail oriented and diligent, however. It's not all glamour.

Editor

Job Description: Editors review, rewrite and edit the work of writers. They may also do original writing. An editor's responsibilities vary with the employer and type and level of editorial position held. Editorial duties may include planning the content of books, technical journals, trade magazines and other general-interest publications. Editors also decide what material will appeal to readers, review and edit drafts of books and articles, offer comments to improve the work and suggest possible titles. In addition, they may oversee the production of the publications. In the book-publishing industry, an editor's primary responsibility is to review proposals for books and decide whether to buy the publication rights from the author.

Training and Educational Qualifications: A college degree generally is required for a position as a writer or editor. Although some employers look for a broad liberal arts background, most prefer to hire people with degrees in communications, journalism or English. For those who specialize in a particular area, such as fashion, business, or law, additional background in the chosen field is expected.

Job Outlook: Employment of salaried writers and editors for newspapers, periodicals, book publishers and non-profit organizations is expected to grow 10 percent, or as fast as the average for all occupations. Magazines and other periodicals are developing market niches that appeal to readers with special interests. Businesses and organizations have newsletters and Web sites, and more companies are experimenting with publishing materials directly on the Internet. Online publications and services are growing in number and sophistication, spurring the demand for writers and editors, especially those with web experience. Advertising and public relations agencies, which also are growing, should be another source of new jobs.

Salary: Median annual earnings for salaried editors are $46,990. The middle 50 percent earn between $35,250 and $64,140. The lowest 10 percent earn less than $27,340, and the highest 10 percent earn more than $87,400. The median annual earnings of those working for newspaper, periodical, book, and directory publishers are $45,970.

Significant Facts:

- Most jobs in this occupation require a college degree in communications, journalism or English, although a degree in a technical subject may be useful for technical-writing positions.

- The outlook for most writing and editing jobs is expected to be competitive because many people are attracted to the occupation.

- Online publications and services are growing in number and sophistication, spurring the demand for writers and editors, especially those with web experience.

INDUSTRY RESOURCES:

American Society of Magazine Editors/ Magazine Publishers of America
810 Seventh Avenue, 24th Floor
New York, NY 10019
Phone: (212) 872-3700
Internet: www.magazine.org

American Society of Newspaper Editors
11690B Sunrise Valley Drive
Reston, VA 20191-1409
Phone: (703) 453-1122
Email: asne@asne.org
Internet: www.asne.org

National Press Club
529 14th Street NW, 13th Floor
Washington, DC 20045
Phone: (202) 662-7505
Internet: http://npc.press.org

Profile: Copy Editor

Name: Bill	**Employer:** *The Washington Post*
Age: 45	**Education: BA, Journalism**
Title: Chief copy editor for national news	**Years in Industry: 22**

CAREER LADDER:

Reporter, the Phoenix Gazette*; copy editor, the* Phoenix Gazette*; design editor, the* Phoenix Gazette*; assistant news editor for design, the* Phoenix Gazette*; assistant copy desk chief, the* Washington Times*; deputy copy desk chief, the* Washington Times*; copy desk chief, the* Washington Times*; copy editor, the* Washington Post*; business copy chief, the* Washington Post*; national copy chief, the* Washington Post.

Did you have an internship in this field prior to starting your job?

I was an intern on the copy desk of the *Phoenix Gazette* the summer after my sophomore year of college. I returned as a reporting intern the summer after my junior year.

Do you know of which companies have the best internships in this field that are known to help launch a successful career?

My employer, the *Washington Post*, has an excellent internship program and is probably the most aggressive among the major papers when it comes to hiring its interns full-time after their internships. Just about all decent-size newspapers have summer interns; the Dow Jones Newspaper Fund has an excellent program that places copy-editing interns at papers large and not-so-large.

Where are the best cities to live to find jobs like yours?

Newspapers are everywhere, of course, but I would say New York and Washington are the best cities for copy editors because, in addition to the multiple newspapers, there are so many other, non-newspaper editing jobs in both cities.

What is your typical day like?

I arrive at work around 4:00 p.m. every weekday to start work on the next day's edition of the *Washington Post*. My first order of business is to log on to the computer system and put my people to work by assigning to them whatever stories are ready to be copy-edited. Then either my deputy or I start to put together the corrections that will appear on Page A2. The rest of the evening is spent mainly assigning stories to copy editors as the stories arrive and then reviewing the stories as well as the headlines and photo captions that the copy editors have written for them. Stories for the first edition have to be finished by 10 p.m. or so. Toward that deadline, I assign every story one more time for proofreading. Each story gets looked at once again, on a photocopy of the actual page, by a different editor from the one who handled it the first time.

Q&A

The editors go into the stories on the computer and make any corrections they decide are necessary and I again review the stories and release them for typesetting. All this is finished by 11:30 p.m. or so for the second edition, and unless there's a major breaking story, I head home at 11:30 or midnight and leave the desk in the hands of a designated late editor.

What are your job responsibilities?

As a copy chief I do the final read on stories that have already been edited by an assignment editor (the reporter's direct supervisor) and by one of the copy editors who report to me. I am responsible for every word that goes on the national-news pages of the Post, including the national stories that make A1. I am also the manager of eight full-time and several part-time copy editors.

What is your favorite part of your job?

It's gratifying to improve writers' work and prevent their mistakes from seeing print, and to craft entertaining and informative headlines and photo captions.

What do you dislike about your job?

The deadline pressure makes the task less creative and more of an assembly line sometimes. To compound that frustration, I have to take responsibility for work that I had almost no time to do—it's easy to look stupid to people who don't understand that reality. I'm also not fond of managerial chores such as performance reviews.

Have you had any turning-point or "light bulb" moments in your career that have helped you get to where you are today?

The move from the *Washington Times* to the *Washington Post* was a big one. I had been in DC for close to eight years and had had only sporadic success at getting the Post to even return my calls, but I decided to make a fresh try after an unpleasant experience one day at the Times. This time I was fortunate enough to find a sympathetic ear at the Post; and before long, there I was on the Post's business desk.

How did you know you wanted to pursue this career?

On my first job application in this industry—applying at the school newspaper as a college freshman—I wrote that I would be obsessive-compulsively editing the paper along with the cereal box every morning, so I might as well get paid for it. Still, I ended up where I am through a series of accidents, like most people, I suppose.

How did you get into this industry and how did you get your most recent job?

I majored in journalism in the hope of becoming a tennis writer, following Bjorn Borg and Jimmy Connors around. This was at the

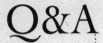

Q&A

University of Arizona, and I actually got a job as a copy editor before I even started my journalism classes. Toward the end of my first semester I saw that the school paper, the *Daily Wildcat*, was advertising for help. They wanted a "copy editor" and "copyreaders," and I think I applied for both. I had never heard of copy editing; I figured it was a proofreading job, and I knew I could do that. It turned out that "copy editor" meant "copy chief," and "copyreader" meant "copy editor." I got called in to take the test, and they handed me this little powder-blue book. That was the first time I had seen an *AP Stylebook*, and I guess I used it well enough to get hired. I spent the rest of my college days working at the *Wildcat*—making a little money and getting an education well beyond what they could offer in the classroom.

I had been copy editing for a couple of semesters before I learned that the job actually existed at "real" papers. I had no idea that reporters and city editors didn't just get things right in the first place! Eventually I became the *Wildcat* copy chief and news editor—learning layout— and one semester I was both news editor and tennis writer. The tennis thing never panned out as a career choice, though—it's tough when you don't want to be a "sportswriter" and other things kept coming along.

I had two summer internships at the *Phoenix Gazette*, an afternoon paper that no longer exists. The first summer I sat on the copy desk and did a little reporting; the next summer I was a reporting intern. The city editor liked me enough to hire me as a reporter right out of college, and for nine months or so I did the night police beat. I wasn't the greatest reporter in the world, but they liked my writing and I got a lot of front-page play. Then there was an illness on the suburban desk and they needed a copy editor. They knew I had the background, and I was drafted. It was a huge career change, but at the time I didn't give it a lot of thought. That's how I became an editor.

I took a detour a few years later when the *Gazette* separated the editing and layout functions. We were going to be a pioneer in electronic layout, designing the pages on a computer screen rather than with pencil and paper, and I wanted to be a part of that. That lasted a couple of years before I decided to accompany my then-girlfriend to Washington, DC because she thought she had landed a job there. It turned out that she hadn't; but I did, at the *Washington Times*. The *Times* was still doing layout the old-fashioned way and its needs were on the word side, so I became a copy chief there and eventually *the* copy chief. That went on for eight years before I finally got the *Post's* attention.

What do you consider your greatest professional accomplishment?

My greatest accomplishment was really outside my day-to-day job: writing two books and getting them published. *Lapsing Into a Comma* (2000) and *The Elephants of Style* (2004) have made me well known within my tiny field.

Profile: Copy Editor

Q&A

If you weren't doing this job, what similar careers might you consider?

I've been a reporter and a page designer, and I could certainly see myself doing those things again. I'd love to just write books full-time, but that would require a significant big break financially.

To what professional associations do you belong?

I belong to the American Copy Editors Society, and I speak at their annual conferences. I've maintained my Society for News Design membership even though I haven't done layout for a while.

What professional Web sites do you read?

I read a bunch of Web sites about copy editing and language in addition to maintaining a couple of them myself.

What advice do you have for others who would like to pursue this career?

I try not to be too much of a cheerleader for copy editing. It's a great fit for a certain type of personality, but a lot of the jobs are low-paying and a real grind. Even the well-paying ones are largely thankless and anonymous. For newspapers in particular, the current climate is full of uncertainty. There will always be editors, but the newspaper appears to be in decline, and so I don't think I'd recommend a career trajectory similar to mine. This might be a better time to start out as a well-rounded word brat, doing some reporting and writing and web technology. Once the journalism world figures out how to make money off web versions of newspapers, there should be plenty of copy-editing jobs at those—I just hope the straight-to-blog phenomenon doesn't make well-edited writing a thing of the past.

If you still decide you want to be a copy editor, I recommend that you read, read, read and write, write, write. You need to be a pretty darn good writer to be a so-so-editor. Learn your style manual backward and forward, but be aware that there is life beyond the stylebook. You need to have a certain amount of empathy and flexibility, and you should never forget that somebody else's name is going on the writing that you're editing.

Profile: Magazine Editor

Name: Kaja Perina
Age: 32
Title: Editor in chief
Employer: *Psychology Today*

Education: BA, English Vassar
College; MS, Journalism
Columbia University
Years in Industry: 10

CAREER LADDER:

Intern, office assistant, fact-checker, associate editor, staff writer, news editor, editor in chief.

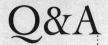

Did you have an internship in this field prior to starting your job? If so, please describe it.

I interned with a literary agency during college and with a British television news channel after graduation from college. Neither experience yielded subsequent employment, but each acquainted me with seasoned professionals so that I was more comfortable when I finally did obtain a job. (I was easily intimidated by authority in my early twenties—luckily this wore off as I gained confidence in my own abilities!)

Do you know of which companies have the best internships in this field that are known to help launch a successful career?

I'm not familiar with the internship opportunities at specific media companies. There is, however, a clear advantage to interning with a small organization: greater exposure and greater responsibility. It's easier to stand out in a small place (though real talent stands out anywhere). I've hired exceptional former interns as editors and retained others as freelance writers.

Where are the best cities to live to find jobs like yours?

New York City.

What is your typical day like?

I work an average of 10 hours per day, closely working with writers and editors on stories for the current issue, as well as researching topics and soliciting writers for future issues.

What are your job responsibilities?

I have creative and managerial oversight of the magazine.

What is your favorite part of your job?

I love taking the germ of an idea—a research finding or just a sentence in passing——and spinning it into a story.

What do you dislike about your job?

I don't always enjoy managing a staff of seven (plus freelancers).

Q&A

Have you had any turning-point or "light bulb" moments in your career that have helped you get to where you are today?

I realized very quickly that you can never be afraid to ask for what you want, whether a job opportunity, creative leeway once you're in the job, or financial remuneration. I believe that assertiveness engenders respect from all but one type of person—those who are frustrated by their own lack of assertiveness. My requests (and occasional) demands have been met with derision and scolding over the years, but I always knew that I was ultimately better off having pleaded my case.

How did you know you wanted to pursue this career?

I've always been drawn to the printed word. I was omnivorous in my taste for fiction and non-fiction as child and teen, but by college I realized I was a better non-fiction writer than writer of fiction. So I came to journalism through a process of elimination. I never set out to become a journalist, and it was only after college that I seriously considered it.

Describe how you got into this industry and how you got your most recent job.

I obtained my first paying job by cold-calling the Associated Press in Washington. They happened to have an office assistant position available (this was at the time the lowest position on the totem pole).

I obtained my job at *Psychology Today* by cold-calling the then-editor and sending him my work. I continued to sporadically check back with the magazine over the course of a year and a half until an opening was available. It turned out that he'd remembered me and was going to ask me to apply for the position. However, I beat him to it, which surely signaled my interest in the job and therefore put me at an advantage. I became editor in chief one and a half years later, at the invitation of the publisher.

What do you consider your greatest professional accomplishment?

I revitalized and greatly improved *Psychology Today*, making it arguably a more alluring magazine than it's been in its 30-year history while still showcasing contemporary psychology. And it continues to evolve.

Of course, I do not take sole credit for improving PT. I work with an excellent editorial and art team. So in terms of individual accomplishments, I am gratified that the last article I wrote for *Psychology Today* before becoming editor was selected for inclusion in the "Best American Science Writing 2004" volume.

If you weren't doing this job, what similar careers might you consider?

I've always been interested in clinical psychology, which drew me to the magazine in the first place. I've toyed with the idea of becoming a

Q&A

licensed professional over the years. I'm also drawn to private investigative work. Journalism involves intellectual and character sleuthing, but detective work raises the stakes on daily foraging for information.

To what professional associations do you belong and what professional?

I do not belong to any guild associations. I read widely—though I don't read "trade" magazines about journalism.

What advice do you have for others who would like to pursue this career?

Figure out where your writing and reporting talents lie (i.e., are you better suited to hard-charging reportage, in which case you might flourish at newspapers or newsweeklies, or are you drawn to ruminative pieces). Then be assertive—even aggressive—in soliciting meetings or jobs from people in your target sphere. Don't take rejection personally, especially when you're starting out. Many people are simply too busy to respond to your inquiries. But it's a numbers game and if you cast a wide enough net and demonstrate aptitude, someone will remember his or her own start and take the time to counsel you.

Force yourself to freelance if your job permits; it will be help you make connections at other companies.

Profile: Supervising Editor, Digital Media

Name: Marc Silver
Age: 54
Title: Supervising editor, digital media

Employer: National Public Radio
Education: BA, English
Years in Industry: 33

CAREER LADDER:

Associate editor, Baltimore Jewish Times
Editor, National Jewish Monthly
Assistant managing editor, U.S. News & World Report
Supervising editor, digital media, National Public Radio (NPR)

Do you know of which companies have the best internships in this field that are known to help launch a successful career?

Many media companies, including National Public Radio, have strong internship programs. Doing an unpaid internship is definitely worthwhile if you can't find a paying one. It's also important to write, write, write for your college newspaper, magazine or Web site.

Where are the best cities to live to find jobs like yours?

The usual list: New York, Washington, DC, Boston, Los Angeles.

What is your typical day like?

Meetings, cooking up project ideas, editing stories.

What are your job responsibilities?

Conceiving and carrying out editorial projects.

What is your favorite part of your job?

Writing and editing. It's always challenging, and it's very gratifying when you're done.

What do you dislike about your job?

Too many meetings!

How did you know you wanted to pursue this career?

I always liked writing and reporting. It gave me a chance to explore many different subjects. And I like the challenge of writing.

How did you get into this industry?

I started writing freelance stories for a pittance and eventually I got hired! I made the leap to online journalism gradually—doing some work at U.S. News. I switched over when I learned of an editing job at NPR, where the goal is to start creating more original content for the Web site. In an era when print is in flux, it seems like digital media is a good place to be. I like the challenge of bringing some of the print sensibilities to electronic media, and using the interactivity and immediacy of the web to expand the kinds of projects I work on.

Profile: Supervising Editor, Digital Media

Q&A

What do you consider your greatest professional accomplishment?
Writing my book, *Breast Cancer Husband*.

What professional Web sites do you read?
Poynter.org.

What advice do you have for others who would like to pursue this career?
You have to really love reporting and writing.

Grant Writer

Job Description: Grant writers find funds for non-profit entities and write proposals that explain and justify potential uses for those funds. They develop resources, research funding sources and prepare contract proposals for a variety of organizations. Grant writers may also administer major contracts and negotiate contractual provisions with potential partners.

Training and Educational Qualifications: A college degree generally is required for a position as a writer or editor. Although some employers look for a broad liberal arts background, most prefer to hire people with degrees in communications, journalism or English. Many grant writers have backgrounds in fundraising/development. Sometimes they enter the field of grant writing as writers who have worked in development communications, including working on grant proposals; other times, they have worked as directors of development or in other development offices in which grant writing was part of their position.

Job Outlook: Employment of writers at non-profit organizations is expected to increase; however, the availability of jobs varies depending on funds available to pay staff as well as the expectations of the organization in how to pursue grants. Some grant writers work as consultants who are independent contractors rather than full-time employees.

Salary: Grant writers earn between $40,014 and $66,379.

Significant Facts:

- Many jobs are located in New York City or Washington, DC where there is a high concentration of non-profit organizations and foundations; however jobs can be found in fewer numbers throughout the country.

- Excellent research skills are normally required for grant writers who must accurately research funders to which they aim to send grant proposals so that they have the highest chance of obtaining funding based on the written proposal.

INDUSTRY RESOURCES:

Association of Fundraising Professionals
4300 Wilson Boulevard, Suite 300
Arlington, VA 22203
Phone: (703) 684-0410
Internet: www.afpnet.org

Sources: Salary.com Salary Wizard® September 4, 2008. Reprinted with permission.

Profile: Grant Writer

Name: Gail
Age: 49
Title: President

Employer: GK Grant Writing (self-employed consultant)
Education: AAS in illustration, BS in biology, MS in zoology
Years in Industry: 7

CAREER LADDER:

Staff analyst and grants specialist, development director, grant writing consultant

Did you have an internship in this field prior to starting your job?

I did not actually have an internship in the traditional sense of the word, but I learned on the job when I worked as the staff analyst and grants specialist for a local elected official. I also took some seminars and workshops and did some reading.

Do you know of which companies have the best internships in this field that are known to help launch a successful career?

The Arts and Business Council of New York has a wonderful Multicultural Arts Management Internship Program for minority students, which may include development work if the intern and the organization for which he or she works choose to do so. This program is sponsored by Con Edison.

Where are the best cities to live to find jobs like yours?

New York City, by far. Many, many foundations are located here, as are many, many non-profits and also The Foundation Center library, although much of this work can be done via Internet, email, phone and fax from wherever someone lives.

What is your typical day like?

I juggle different clients and their needs on a daily basis. Some need me to research potential funding sources and this mostly involves doing searches on the Internet. In particular, I use The Foundation Center's online database, to which I am a subscriber. Once these funders are identified, I confer with the client to narrow the list to the ones that best fit their organization's needs.

At this point I then carefully read each funder's guidelines to see how they would like to be approached initially by a non-profit organization. There is a lot of give and take with the client at this point via email and phone to gather the information I will need to write the grant proposal.

The final step is writing the actual proposal, letter or application, which may include doing additional research to gather statistics relevant to the proposal. I then email the proposal to the client with a list of additional attachments that must included and any other steps that must be taken.

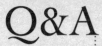

Q&A

On a given day I might be working on any of the tasks listed above, as well as attending meetings with current or potential clients, doing administrative work for my business (such as bookkeeping or marketing), returning calls and emails and attending educational or networking events.

What are your job responsibilities?

To identify and help secure funding from foundation, corporate and government sources for my non-profit clients.

What is your favorite part of your job?

Writing the actual proposals.

What do you dislike about your job?

The length of time it sometimes takes to cultivate a client and then to get to the point where there is a signed contract and I am able to start.

Have you had any turning-point or "light bulb" moments in your career that have helped you get to where you are today?

When I worked for a local elected official providing technical assistance regarding fundraising to non-profits, I realized how much I enjoyed doing that sort of work. I decided to leave that position because I was ready to enter the development field ("development" is the technical name for fundraising).

How did you know you wanted to pursue this career?

I enjoyed helping various organizations that were all trying to make the world a better place in one way or another. I felt I was directly contributing to their success. In particular, I enjoy helping organizations in the arts, environment, education and science fields.

How did you get into this industry and how did you get your most recent job?

I met the executive director of a non-profit theater when I was working for the local elected official. That led to my working as the development director (chief fundraising manager) for the theater for six and a half years. When I decided I wanted to leave my previous job and find a position doing development work full-time, I contacted the executive director myself. He was looking for someone and hired me. I left this position as development director in June 2006 to start my own business. As a working mother of an eight year old child, I needed to balance work and family life better. By consulting as a grant writer I am able to do so.

Q&A

What do you consider your greatest professional accomplishment?

Along with the theater's Artistic Director of Latino Programming, I helped initiate a program at the theater that commissioned new dance work from Latino and Latin American choreographers. We received funding for the program from the very start, including some funding from the NEA. The program continues to this day and most of the choreographers have been reviewed by the *New York Times* for their work, which is a major accomplishment for them. In fact, one of the choreographers is now one of my clients.

If you weren't doing this job, what similar careers might you consider?

Someday I want to start a "green" business that helps people help the environment. I just don't know exactly what kind of business yet!

To what professional associations do you belong?

I belong to the Association for Fundraising Professionals (AFP). I also recently joined the National Association of Female Executives (NAFE).

What professional publications and Web sites do you read?

I regularly use The Foundation Center's Web site and am a subscriber to some of their online newsletters. I don't get much time to read any other publication regularly.

What advice do you have for others who would like to pursue this career?

There are now programs offered by some colleges if you are interested in fundraising as a career. For example, New York University's George H. Heyman, Jr. Center for Philanthropy and Fundraising offers both a Master of Science in Fundraising and Certificates in Fundraising or Grantmaking and Foundations.

If you do not want to go this new route, be sure your writing and researching skills are top notch. Read fundraising journals such as the *Chronicle of Philanthropy*. In addition, AFP has more than one conference per year where you can learn the basics of fundraising if you are new to the profession.

Literary Agent

Job Description: A literary agent represents writers to publishers. An agent gets an author's manuscripts read and published, negotiates contracts and protects the author's rights. Agents usually specialize in the types of manuscripts they represent such as nonfiction (and particular categories like business, careers, education, popular psychology, or self-help) and/or fiction. Some fiction agents specialize in different genres like literary fiction, fantasy, historical, popular fiction, romance, science fiction, or young adult.

Training and Educational Qualifications: Most literary agents have college degrees. In many cases, agents majored in English or journalism or studied in humanities. They must have a good understanding of what makes good literature. However, agents come from a variety of academic backgrounds. One thing that is common to literary agents is a love for reading.

Job Outlook: The job outlook for literary agents is difficult to determine. Book publishing in general is currently competing for attention from the public due to the growth of entertainment industries such as television, film and digital media. Nonetheless, thousands of books continue to be published year after year and the majority of published books are produced through agents contacting appropriate editors at publishing houses rather than writers representing themselves.

Salary: Salaries vary greatly. There are so few literary agents compared to other occupations that there is no solid salary data available.

Significant Facts:

- Many literary agents start as interns or assistants in established literary agencies and some begin in book publishing before transitioning to agenting.

- There are very few literary agents in the United States—fewer than 500.

- Most positions are in New York City.

INDUSTRY RESOURCES:

Association of Authors' Representatives
www.aar-online.org

Profile: Literary Agent

Name: Scott
Age: 32
**Title: Literary Agent and
    Managing Member, FolioLit**

**Education: BA Government, MBA
    Finance**
Years in Industry: 4

CAREER LADDER:

My story is not typical of the average literary agent. I began my career in politics and was a partner with a lobbying firm in Washington, DC. I went to graduate school to get my MBA, intending to work in finance before finding the world of literary agenting. So I went from lobbyist, to graduate student, to literary intern, to literary agent, to literary agent/agency owner.

Did you have an internship in this field prior to starting your job?
Yes. I was an intern at a literary agency before being offered a full-time job.

Do you know of which companies have the best internships in this field that are known to help launch a successful career?
There are several ways to get into the profession and yes, interning at a literary agency is one of them. Many agents started out on the editorial side of publishing houses and later became agents; many others started out as assistants to established literary agents. Also, some book scouts become agents—they are people hired by foreign publishers to find books published in the United States that would sell well in other countries. Getting an internship is a good way to start at some agencies. We have about ten interns right now.

Where are the best cities to live to find jobs like yours?
New York. But once you've made contacts, you can live in other cities.

What is your typical day like?
It really varies depending on the time of year. But overall the breakdown is this: 25 percent editorial, 25 percent deal-making, 25 percent reading and 25 percent administration.

What are your job responsibilities?
I read submissions to determine who I want to take on as a client (I get about 300 to 500 submissions a week), decide which editor or publishing house to seek to sell manuscripts, and travel to speak at conferences. And like any other small business, there is the administrative component of managing finances and staff, and running an office.

What is your favorite part of your job?
I have two favorite parts. Having been a lifelong "book junkie," there is nothing like seeing a project you worked on actually in bookstores

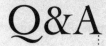

Q&A

and imagining how many people's lives you can touch through books. Plus, I meet a lot of people so I learn something new all the time.

What do you dislike about your job?

The publishing business is archaic in a lot of ways; the amount of time it takes to get a book published can be frustrating and it's not a huge growth industry

How did you know you wanted to pursue this career?

I spent 10 years as a working partner at a lobbying firm and I realized that it wasn't for me. I had to get out of that soul-sapping business. I needed a career change. I sold my firm and decided to pursue an MBA in finance. I thought I'd be working in that arena, but I discovered that I did not want to spend 18 hours a day working in a cubicle no matter what they paid me. I knew someone whose husband was an author and asked how he got his books published. It was at that point I found out that literary agenting was actually a job. I've always loved books and making deals, and being a literary agent combined my two interests so it seemed to be a perfect career fit for me.

How did you get into this industry?

During my last semester of graduate school, I sent out blind resumes to literary agencies. I told an agent that I would "work for free if you teach me the business." I interned there for about 6 to 8 weeks before joining the agency as a full-time agent.

Have you had any turning-point or "light bulb" moments in your career that have helped you get to where you are today?

I worked as an agent where I interned for about a year while I built up my own agenting practice. I am an entrepreneurial person and I was becoming dissatisfied working for someone else. So I determined that I would start a new firm. As of January 2007, with three partners in the business, we have sold about 100 books. I wake up every morning with a thrill to go the office. I feel like I have the best job in the world.

What do you consider your greatest professional accomplishment?

I've sold probably 45 books. Each one is a real accomplishment. Each author is like my family. Their books are like their children. It's terrifically rewarding.

If you weren't doing this job, what similar careers might you consider?

I'd probably be doing another "making deals" sort of job like management consulting or working private equity. Eventually, I'd like to own a small Irish pub in a small town.

Profile: Literary Agent

Q&A

To what professional associations do you belong?

I'm in the process of joining the Association of Artists' Representatives (AAR).

What professional publications do you read?

Publishers Weekly, Kirkus Reviews, Publisher's Marketplace and general interest publications.

What advice do you have for others who would like to pursue this career?

You have to really love books and really love reading. It takes a long time to build a practice and sustain yourself doing this. There is a very steep learning curve. It's not something you can really dabble in for a short amount of time; you have to budget between five to seven years to see if you can make it. Not a lot of people do this job—only about 300 in the whole country because it takes a long time to find out if you can build a career out of it. You must have a firm commitment to succeed.

Public Relations Specialist

Job Description: Public relations specialists handle organizational functions for groups in areas of media, community, consumer, industry, and governmental relations. They also can be involved in political campaigns, interest-group representation, conflict mediation and employee and investor relations. Public relations specialists do more than "tell the organization's story." They must understand the attitudes and concerns of community, consumer, employee, and public interest groups and establish and maintain cooperative relationships with them and with representatives from print and broadcast journalism.

Training and Educational Qualifications: There are no defined standards for entry into a public relations career. A college degree combined with public relations experience, usually gained through an internship, is considered excellent preparation for public relations work; in fact, internships are becoming vital to obtaining employment. The ability to communicate effectively is essential. Many entry-level public relations specialists have a college major in public relations, journalism, advertising or communication.

Job Outlook: Employment of public relations specialists is expected to grow 18 percent faster than average for all occupations through 2016. The need for good public relations in an increasingly competitive business environment should spur demand for public relations specialists in organizations of all types and sizes. However, keen competition likely will continue for entry-level public relations jobs, as the number of qualified applicants is expected to exceed the number of job openings.

Salary: Median annual earnings for salaried public relations specialists are $47,350. The middle 50 percent earn between $35,600 and $65,310; the lowest 10 percent earn less than $28,080, and the top 10 percent earn more than $89,220.

Significant Facts:

- Although employment of public relations specialists is projected to grow faster than average, keen competition is expected for entry-level jobs.

- Opportunities should be best for college graduates who combine a degree in public relations, journalism or another communications-related field with a public relations internship or other related work experience.

- Creativity, initiative and the ability to communicate effectively are essential.

INDUSTRY RESOURCES:

Public Relations Society of America, Inc.
33 Maiden Lane
New York, NY 10038-5150
Phone: (212) 460-1400
Internet: www.prsa.org

International Public Relations Association (IPRA)
1 Dunley Hill Court
Ranmore Common
Dorking, Surrey, RH5 6SX
United Kingdom
Phone: +44 1483 280 130
Email: iprasec@btconnect.com
Internet: www.ipra.org

Profile: Public Relations Executive

Name: Helen

Title: Executive Vice President, Arts and Communication Counselors Division

Employer: Ruder Finn

Education:
BA Art History and Government; MS Journalism and Communication

Years in Industry: 15

CAREER LADDER:

Promotions Intern, KISS FM radio, New York

Executive Trainee, Ruder Finn

Account Executive, Ruder Finn

Appointed to Assistant to Commissioner for Cultural Affairs, City of Chicago

Director of Public Affairs, Human Resources Development Institute

Public Relations Executive, Mingo Group

Vice President, Ruder Finn

Senior Vice President, Ruder Finn

Executive Vice President, Ruder Finn

Did you have an internship in this field prior to starting your job?

I had several. I interned at *Seventeen* magazine in the fashion department, at a museum doing research for a blockbuster expedition on the Harvard renaissance, at KISS FM radio in New York, and I did the training program at Ruder Finn.

Do you know of which companies have the best internships in this field that are known to help launch a successful career?

The Ruder Finn program is renowned throughout the industry. If you get into the program, which is not the easiest, you are immediately immersed into the business of the agency.

Where are the best cities to live to find jobs like yours?

It depends on your area of interest. For example, in the hi-tech industry, I imagine a lot jobs are in Silicon Valley. Most major cities have cultural institutions for someone interested in public relations for arts and cultural organizations. Overall, the cities that have the most opportunities are generally known to be New York, Chicago, Los Angeles and Washington, D.C.

What is your typical day like?

In a word, busy. I deal with client demands. This includes doing reports, doing research, writing and brainstorming.

What are your job responsibilities?

When you are coming up in this business, you are charged with execution in terms of research and drafting materials. The agency side of public relations is entrepreneurial and in management, it's exciting to bring in income for the agency doing what you enjoy.

Profile: Public Relations Executive

Q&A

What is your favorite part of your job?

Interacting with clients and coming up with different initiatives, plans, and programs for them to do. That is the most exciting part. Also, I have to stay on top of different trends happening in the field.

What do you dislike about your job?

It's constantly nonstop, so things that people do for fun are work for me. People say things like, "Did you see the exhibition at the Met?" A lot of those things I don't do because I do them for a living.

Have you had any turning-point or "light bulb" moments in your career that have helped you get to where you are today?

I moved to Chicago and was immediately embraced by a lot of good people. That was a good turning point for my career. Ultimately, coming back to Ruder Finn where I began, has been wonderful. I work in an environment where creativity is appreciated and encouraged. And working with David Finn, a giant in the industry, is fantastic—being in his presence is an honor.

How did you know you wanted to pursue this career?

In the beginning, I didn't really know what this career was. My peers were going to be lawyers or investment bankers. I applied to law school but decided I didn't want to pursue that career. Then I signed up for a presentation at Boston University and I was the only person who showed up to the event. I ended up having a one-on-one conversation with the speaker about a career in public relations. I got a scholarship to Boston University and the rest is history. This career combined what I love to do: writing, working with creative people and being around the arts.

What do you consider your greatest professional accomplishment?

My greatest professional accomplishment has been the innovations I have brought to the field. I have done things that have never been done before in the spirits industry. I am proud of promotions I personally created for certain brands. Finding and creating new ways to promote my clients' products and services continues to drive me.

If you weren't doing this job, what similar careers might you consider?

Journalism or law.

To what professional associations do you belong?

I don't belong to professional associations but I do participate in non-profit organizations. I am on the board of a few charitable organizations. I am active in supporting minority scholarships and neonatal wellness and literacy.

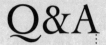

Profile: Public Relations Executive

Q&A

What advice do you have for others who would like to pursue this career?

Learn as much about the field as you can. Be open to opportunities. Be committed to being very professional. Sometimes people have an image of doing parties and events and hanging out with people; there's much more to it than that. Get a strong foundation with skills like writing and understanding media trends.

Reporter

Job Description: In covering a story, reporters investigate leads and news tips, look at documents, observe events at the scene and interview people. Reporters take notes and also may take photographs or shoot videos. At the office, they organize the material, determine the focus or emphasis, write their stories and edit accompanying video material.

Training and Educational Qualifications: Most employers prefer individuals with a bachelor's degree in journalism or mass communications, but some hire graduates with other majors. They look for experience at school newspapers or broadcasting stations and internships with news organizations. Large-city newspapers and stations may prefer candidates with a degree in a subject-matter specialty such as economics, political science or business. Some large newspapers and broadcasters may hire only experienced reporters.

Job Outlook: Competition will continue to be keen for jobs on large metropolitan and national newspapers, broadcast stations and networks, and magazines. Most job opportunities will be with small-town and suburban newspapers and radio and television stations. Newspapers are increasingly hiring stringers and freelancers.

Salary: Median annual earnings of reporters and correspondents are $33,470. The middle 50 percent earn between $24,370 and $51,700. The lowest 10 percent earn less than $19,180, and the highest 10 percent earn more than $73,880.

Significant Facts:

- Competition will be keen for jobs at large metropolitan and national newspapers, broadcast stations and magazines; most entry-level openings arise at small broadcast stations and publications.

- Most employers prefer individuals with a bachelor's degree in journalism or mass communications and experience gained at school newspapers or broadcasting stations or through internships with news organizations.

- Jobs often involve irregular hours, night and weekend work, and pressure to meet deadlines.

INDUSTRY RESOURCES:

Society of Professional Journalists
Eugene S. Pulliam National Journalism Center
3909 N. Meridian Street
Indianapolis, IN 46208
Phone: (317) 927-8000
Internet: www.spj.org

Dow Jones Newspaper Fund, Inc.
P.O. Box 300
Princeton, NJ 08543-0300
Phone: (609) 452-2820
Email: newsfund@wsj.dowjones.com

Profile: Reporter

Name: Jay	**Employer:** *The Washington Post*
Age: 62	**Education: BA Government, MA in**
Title: Education Reporter and	**East Asian regional studies**
Columnist	**Years in Industry: 40**

CAREER LADDER:

Summer intern reporter, Associated Press, New York City (NYC), information specialist, US Army, Vietnam; summer intern reporter Washington Star, (all the rest are Washington Post) night meetings reporter, Arlington County reporter, assistant foreign editor, DC political reporter, Virginia roving reporter, assistant foreign editor, Hong Kong bureau chief, Beijing bureau chief, LA bureau chief, wall street correspondent, Alexandria-Arlington schools reporter, metro education reporter (which I still am), education columnist.

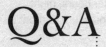

Did you have an internship in this field prior to starting your job?

I spent a summer as a reporter in the NYC bureau of the Associated Press after my junior year of college and one summer as an intern reporter at the *Washington Star* between my two years of graduate school. In both cases, I worked as a full-time reporter since I had experience as a very active reporter and editor on my college paper.

Do you know of which companies have the best internships in this field that are known to help launch a successful career?

The *Post* has the best program, but there are still some good internships at the *Boston Globe*, the *LA Times* and maybe a few other papers. The best thing to do is write to any and all papers you want to work for.

Where are the best cities to live to find jobs like yours?

New York, Washington, Houston, Los Angeles, Chicago. The bigger the city, the more opportunities.

What is your typical day like?

I get up at 7:30 a.m., read the papers, and get to work by 11:00 am. I check my email and send emails to sources on upcoming stories, talk to my editor on the phone (I work in our Alexandria, Virginia bureau and he is in the main newsroom in DC), write a column or story, check email, maybe make a phone call or two, go home to read accumulated work mail and transcribe tapes or work on book manuscript (I usually try to do 1,000 words a day on such projects). I interview someone in-person or watch a classroom in action about twice a week.

What are your job responsibilities?

I write stories for the Schools and Learning page of the *Post* every other week and do a weekly column for our Web site as well as a quarterly column for our magazine. I also write weekly Q&A columns in the

Q&A

neighborhood sections of the *Post* for Fairfax and Montgomery Counties, our two biggest school districts.

What is your favorite part of your job?

Interviewing successful educators, transcribing the tapes of those interviews (I always hear something I missed) and writing articles, columns or books about them.

What do you dislike about your job?

It is hard to keep control of the enormous amount of email I get. I am now mostly an email reporter, and that makes me much more efficient and productive, but I always feel like I am way behind.

Have you had any turning-point or "light bulb" moments in your career that have helped you get to where you are today?

My earlier career as a China correspondent began when I was taking a shower at age 16, thinking about my life, and realizing I was fascinated with that growing power in the East. But another experience actually got me where I am now in education writing. On December 7, 1982, while working as LA bureau chief for the *Post*, I went to Garfield High School to interview AP math teacher, Jaime Escalante. That interview led to several books and hundreds of articles, as well as the high school rating system used by *Newsweek*, on my favorite subject, how to make high schools more challenging.

How did you know you wanted to pursue this career?

I wanted to go to China. I first studied to be a diplomat but discovered that was a huge bore—too many rules, too much emphasis on social chit chat. My dad had been a reporter for a while, so I thought that would be a more enjoyable way to get to China.

How did you get into the industry?

I joined the *Harvard Crimson*, the daily student paper at my college. That was an important move, and I recommend that to everyone. Go to a large university that has a daily paper and make that your prime extra-curricular activity. It's fun, you learn a very useful trade and you meet some very interesting people. I married the managing editor the day we graduated.

What do you consider your greatest professional accomplishment?

I have been able, through the *Post* and my books and the *Newsweek* list, to spotlight one of the worst facets of high school education—the persistent refusal to open up our best courses, Advanced Placement (AP) and International Baccalaureate (IB), to all students who want to take them. Far more people are aware of this now and are doing something about it than before I started.

Profile: Reporter

Q&A

If you weren't doing this job, what similar careers might you consider?

I would probably be a high school teacher and then a principal.

To what professional associations do you belong?

I am on the board of Editorial Projects in Education, the non-profit organization that publishes *Education Week*, the newspaper. I belong to the Education Writers Association.

What professional publications do you read?

I read *Education Week* and an assortment of education publications.

What advice do you have for others who would like to pursue this career?

Good writing and reporting starts with lots of reading. Get in the habit of reading a good newspaper every day and study deeply those subjects that interest you. The happiest journalists, like me, are specialists.

Screenwriter

Job Description: Screenwriters create original scripts to be performed by actors for television and film. In addition to crafting the story and dialogue, screenwriters also provide descriptions of setting, mood and character to give readers a visual impression of what the finished work might look like on screen.

Training and Educational Qualifications: A college degree generally is helpful for a screenwriter but it is not necessarily required. Some people pursue master's of fine arts degrees (MFA) in screenwriting to learn their craft.

Job Outlook: Because screenwriting is such a unique profession and few people make a living at it, it is difficult to determine a "job outlook" for this particular type of writing. As Richard Walter, the head of the UCLA's Department of Film and Television says, "Your day job is your friend."

Salary: Salaries for screenwriters vary greatly by project. There is no annual salary for screenwriters unless they are employed as full-time writers for studios, and this is normally for television writing rather than for films.

Significant Facts:

- It is often helpful to study communications, journalism, or English at the college level and take screenwriting courses to learn how to write a script.

- Most screenwriters have agents who represent them.

- Screenwriting is an extremely competitive field.

INDUSTRY RESOURCES:

Writers Guild of America, East
555 West 57th Street, Suite 1230
New York, NY 10019
Phone: (212) 767-7800
Internet: www.wgaeast.org

Writers Guild of America, West
7000 West Third Street
Los Angeles, CA 90048
Phone: (800) 548-4532
Internet: www.wga.org

Profile: Screenwriter

Name: Jessica Bendinger
Title: Screenwriter

Education: BA English
Years in Industry: 11

CAREER LADDER:

Intern, SPIN magazine
Freelance writer, SPIN magazine
Writer, MTV News
Editor, SPIN magazine
Music video director
Freelance writer (corporate and technical)

Freelance producer for corporate events
Scriptwriter, Sous Le Soleil
Screenwriter (my first screenplay was
   Bring it On)
Screenwriter/Script Doctor/Director

Where are the best cities to live to find jobs like yours?

Los Angeles is the best for film, at least in the beginning of a career, because it is easier to learn the rules of the business living in Los Angeles. There are many opportunities in New York for television. But after you've navigated Hollywood and have achieved some success as a screenwriter, you can live anywhere.

What is your typical day like?

Being a screenwriter provides an enormous amount of freedom. If I am not on assignment for a studio, I choose my own hours and work when my inspiration strikes. But at the times I am working on assignment or doing a production rewrite, then I keep strict hours. I go to my office and work from 8:00 a.m. to noon and get a lot done before lunch. I set little goals for myself; for example, I try to get a certain numbers of pages done per day and things like that.

Depending on how urgent a project is, I log the "man hours" which can be as many as 10–12 hours. Other times, it might just be two hours. In the last 10 years, I've actually worked on 20 projects, which means that I've worked on a lot of movies that have employed numerous scriptwriters. However, just because I work on a project doesn't ultimately mean I have my name on the finished product.

What are your job responsibilities?

As a screenwriter, I write an original script, then edit and polish it. I also rewrite scripts for studios, which entails getting notes from the studio and producers. I have to read previous scripts and make sure I am incorporating the right pieces of existing drafts. This work is sometimes explained as being a "script doctor" and it means creating a new script from pre-existing ones. Often, there are multiple drafts. I have to make sure I am omitting the right things and folding in new changes—I piece together a new script from old versions, however, the final product has to be seamless. If I am rewriting a script and the film is in production or pre-production, it can be a very tight schedule.

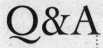

Q&A

What is your favorite part of your job?

The opportunity to access my imagination and creatively go wherever I want to go—I get to be an emotional and psychological explorer.

What do you dislike about your job?

Every business has a certain amount of rules of the road you have to learn and master. The politics of Hollywood is fascinating—it's some common sense and some ego—but the power dynamic can be arbitrary. Screenwriters have to learn to take it with a big grain of salt.

Have you had any turning-point or "light bulb" moments in your career that have helped you get to where you are today?

Writing and screenwriting are such cumulative processes and the journey is such that you can't pin down one moment. Screenwriters can get attached to their work; sometimes we think we are the work. But you must discover that screenwriting is a collaborative medium; it is a recipe for the actors, director and crew to use in making that dish. That's an important realization for screenwriters to have—a healthy sense of collaboration and yet detachment from the work. Words on a page are suggestions for the ingredients of the dish that is going to be made, but it might not be concocted exactly the way a screenwriter envisions. In filmmaking, there are really three different movies: the one that is written, the one that is shot, and the one that is cut for audiences to see.

How did you know you wanted to pursue this career?

It was unconscious more than conscious. I was watching movies and thought, "Maybe I could do this!" Movies like *Diner* by Barry Levinson and movies by John Hughes and Cameron Crowe spoke to me. I could relate to the conversational dialogue. I could see myself writing those conversations. I studied some books about screenwriting, got my hands on some screenplays and I met a working screenwriter in college. All of those things helped to demystify the process for me.

How did you get into this industry?

Everyone's story of getting into Hollywood is different. My first writing job was doing an internship at *SPIN* magazine in college. The magazine was understaffed, so it was a great opportunity to get assignments. I was fortunate enough to interview some hip hop artists, so I was published before I graduated.

Actually getting to Hollywood took a while. I had taken some film classes at Columbia. I wanted to try it, but it seemed like a difficult goal to achieve. I applied to the Sundance Screenwriter's Lab, but I was rejected.

I decided to write a TV sitcom spec, and I was able to find a TV agent. I had a lot of meetings in Los Angeles but I couldn't get a television writing job. I supported myself doing technical writing, PR and

freelance writing. I'd given notes to a writer in New York who had written a TV spec script. He eventually sold a TV series in France. He asked if I wanted to work on the show, so I moved to Paris to work on *Sous le Soleil*.

When I came back to Hollywood, no one cared about my scriptwriting experience in France, so I wrote a spec feature film script and it went to "auction," which means an agent sends it to potential buyers. No one wanted it because a similar movie was about to come out, but everyone loved the writing so I got meetings from the sample. I pitched *Bring It On* at my first meetings—29 times. I got 28 "no's" but one "yes," and that was all it took. That sale got me into the Writer's Guild. So it was kind of a "10-year overnight" success story.

What do you consider your greatest professional accomplishment?

I have a couple. The first script I sold was produced and that was a wonderful accomplishment. In Hollywood, not all scripts that are sold become movies—so it is a great achievement to have the first one sold actually become a movie. Another milestone was that I sold the script *Stick It!* for $1.5 million, also was attached to direct it (my directorial debut) and received a "progress-to-production deal." This means the studio was required to "green light" the movie within six months, which is rare in Hollywood. As both a screenwriter and director, to see your ideas come to fruition as a movie is extraordinary.

If you weren't doing this job, what similar careers might you consider?

I love people and the processes of change that people go through over time. I might be a therapist, guidance counselor or teacher.

To what professional associations do you belong?

Writers Guild of America, Director's Guild of America, and SACD, which is the French Writers' Union.

What trade publications do you read?

I don't subscribe to industry trades like *Hollywood Reporter* or *Variety*. I think reading them too much can engender an unhealthy sense of competition. I believe creativity should come from inspiration. It's important to know what's going on in one's field, but I don't want to know every single deal that's made every single day. If there is something I know I need to find out, I will research it and find the information that way. When I do read the trade publications on occasion, I read them in a targeted way.

Profile: Screenwriter

Q&A

What advice do you have for others who would like to pursue this career?

For people who aspire to be writers, make sure you are good. Writing can be an isolated and lonely endeavor. Get feedback through a class, a professional mentor, or you can even pay a script reader to give you "coverage," (which is a professional analysis from the Hollywood perspective). After you've taken classes, studied, read your books and written drafts, it's very important to get feedback—but not just any feedback—it's important to use discernment about whom you get feedback from. Without feedback from sources who understand the medium, it's hard to gauge where you are on the playing field. Give your samples to people who are accustomed to reading scripts.

How do screenwriters get agents?

Relationships with agents begin by having strong writing samples combined with the legwork of networking. Some people start networking at film schools. Some people meet industry contacts through friends or festivals. But getting an agent is the least of a potential screenwriter's problems. The biggest challenge is to become a great screenwriter. It's not enough to be good. It's very different than most forms of creative writing. About 98 percent of most scripts aren't done well. As a result, it's hard to get people to read material for free. If the first two to ten pages aren't good, the reader won't read any further. If you are talented and work hard to cultivate your abilities to become a great screenwriter, you have an excellent chance of finding an agent.

Jessica Bendinger Filmography

Stick It *(2006, written and directed by)*
Aquamarine *(2006, screenplay)*
First Daughter *(2004, screenplay, story)*
The Truth About Charlie *(2002, screenplay)*
"Sex and the City" *(2001, season 4)*
Time and Punishment *(2001, TV episode)*
Bring It On *(2000, written by)*

Speechwriter

Job Description: Speechwriters assess facts and opinions that are to be presented by a client and then compose speeches for the client, or a representative of the client, to deliver in both the public and private sectors of business, non-profit, government and higher education settings.

Training and Educational Qualifications: A college degree generally is required for a position as a writer or editor. Although some employers look for a broad liberal arts background, most prefer to hire people with degrees in communications, journalism or English. For those who specialize in a particular area, such as fashion, business, or law, additional background in the chosen field is expected. Knowledge of a second language is helpful for some positions.

Job Outlook: In general, employment of salaried writers is expected to increase. Large businesses and organizations often hire speechwriters to write for their executives.

Salary: Speechwriters earn between $48,929 and $107,200.

Significant Facts:

- Most speechwriters are experienced writers—many of them have backgrounds in journalism and public affairs.

- Sometimes speechwriting is one duty of a top-level manager in public affairs, public relations or communications.

- Positions for full-time speechwriters (as the primary or sole job function) are available in government, large companies and non-profit organizations and periodically, in universities for university presidents.

Salary Source: Salary.com Salary Wizard® September 4, 2008. Used with permission.

Profile: Speechwriter

Name: Ed
Age: 62
Title: Speechwriter/Owner, Vilade
**   Communications**
Employer: Self-employed

Education: BA, Public
**   Communications; MA, Speech**
**   Communications**
Years in Industry: Professional
**   writer, 41; Speechwriter, 26.**

CAREER LADDER:

Sportswriter, Morris County Record, Plainfield Courier News, *1965–68; Sports Editor,* Somerset Messenger-Gazette, *1968–69; News Editor, Editorial Page Editor,* Morris County Record, *1969–72; Staff Editor,* National Petroleum News *(McGraw-Hill), 1972; Editor-in-Chief, U.S.* Oil Week, *1972–74; Public Information Officer, Federal Energy Office/Administration, 1974–76; Director of General News (media relations), Special Assistant to Deputy Secretary, Chief Speechwriter, US Department of Energy, 1976–84; Publisher, Arrival Magazine, 1984; Executive Writer, Pacific Gas & Electric, 1984–87; Executive Writer, Virginia Power, 1987–89; Owner, Vilade Communications, 1989–91; Manager, Public Policy Issues, Niagara Mohawk Power, 1991–97; Owner, Vilade Communications, 1997–2001; Chief Speechwriter, Nuclear Energy Institute, 2001–2003; Owner, Vilade Communications, 2003–present.*

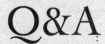

Do you know of which companies have the best internships in this field that are known to help launch a successful career?

There are no internships that I know of, as speechwriting isn't really an entry-level position. Some large companies might have research internships that would help. The best training is editorial writing for newspapers—any kind of opinion writing. Capitol Hill is a good place to get training, which would be writing for a Senator or Congressperson.

Where are the best cities to live to find jobs like yours?

Washington, DC is probably best because there are so many legislators and executive branch officials giving speeches. There are also many trade associations and Non-Governmental Organizations (NGOs) that need speechwriters. Other than that, New York City or any other major city.

What is your typical day like?

When I'm working out of my home office, what I do with my day depends on whether or not I have an assignment. A speech can take anywhere from half a day to a whole week to write. Early in the process, I do research and read through the materials a client has provided. I also try to interview the client personally, using a tape recorder. Once the research and interviewing are done, I just sit down at my computer and write until I get a draft done. Once I send off a draft, I wait for comments and/or revisions, and then I make them.

When I'm looking for assignments, I might use the day to call or visit prospective clients, or network with other speechwriters to see what is happening and find out if they have any leads. For the past several months, though, I have been (atypically) working out of my client's

Profile: Speechwriter

office on a contract. So I put on a coat and tie and drive to the office, where I work on speeches much as I would from my home office.

What are your job responsibilities?

I write speeches, stay up on what's going on in the world so I can make topical references, read up on the subject matter about which I write (energy, environment, world trade, international finance, etc.) so I can help my speaker sound erudite.

What is your favorite part of your job?

Writing—crafting a speech that helps my speaker achieve his or her communication objective.

What do you dislike about your job?

The speaker's inevitable cadre of assistants and other gatekeepers who destroy my best lines before the Secretary/CEO/Chairman/President gets to read them.

Have you had any turning-point or "light bulb" moments in your career that have helped you get to where you are today?

I have had several. One of the first came when I was given an assignment to write a speech before I formally became a speechwriter. Several colleagues commiserated, to the tune of "Man, I could never write a speech. It's too tough." I realized that the more people felt that way, the less competition I would have. I also realized that if clients thought it was tough, they would pay more. Both have proven to be true—there's competition, but there's enough business to go around. And it does pay well.

My second light bulb moment came when I realized, after writing speeches for years, that what I did was an actual academic discipline called "rhetoric" or "speech communication." I went back for my master's and learned why I was doing what I was doing. My academic study of speech communication has made me a much better speechwriter.

How did you know you wanted to pursue the career?

The Department of Energy made me a manager, and eventually I had to decide which 15 of the 30 people I managed would be laid off. I decided that I didn't want to be a manager any more, and that I wanted to go back to what I did best—writing. Speechwriting pays more than any non-managerial position in corporate communications, and more than any other type of freelancing, in my experience.

How got into the industry and how got most recent job?

I was originally hired into the government as a speechwriter, despite never having written a speech. It was a convenience used to get me on board during the Arab Oil Embargo. When they discovered my newspaper background, they threw me into the breach in media relations.

Profile: Speechwriter

Q&A I became a high-profile spokesperson for the Department of Energy during the energy shocks of the '70s under the Carter Administration. When the Reagan Administration came in, they abolished my job. I had Republican as well as Democratic friends, however. Since I had been initially hired as a speechwriter, the new administration simply shifted me over to be chief speechwriter for the Department of Energy. It was what I wanted anyway and I have been doing it ever since.

I got my most recent job when I decided I didn't want to be a corporate speechwriter any more, and I began freelancing. I value the freedom—the opportunity to work out of my basement office wearing sweats or take off in the middle of the week to play golf.

What is your greatest professional accomplishment?

I have written speeches for three United States presidents, senators, governors, more than 100 CEOs, university and association presidents and others. My greatest accomplishment is probably lasting more than 25 years as a speechwriter. I have written many speeches of which I am proud, and it is hard to single out any one of them.

What other career might I have considered?

Author. I'm going to phase out of speechwriting someday soon and just write books for the rest of my life. I have two in the works now. At 62, I'm overdue to publish a book.

To what professional associations do you belong?

I belong to Washington Speechwriters Roundtable and Washington Independent Writers.

What professional publications do you read?

I subscribe to *The Speechwriters Newsletter* and the *Economist*.

What advice do you have for others who would like to pursue this career?

If you want to be a speechwriter, study speech communication—learn your craft. There are dozens of excellent speech communication programs around the country. Otherwise, go into newspaper work and become an editorial writer. It's an excellent way to learn opinion writing, which is the core of speechwriting.

Technical Writer

Job Description: Technical writers put technical information into easily understandable language. They prepare operating and maintenance manuals, catalogs, parts lists, assembly instructions, sales promotion materials and project proposals. Many technical writers work with engineers on technical subject matters to prepare written interpretations of engineering and design specifications and other information for a general readership.

Training and Educational Qualifications: A college degree often is required for a position as a writer or editor. Although some employers look for a broad liberal arts background, most prefer to hire people with degrees in communications, journalism or English. Increasingly, technical writing requires a degree in, or some knowledge about, a specialized field—for example, engineering, business or one of the sciences. In many cases, people with good writing skills can acquire specialized knowledge on the job. Some transfer from jobs as technicians, scientists or engineers.

Job Outlook: Demand for technical writers and writers with expertise in areas such as law, medicine or economics is expected to increase because of the continuing expansion of scientific and technical information and the need to communicate it to others. Rapid growth and change in the high-technology and electronics industries has resulted in a greater need for people to write users' guides, instruction manuals and training materials.

Salary: Median annual earnings for salaried technical writers are $58,050. The middle 50 percent earn between $45,130 and $73,750. The lowest 10 percent earn less than $35,520, and the highest 10 percent earn more than $91,720. Median annual earnings in computer systems design and related services are $59,830.

Significant Facts:

- Technical writers must exhibit a familiarity with electronic publishing, graphics and video production equipment. Use of electronic and wireless communications equipment to send email, transmit work and review copy often is necessary as well.

- Demand for technical writers and writers with expertise in areas such as law, medicine or economics is expected to increase because of the continuing expansion of scientific and technical information and the need to communicate it to others.

- Technical writers may serve as part of a team conducting usability studies to help improve the design of a product that still is in the prototype stage.

INDUSTRY RESOURCES:

Society for Technical Communication, Inc.
901 N. Stuart Street, Suite 904
Arlington, VA 22203
Phone: (703) 522-4114
Email: stc@stc.org
Internet: www.stc.org

Profile: Technical Writer

Name: Linda
Age: 58
Title: Manager, Technical Publications

Employer: Hewlett-Packard
Education: BA, English Literature
Years in Industry: 30

CAREER LADDER:

I began as a fruit seller, then clerk, then accounting tech. Next, I was a clerk/administrative assistant, then finally, editorial assistant, tech writer/editor, followed by becoming a manager of tech writers. After those jobs, I went back to being a writer, then manager again. I filled a position as a VP of a techcom consulting firm, and then became senior editor for software, then consultant, then manager of tech publications again.

Where are the best cities to live to find jobs like yours?
Where high tech, biomed, government research, banking and finance, and medical services abound, so do tech communicators.

What is your typical day like?
Mentoring, administering, collaborating, attending meetings, team leading, writing, editing and more meetings!

What are your job responsibilities?
As manager, I lead a team of six information developers who write online software documentation, white papers, and other docs to support the software our area of HP develops.

What is your favorite part of your job?
People—always the people!

What do you dislike about your job?
Bureaucracy and lack of people for support of a huge company (support is all through a portal, and we seldom see real people to support our HR, IT, needs, etc.).

Have you had any turning-point or "light bulb" moments in your career that have helped you get to where you are today?
Absolutely! I've had many. In a nutshell, I believe that professional organizations like Society for Technical Communication (STC) keep us sane, integrity to self keeps us whole, and it can't only be about the money! You have to have passion for what you do.

How did you know you wanted to pursue this career?
I was a single mom trying to put myself through school in order to earn an English degree. I was offered amazing training opportunity through my employer (the Department of Defense at the time) and with their help, I finished school.

Profile: Technical Writer

Q&A

I chose becoming a tech writer as my goal because it was the only thing the lab did that supported my interest and abilities in writing and language.

How did you get your most recent job?

I got my current job through positive thinking, the help of the Society for Technical Communication and friends, and being proactive when an online resume/application process didn't work. By calling the company and complaining, I was brought to their attention, and the job became mine. (We were not HP at the time, but a smaller software company. HP has since acquired us.)

What do you consider your greatest professional accomplishment?

Becoming a Society for Technical Communication Fellow.

If you weren't doing this job, what similar careers might you consider?

Teaching, mediation, child advocacy.

To what professional associations do you belong?

Society for Technical Communication (STC) and Women in Technology International (WITI).

What professional publications do you read?

I read materials from both organizations I belong to as well the *Harvard Business Review*.

What advice do you have for others who would like to pursue this career?

Love it; do it well, believe in yourself, and roll with the punches.

English/Journalism: Creative Writing Professor

Job Description: Creative writing professors teach various forms of creative writing such as fiction, nonfiction, playwriting, and screenwriting, at both the undergraduate and graduate levels in colleges and universities. Creative writing professors are often expected to publish their own literary works while teaching. Creative writing faculty are usually faculty members in a larger campus English department.

Training and Educational Qualifications: The terminal degree in creative writing is the master of fine arts (MFA) degree, which is normally required for a full-time, tenure-track position at a college or university. A few doctoral programs in creative writing, or a combined doctorate in creative writing and literature, do exist. Some of those degree holders also seek jobs teaching creative writing positions in academia; however, the MFA is still the most common degree in the field.

Job Outlook: Overall, employment of postsecondary teachers is expected to grow much faster than the average for all occupations through 2016. A significant proportion of these new jobs will be part-time positions. Job opportunities are generally expected to be very good—although they will vary somewhat from field to field—as numerous openings for all types of postsecondary teachers result from the retirement of current postsecondary teachers and continued increases in student enrollment.

Finding a job teaching creative writing is one of the most competitive academic fields in higher education. Prospective candidates should have both excellent academic credentials and a well-regarded record of publication. Without at least one published book (and sometimes more than one), a prospective applicant will not be competitive with other applicants seeking a position teaching creative writing at the college level.

Salary: Earnings for college faculty vary according to rank and type of institution, geographic area, and field. According to a 2006-07 survey by the American Association of University Professors, salaries for full-time faculty averaged $73,207. By rank, the average was $98,974 for professors, $69,911 for associate professors, $58,662 for assistant professors, $42,609 for instructors and $48,289 for lecturers.

Significant Facts:

- Opportunities for postsecondary teaching jobs are expected to be good, but many new openings will be for part-time or non-tenure track positions.

- Creative writing is one of the most competitive academic fields.

- Most applicants will need to have an MFA in creative writing and a record of publication to be competitive for vacancies.

INDUSTRY RESOURCES:

American Association of University Professors (AAUP)
1012 Fourteenth Street, NW, Suite 500
Washington, DC 20005-3465
Phone: (202) 737-5900
Internet: www.aaup.org

The Association of Writers and Writing Programs
Mail Stop 1E3
George Mason University
Fairfax, VA 22030-4444
Phone: (703) 993-4301
Internet: www.awpwriter.org

Profile: Creative Writing Professor

Name: Jim Daniels
Age: 50
Title: Thomas Stockham Baker Professor of English/Director, Creative Writing Program

Employer: Carnegie Mellon University
Education: BA, English, MFA, Creative Writing
Years in Industry: 27

CAREER LADDER:

Thomas Stockham Baker Professor of English
Professor, English Department, Carnegie Mellon University
Field Faculty, Vermont College of Norwich University
Visiting Professor, Northern Michigan University

Writer in Residence, Alma College, Spring Term
Associate Professor, English Department, Carnegie Mellon University
Visiting Professor, Florida International University
Assistant Professor, English Department, Carnegie Mellon
Visiting Writer in Residence, Carnegie Mellon
Lecturer, English Department, Bowling Green State University

Where are the best cities to live to find jobs like yours?

It depends on where the universities are. Bigger cities tend to have clusters of universities, which means more jobs in the field.

What is your typical day like?

I teach creative writing classes two days a week. On the days I teach, I go in and teach, then maintain my office hours in which I meet individually with students, and I also attend various meetings connected to the English department and creative writing program.

What are your job responsibilities?

Teaching creative writing classes and overseeing a program that contains eight faculty members and approximately one hundred majors.

What is your favorite part of your job?

Teaching. I teach what I love, and working with young writers continues to feed my enthusiasm for my own writing.

What do you dislike about your job?

The bureaucracy that I sometimes have to deal with in terms of scheduling classes, etc.

Have you had any turning-point or "light bulb" moments in your career that have helped you get to where you are today?

When I read a book called *A Government Job at Last* edited by Tom Wayman, it convinced me that I could write about things that mattered to me, things that I knew and cared about such as factory work and working-class life, and find places that might publish my work.

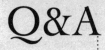

Profile: Creative Writing Professor

Q&A

How did you know you wanted to pursue this career?

When I was in high school, I became hooked on writing. I had the encouragement of a couple of teachers who helped give me the confidence to pursue a career in the arts.

Describe how you got into this industry and how you got your most recent job.

I had published enough in graduate school to get an interview for the job at Carnegie Mellon. I had experience editing literary magazines and running a reading series, which also helped.

What do you consider your greatest professional accomplishment?

Getting an endowed chair at Carnegie Mellon.

If you weren't doing this job, what similar careers might you consider?

Perhaps journalism or publishing.

To what professional associations do you belong?

I belong to the Associated Writing Programs and the Academy of American Poets.

What professional publications do you read?

I read many, many literary journals. Two journals I read for information on writing are *Poets & Writers* magazine and the *Writer's Chronicle*.

What advice do you have for others who would like to pursue this career?

As soon as you think your work is polished/finished, begin working on getting it published. It is extremely difficult to find a job teaching creative writing if you have not published anything.

English/Journalism Teacher (K-12)

Job Description: English teachers teach grammar, writing and literature. Some English teachers also teach creative writing electives or journalism classes. Many advise students in related extra-curricular activities such as publishing a school newspaper or literary magazine.

Training and Educational Qualifications: Requirements for licenses to teach kindergarten through grade 12 vary by state. However, all states require general education teachers to have a bachelor's degree and to have completed an approved teacher training program with a prescribed number of subject credits as well as supervised practice teaching. Some states also require technology training and the attainment of a minimum GPA. A number of states require that teachers obtain a master's degree in education within a specified period after they begin teaching.

Job Outlook: Through 2016, overall student enrollment in elementary, middle, and secondary schools—a key factor in the demand for teachers—is expected to rise more slowly than in the past as children of the baby boom generation leave the school system. Projected enrollments will vary by region. Fast-growing states in the West—particularly California, Idaho, Hawaii, Alaska, Utah, and New Mexico—will experience the largest enrollment increases. Enrollments in the South will increase at a more modest rate, while those in the Northeast and Midwest are expected to hold relatively steady.

Salary: Median annual earnings of kindergarten, elementary, middle, and secondary school teachers range from $43,580 to $48,690; the lowest 10 percent earn $28,590 to $33,070; the top 10 percent earn $67,490 to $76,100.

According to the American Federation of Teachers, beginning teachers with a bachelor's degree earned an average of $31,753.

The estimated average salary of all public elementary and secondary school teachers was $47,602. Private school teachers generally earn less than public school teachers, but may be given other benefits such as free or subsidized housing.

Significant Facts:

*   In addition to conducting classroom activities, teachers oversee homerooms, supervise extra-curricular activities, and accompany students on field trips.

*   Public school teachers must have at least a bachelor's degree, complete an approved teacher education program and be licensed.

*   Many states offer alternative licensing programs to attract people to the field of teaching.

INDUSTRY RESOURCES:

American Federation of Teachers
555 New Jersey Avenue, NW
Washington, DC 20001
Phone: (202) 879-4400
Internet: www.aft.org

National Education Association
1201 16th Street, NW
Washington, DC 20036-3290
Phone: (202) 833-4000
Internet: www.new.org

National Council of Teachers of English
1111 W. Kenyon Road
Urbana, IL 61801-1096
Phone: (217) 328-3870
Internet: www.ncte.org

Journalism Education Association
Kansas State University
103 Kedzie Hall
Manhattan, KS 66506-1505
Phone: (866) 532-5532
Internet: www.jea.org

Profile: English Teacher

Name: Tomm
Age: 39
Title: High School English Teacher
Employer: North Pocono High School/The University of Scranton

Education: BS Secondary Education, BA English, MS Educational Strategy,
MS Educational Technology
Years in Industry: 14 teaching /15 coaching

CAREER LADDER:

English teacher, assistant coach to head coach

Did you have an internship in this field prior to starting your job?

Student teaching during college—a college senior assumes duties and responsibilities of classroom teacher over the course of a semester as part of becoming a teacher.

Where are the best cities to live to find jobs like yours?

Everywhere.

What is your typical day like?

I teach English and Shakespeare through Performance from 8:00 a.m. to 3:30 p.m. Then I coach a two-hour practice as a part-time college swimming coach. I teach four sections of eleventh grade English literature as well as two honors classes.

What are your job responsibilities?

All facets of English education. I teach grammar, writing, literature, vocabulary and understanding Shakespeare through performing his plays on the stage.

What is your favorite part of your job?

I get paid to talk about my favorite things to people who have to listen. When students are open, willing, and ready to learn, giving them the opportunity to make a connection between the characters from a Shakespeare play and modern society today is a great feeling.

What do you dislike about your job?

Paperwork, forms, bureaucracy.

Have you had any turning-point or "light bulb" moments in your career that have helped you get to where you are today?

I studied with Shakespeare and Company, a theater company in Lenox, Massachusetts, in the summer of 2003. That experience affected both my teaching and coaching. It was a performance company that had a strong education philosophy and taught how to teach Shakespeare through performance; specifically, the experience taught me how to take

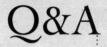

Q&A

Shakespeare's language and remove the ostentatiousness to see it in a different light. His plays were never intended to be read silently—it is an interesting literary pursuit to read them—but someone reading the lines is more true to the meaning of his plays.

How did you know you wanted to pursue this career?

I took education classes in college because they came easy to me and helped keep my GPA up. By the end of school, I realized that I only needed to student teach and pass a few tests to get certified. The district where I student taught had some openings over the next few years and the rest is history.

What do you consider your greatest professional accomplishment?

Getting the Shakespeare class going has also been a highlight for me. It was passed over three times before acceptance. We changed principals and the new principal was intrigued by the class. He allowed me to go into the classroom and pitch the class to the kids. Many people said "No kid is willing to study Shakespeare." But they were. And they did choose to study this with me. They are very happy to be in the class; they are having fun and learning. Since the goal of the class is to better understand Shakespeare through performing the plays and scenes, we do memorize the lines and perform in class everyday. The first quarter they only perform in front of classmates. The second quarter they perform in front of an audience without costumes or scenery. They learn that the language can convey the meaning when it is spoken correctly and enacted on the stage.

If you weren't doing this job, what similar careers might you consider?

I think that I need to interact with people and teach or show them something. I would be very poor at sales, but I probably would be a good presenter or something similar to that. I'd certainly perish in an office and would love, love, love to be an actor.

To what professional associations do you belong?

The Pennsylvania Teachers' Union.

What advice do you have for others who would like to pursue this career?

Teaching is much more difficult than it appears. The part we all remember as students is the easy part. The planning and grading along with the adapting to changes is far more challenging.

Profile: High School Journalism Teacher/Advisor

Name: Christine	**Education:**
Age: 30	**BA in English; MEd English**
Title: Journalism Adviser	**Education with emphasis in**
Employer: School District of	**Journalism Education**
Clayton	**Years in Industry:** 7

CAREER LADDER:

Newspaper advisor and communication arts (English) teacher, yearbook advisor, broadcast news advisor, photojournalism teacher

Do you know of which companies have the best internships in this field that are known to help launch a successful career?

To be a journalist or a journalism teacher, the best place to intern would be at a specific media company. I think radio is probably one of the easier internships to get, but all forms of media need and use interns, whether it's TV, newspapers, magazines or publishing companies.

Where are the best cities to live to find jobs like yours?

States with strong university journalism programs probably also have strong high school journalism programs. For example, the University of Missouri has one of the top-rated journalism schools in the United States, so scholastic journalism is very strong in high schools in St. Louis, Kansas City and even in smaller towns in Missouri. Other states that have strong scholastic journalism traditions are Kansas, Texas, Indiana, California, New York and Virginia, but journalism teachers are needed in every high school in the US. Public schools are likely to have more extensive journalism programs than private schools. Each high school usually only has one or two journalism advisors.

What is your typical day like?

Many journalism advisors teach English classes, and though I have in the past, I do not now. I usually arrive at school about 1.5 hours before it begins and work with students on their layouts, stories or photo assignments. I teach a photojournalism class, a yearbook class, and a broadcast news class that produces an eight-minute news and feature show once a week. I usually stay after school to work with students or allow them time to work on their assignments.

What are your job responsibilities?

I teach journalism lessons to students on such topics as journalism law and ethics, writing, photography and digital video/photo editing. I help students one-on-one with their tasks. I manage the budgets of the yearbook and the broadcast news class.

Profile: High School Journalism Teacher/Advisor

Q&A

What is your favorite part of your job?
Working one-on-one with students in a more relaxed environment.

What do you dislike about your job?
The pressure of deadlines.

Have you had any turning-point or "light bulb" moments in your career that have helped you get to where you are today?
When I moved from Kansas City to St. Louis, I applied for both English and journalism teaching jobs. I was offered a job at a school teaching only English and a job teaching only journalism. I realized that I had developed a passion for teaching journalism, more so than English, so that's the path I took.

How did you know you wanted to pursue this career?
I really like the significance of journalism, the idea of sharing human stories and helping people understand each other. I feel that journalism is a wonderful way to learn about so many fields of study, from politics to sociology to sports. It's also a great way to teach organization, writing and creativity. Kids love journalism classes because they are so hands-on. I just see so much purpose in teaching students to be journalists.

How did you get into this industry?
I wanted to teach English and when I was offered a job at a good school on the condition that I would advise the newspaper, I agreed. I had no journalism experience except writing for the yearbook in high school.

What do you consider your greatest professional accomplishment?
I've had several: helping a student get an internship at a radio station that turned into a career for him; watching one of my students spend all of her extra time making a documentary just for her own satisfaction; knowing that one of my students wants to be a journalism teacher just like me; watching my students win awards at conferences; and earning my master's degree in journalism/English education.

If you weren't doing this job, what similar careers might you consider?
I would try to write for magazines, work behind the scenes in television news, copy edit or do photography. I also coach volleyball and would definitely explore a coaching job.

To what professional associations do you belong?
I'm the co-president of the local scholastic journalism advisor's organization, Sponsors of School Publications (SSP). I also belong to the Journalism Education Association (JEA), Missouri Interscholastic Press

Profile: High School Journalism Teacher/Advisor

Q&A

Association (MIPA), National Scholastic Press Association (NSPA), and Student Television Network (STN).

What professional publications do you read?

I subscribe to *Communication: Journalism Education Today*, JEA's publication, as well as the Student Press Law Center's (SPLC) publication on press law. I frequent Poynter.org, a resource for journalists; http://jea.org, JEA's Web site; www.rtndf.org, Radio and Television News Directors Foundation's Web site; http://www.studenttelevision.com, STN's Web site; http://splc.org, SPLC's Web site; and http://www.nationalgeographic.com for photography ideas. Our local organization also has a Web site, http://ssp-stl.org. I used to frequent http://highschooljournalism.org, the Web site of the American Society of Newspaper Editors.

What advice do you have for others who would like to pursue this career?

Major in journalism in a state that provides journalism certification for teachers (not all states do). Definitely get some real-life experience in the field of journalism.

English Professor

Job Description: Every college and university has an English department; therefore, there are numerous faculty members teaching English at the postsecondary level. English department faculty members are expected to teach classes and conduct scholarly research in their area of specialty as well as publish.

Training and Educational Qualifications: Four-year colleges and universities usually consider PhDs for full-time, tenure-track positions, but they may hire master's degree holders or doctoral candidates for part-time and temporary (adjunct) jobs.

Obtaining a PhD in this field usually takes five to seven years of full-time study. Graduate students choose a major field in which to earn their PhD and as a result, the jobs that they will be qualified for when they finish their PhD are limited to that specialty (for example, a PhD might be in American literature, comparative literature, postcolonial literature, etc. It is not uncommon to see an English professor job advertised as "assistant professor of Victorian Literature," meaning someone who has a PhD in English literature and specialized in the nineteenth century). Besides positions in literature, those who earn PhD degrees in rhetoric and composition prepare to teach writing rather than literature.

In 2-year colleges, master's degree holders fill most full-time positions. However, in certain fields where there may be more applicants than available jobs, master's degree holders may be passed over in favor of candidates holding PhDs.

Job Outlook: Overall, employment is expected to grow much faster than the average for all occupations through 2016. A significant proportion of these new jobs will be part-time positions. Job opportunities are generally expected to be very good—although they will vary from field to field—as numerous openings for all types of teachers will result from retirements of current postsecondary teachers and continued increases in student enrollments.

Salary: Earnings for college faculty vary according to rank and type of institution, geographic area, and field. According to a 2006-07 survey by the American Association of University Professors, salaries for full-time faculty averaged $73,207. By rank, the average was $98,974 for professors, $69,911 for associate professors, $58,662 for assistant professors, $42,609 for instructors and $48,289 for lecturers.

Significant Facts:

- Opportunities for postsecondary teaching jobs are expected to be good, but many new openings will be for part-time or non-tenure track positions.

- A PhD is required for tenure-track jobs at colleges and universities; a master's degree is the minimal requirement for tenure-track jobs at community colleges but many community college professors in English departments also have PhDs.

- There are numerous openings for adjunct faculty in English, especially in teaching composition; but these jobs are often contracted by the semester, do not usually come with benefits, and are only renewable semester to semester.

INDUSTRY RESOURCES:
American Association of University Professors (AAUP)
1012 Fourteenth Street, NW, Suite 500
Washington, DC 20005-3465
Phone: (202) 737-5900
Internet: www.aaup.org

Modern Language Association (MLA)
26 Broadway, 3rd floor
New York, NY 10004-1789
Phone: (646) 576-5000
Internet: www.mla.org

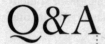
Profile: English Professor

Name: John	**Employer: George Mason University**
Age: 61	
Title: Professor of English and Cultural Studies	**Education: PhD**
	Years in Industry: 39 (including graduate school)

CAREER LADDER:

Acting assistant professor (2 years), assistant professor (8 years), associate professor (8 years), professor (16 years)

Q&A

Did you have an internship in this field prior to starting your job?

I was a teaching assistant two different semesters at my graduate institution.

Where are the best cities to live to find jobs like yours?

To get established as a professor, you really have to be prepared to move anywhere. That said, certainly the Boston area, the San Francisco Bay Area, and the Baltimore-Washington areas are among the best, and I've been lucky to have been connected with all three at different points in my life. I've also heard that college towns like Madison, WI; Ann Arbor, MI; Austin, TX or Chapel Hill, NC can work out very well.

What is your typical day like?

I get up around 9:00 a.m. after a night class the evening before, get to school around 10:30 a.m. and work through my email. I may contact a student about a make-up exam and design the exam, send messages to a couple of colleagues at other institutions about a prize competition for graduate students that we are judging or consult with the department chair about upcoming tenure cases. I usually read for an hour or so in preparation for a 4:30 p.m. class (most of the reading was done earlier in the week), eat lunch at my desk and both review and update my teaching notes for the class (on the computer). I also might draw up a reading list and course schedule for a class to be taught next semester, locate and download a couple of pictures from the Internet as enrichment for my class, write a letter of recommendation for a student going to law school and talk to two students during office hours, giving one advice on her course paper and explaining to the other what courses will fulfill his self-designed major. I could also talk to a colleague about a new publishing program that I need to learn to use. Then I go to my class and teach it from 4:30 to 7:10 p.m. My teaching style includes lecturing, but I spend much of the time asking questions and getting the students to think more deeply and imaginatively about the reading. After class, I'll grab dinner at the campus cafeteria before it closes at 7:30 p.m. and then meet a thesis-writing student at 7:45 p.m. and comment on the most recent chapter of her project. I could drop in at the library at 8:30 p.m. and spend an hour researching various items before heading home.

Profile: English Professor

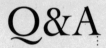

I should add that this is a typical busy day on campus; there are also days when I can actually concentrate on a good book, or spend most of the time between 9:00 and 5:00 writing an article or listening to papers at a conference and discussing them with colleagues.

What are your job responsibilities?

My responsibilities are varied and include the following: research as measured by publication of books and articles; curriculum development, as shown by new and substantially redesigned courses and verified by the syllabi for the courses; teaching three classes per semester (general education, undergrad major, grad students); evaluation of student performance; department administration (hiring new faculty, evaluating junior faculty for tenure, advising students, etc.).

What is your favorite part of your job?

I have several favorites: a class with lively, interested students; the satisfaction of getting good work published; friendly relations with bright, stimulating colleagues; reading good books and being inspired by them.

What do you dislike about your job?

Too much grading, heavy crush of work just before the Christmas holidays, and conducting class with tired, uninterested students.

Have you had any turning-point or "light bulb" moments in your career that have helped you get to where you are today?

Publishing my first book; publishing my second book; living abroad for a full year each in Germany, Italy, and France; moving from an elite school for 18 to 21 year olds with most students housed on campus to an ethnically very diverse, commuting school with students of all ages.

How did you know you wanted to pursue this career?

I was fascinated by the particular field—comparative literature—within the broader domain of literary studies. I took several courses as an undergraduate, planned a program of study that met the requirements for graduate school and was lucky to be admitted to good programs. Had I not been accepted into one of the very limited programs, I probably would not have gone into university teaching at all. It was the intellectual challenge of the particular field that really got my attention. I've discovered in my subsequent career that I enjoy teaching and that I can be very good at it; but back then, I didn't know that side of the field at all.

How did you get into this field?

I was lucky to interview well after getting my degree and was hired right away—in 1971, university hiring was still relatively easy. The transition to tenure in the early 1980s was more difficult since there was

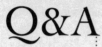

Q&A

something close to a freeze on hiring at that time. I just kept at it—I wrote hundreds of letters that eventually paid off with several good job offers.

What do you consider your greatest professional accomplishment?

The books I've written, the scholarly journal that I edited in one capacity or another for 13 years, the really successful classes that I've had from time to time, the new courses that I've launched and enjoyed the challenge of developing and making into a success. Also, some of the team efforts, such as organizing a large, international conference, managing the affairs of a scholarly organization in my field, winning a group research and teaching grant, and then going through with the project with four colleagues.

If you weren't doing this job, what similar careers might you consider?

I had wanted to go into publishing, but it wasn't an option when I graduated from college. I might also have liked some line of work that would have taken me abroad more often—the foreign service, for example, or some kind of international business career.

To what professional associations do you belong and what do you read?

I must belong to close to ten scholarly organizations, all connected with literary study in some way. I read widely, without sticking to any small group of sources, especially now, when I'm working on a world literature curriculum.

What advice do you have for others who would like to pursue this career?

Be sure you want to do this. You don't make "big bucks," but there can be a tremendous amount of "psychic income." Also, there really is a "publish or perish" criterion; you have to enjoy research and writing, and the amount of solitary effort that comes with that, as well as the "self-starter" mentality that is required.

Journalism Professor

Job Description: Journalism professors teach the next generation of reporters and editors to prepare them for careers in journalism. Courses that journalism professors teach are varied but some of the most frequent courses taught are news reporting, editing, investigative journalism, feature writing, and ethics in journalism. Many journalism professors advise student newspapers and if they are concentrated in broadcast journalism, they could advise a student-run radio or television station. (However, at some college campuses, student media advisors, rather than professors, perform the duties of advising student-run newspapers, television stations and radio stations.)

Training and Educational Qualifications: Four-year colleges and universities usually consider PhDs for full-time, tenure-track positions, but they may hire master's degree holders or doctoral candidates for certain disciplines, such as the arts, or for part-time and temporary jobs.

In 2-year colleges, master's degree holders fill most full-time positions. However, in certain fields where there may be more applicants than available jobs, master's degree holders may be passed over in favor of candidates holding PhDs.

Most journalism professors have also had a professional career in journalism in addition to academic credentials.

Job Outlook: Overall, employment of postsecondary teachers is expected to grow much faster than the average for all occupations through 2016. A significant proportion of these new jobs will be part-time positions. Job opportunities are generally expected to be very good—although they will vary somewhat from field to field—as numerous openings for all types of postsecondary teachers will result from retirements of current postsecondary teachers and continued increases in student enrollments.

Salary: Earnings for college faculty vary according to rank and type of institution, geographic area, and field. According to a 2006-07 survey by the American Association of University Professors, salaries for full-time faculty averaged $73,207. By rank, the average was $98,974 for professors, $69,911 for associate professors, $58,662 for assistant professors, $42,609 for instructors, and $48,289 for lecturers.

Significant Facts:

- Opportunities for postsecondary teaching jobs are expected to be good, but many new openings will be for part-time or non-tenure track positions. Prospects for teaching jobs will be better and earnings higher in academic fields in which many qualified teachers opt for nonacademic careers, such as health specialties, business, and computer science, for example.

- Educational qualifications for postsecondary teacher jobs range from expertise in a particular field to a PhD, depending on the subject being taught and the type of educational institution.

- Most journalism professors are experienced journalists as well as academicians but the qualifications vary by institution.

INDUSTRY RESOURCES:

American Association of University Professors (AAUP)
1012 Fourteenth Street, NW, Suite 500
Washington, DC 20005-3465
Phone: (202) 737-5900
Internet: www.aaup.org

Profile: Journalism Professor

Name: Loren

Age: 65

Title: Professor, Medill School of Journalism and President, Association of Schools of Journalism and Mass Communication

Employer: Northwestern University

Education: BA, History and English; Master of Urban Studies, J.D.; PhD, American Civilization

Years in Industry: 26 in journalism, 10 in journalism education

CAREER LADDER:

Reporter, Claremont Courier
Freelance Writer
Intern, The Washington Post
English Instructor
Congressional Fellow/Legislative Assistant
Assistant to the Director, National Endowment for the Humanities

Editor and Publisher, The News, *Southbridge, MA*
Professional-in-Residence, The Newseum
Director, Annenberg School of Journalism
Dean, Medill School of Journalism

Q&A

Did you have an internship in this field prior to starting your career?

I had internships at the twice-weekly *Claremont Courier* and *The Washington Post.* My experience at the *Courier* helped persuade me that I wanted to put out my own newspaper.

Do you know of which companies have the best internships in this field that are known to help launch a successful career?

It depends on what you define as "best." I would want to intern at an organization that would let me do the most and gain the greatest experience. In that respect, the *Courier* offered a better internship than the *Post*.

Where are the best cities to live to find jobs like yours?

In journalism, jobs are everywhere, small towns to big cities and around the globe.

What is your typical day like?

I'm on sabbatical, so nothing is typical. I try to write in the early morning (get to the office by 7:00 a.m.), then conduct regular business the rest of the working day (teaching, mentoring, etc.); then I read at night (two dailies, many magazines and Web sites, books on the subject of my next book I'm writing, etc.).

What are your job responsibilities?

Teaching, writing, researching.

Q&A

What is your favorite part of your job?
Helping students.

What do you dislike about your job?
Not much, though faculty committee meetings can wear thin after years.

Have you had any turning-point or "light bulb" moments in your career that have helped you get to where you are today?
Teaching at historically black Rust College in Holly Springs, Mississippi during "Freedom Summer" in 1964.

How did you know you wanted to pursue this career?
I wanted to change America for the better and I wanted to report and write.

How did you get into this industry?
After my two internships, at age 28, I bought a tiny daily that had been losing money, the *Southbridge (MA) News*.

What do you consider your greatest professional accomplishment?
I've had two: the New England Daily Newspaper Survey and election to presidency of American Society of Newspaper Editors.

If you weren't doing this job, what similar careers might you consider?
Editorial writing or high school teaching.

To what professional associations do you belong?
American Society of Newspaper Editors, Society of Professional Journalists, and the Council on Foreign Relations.

What professional publications do you read?
I like to think I read everything, from *American Journalism Review* and *Columbia Journalism Review*, to Romensko, to the *American Editor, The Economist, Journal of Mass Media Ethics, Wired*—too many publications.

What advice do you have for others who would like to pursue this career?
Be eager to move beyond your comfort zone. Experience the world.

Chapter 6

Careers in Arts Administration

If you love the arts but choose not to be become a professional actor, artist, dancer, musician, or writer, there are plenty of opportunities to do work promoting the arts for non-profit organizations. Directing and managing arts programs for arts councils and organizations and professional dance, music, or theater companies, can be a fulfilling job that involves surrounding yourself with artists and working with them to further their artistic goals. This career path is commonly known as arts administration. Careers in arts administration can be divided into four primary categories: (1) development/fundraising, (2) educational programming and outreach, (3) general administration and (4) marketing and sales, which sometimes includes communications functions.

Arts administration often combines many of the principles of business to effectively promote an organization and its mission. Consequently, knowledge of the arts in general, or more specifically, the art form on which the organization is focused, is advantageous to an arts administrator, as is knowledge of business principles. Effective written and oral communication skills are often necessary for almost all jobs in arts administration.

While arts administration jobs are abundant in large metropolitan areas with established arts "scenes," there are opportunities for arts administrators in almost any mid- to large-size urban or suburban area in the nation. Where there are people, there is an interest in the arts. Most new jobs exist in areas with growing economies as larger numbers of people relocating to such areas usually increase the opportunities to promote the arts to newer and greater audiences.

For an artist seeking a real-world job that utilizes skills in business, a career in arts administration might be the perfect fit.

Development

Job Description: Arts organizations such as symphony orchestras, ballet, theater and opera companies often rely heavily on the generosity of benefactors to supplement their operating budgets. Development departments are responsible for establishing relationships with donors.

In small companies there may be only one staff person dedicated to development. However, in larger organizations, there can be a variety of specialized positions under the development umbrella including the following: individual giving, special events, corporate partnerships, donor relations, donor services, and foundation relations.

Training and Educational Qualifications: Almost all arts administrators have completed four years of college, and the majority possess a master's or a doctoral degree. Experience in marketing and business is helpful because promoting events is a large part of the job. Many higher education institutions offer master's degrees in arts administration or master's of business (MBA) degrees with a concentration in arts administration.

Job Outlook: Wage and salary jobs in arts, entertainment, and recreation, in general, are projected to grow about 31 percent over the 2006-16 period, compared with 11 percent for all industries combined. However, the exact job outlook for arts administrators in particular is not provided.

Salary: Salaries vary greatly depending on the size of the hiring organization. *The Nonprofit Times* Annual Salary Survey reported that development directors earned a median salary of $76,770 in 2006.

INDUSTRY RESOURCES:

Association of Fund Raising Professionals
4300 Wilson Boulevard, Suite 300
Arlington, VA 22203
Phone: (703) 684-0410
Internet: www.afpnet.org

Association of Arts Administration Educators
975 University Avenue
Madison, WI 53706
Phone: (608) 263-4161
Internet: www.artsadministration.org

Profile: Development Director

Name: Rebecca	**Employer:** Duke University
Age: 37	**Education:** BFA Design, MA Arts
Title: Director of Development and External Relations, Nasher Museum of Art at Duke University	Administration **Years in Industry:** 10

CAREER LADDER:

Director of Development and External Affairs
Director of Development
Assistant Director for Phone and Mail
   Programs for the Annual Fund
Development and Outreach Coordinator

Development Officer
Director of Annual Programs
Curatorial Assistant
Student Administrative/Curatorial Assistant

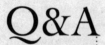

Did you have an internship in this field prior to starting your job?
Yes, I had several. I interned at a commercial art gallery and realized the commercial world wasn't for me. I also interned at an arts educational non-profit, which was a great experience and seemed a better fit.

Where are the best cities to live to find jobs like yours?
Any place that is growing is likely to have a lively arts scene. Of course, there are plenty of jobs in cities like New York, Chicago, Los Angeles and Seattle, but a lot of smaller cities like Raleigh will have plenty of opportunities to work in the arts as well.

What is your typical day like?
There is nothing typical about it. I usually plan about four major tasks to accomplish but then three other things hit my desk that all need my attention. So I have to balance my priorities.

What are your job responsibilities?
I tackle everything from grant and proposal writing, to working with the corporate community, to drafting endowment agreements, to stewarding individual donors. I also oversee our external relations team which encompasses marketing and communications, annual fund and membership, and special events.

What is your favorite part of your job?
The people—you have to like working with people to succeed in development and you need strong negotiating skills to build and maintain good relationships.

What do you dislike about your job?
The pressure. It can be a high-pressure job. Financial goals must be met as well as strict deadlines for proposals and grant applications.

Q&A

Have you had any turning-point or "light bulb" moments in your career that have helped you get to where you are today?

I took a job in development, working in an environment without an arts focus. I realized that there was a lack of spark for me and I didn't really want to work in development if it wasn't in the arts. Also, through working in smaller organizations, I learned that I didn't enjoy grassroots fundraising: I prefer working for an organization that has established a solid identity and vision rather than one that is still in its seedling stage.

Another light bulb for me was realizing from my work and internship experience that I wanted to work for an organization that has a staff of about 10 to 30 people. When an organization is small, you end up doing everything by yourself, which is overwhelming; and when it is really large, don't have the opportunity to be involved in related areas of the institution's work, finding yourself assigned to a narrow aspect of development such as the annual fund vs. corporate relations. At large institutions, job titles can get very specific so I knew I wanted to work in a mid-size organization.

I realized it was important to me to work somewhere that had a strong educational outreach component as part of its mission. As a fundraiser, it is very beneficial to talk about something that raising money accomplishes beyond just presenting art at its highest level—and educating children or communities is something that can inspire donors to become involved.

How did you know you wanted to pursue this career?

I thought to myself, "If I am not going to be a famous artist, I'd better find a career." I was working at an art museum and considered becoming a curator, but my mentor said I'd probably need to consider getting a PhD and I would need to write scholarly articles to excel in that field. I didn't see myself completing a doctorate or writing exhibition catalogues. However, my mentor recognized my strength in organizing material and working with people and suggested arts administration and I took that path.

How did you get into this industry?

My first job was working as a student assistant at the art museum on my college campus. I then decided to pursue my graduate degree in arts administration, interning while I pursued that program. Afterward I continued to work in the field.

What do you consider your greatest professional accomplishment?

Being a part of a team that closed a million dollar corporate gift for sponsorship of an exhibition.

Profile: Development Director

Q&A

If you weren't doing this job, what similar careers might you consider?

I might be a librarian or weaver.

To what professional associations do you belong?

Association of Fundraising Professionals (AFP), the Art Museum Development Association (AMDA), Rotary International.

What publications do you read?

Triangle Business Journal (local paper) and the *Chronicle of Philanthropy*.

What advice do you have for others who would like to pursue this career?

Do internships to get your foot in the door. Learn what you do and don't like. Choose an internship where you can get the best experience that is meaningful to you—knowing that there will be real work involved in an internship allows you to walk away from it with a sense of professional accomplishment. If you want to be in senior management, you will probably need a graduate degree, so that is worth contemplating as part of your educational plans if you see yourself working in a senior management position one day.

Education and Outreach

Job Description: In addition to running schools affiliated with their companies, large arts organizations often have educational and outreach programs. The focus of such a department or program is to introduce new audiences to the organization's chosen art form. Many such departments produce educational print materials for teachers, coordinate special performances for schools, sponsor visiting artist programs and arrange lecture demonstrations.

Training and Educational Qualifications: Almost all arts administrators have completed four years of college, and the majority possess a master's or a doctoral degree. Experience in marketing and business is helpful because promoting events is a large part of the job. Many higher education institutions offer master's degrees in arts administration or master's of business (MBA) degrees with a concentration in arts administration.

Job Outlook: Wage and salary jobs in arts, entertainment, and recreation, in general, are projected to grow about 25 percent over the 2004-14 period, compared with 14 percent for all industries combined. However, the exact job outlook for arts administrators in particular is not provided.

Salary: Salaries vary greatly depending on the size of the hiring organization. Average earnings for education administrators in the performing arts are $71,360.

INDUSTRY RESOURCES:

Association of Arts Administration Educators
975 University Avenue
Madison, WI 53706
Phone: (608) 263-4161
Internet: www.artsadministration.org

Profile: Education and Outreach Officer

Name: Kushana

Age: 27

Title: Education and Outreach Officer

Employer: National Gallery of the Cayman Islands

Education: BFA Painting

Years in Industry: 2 years

CAREER LADDER:

Clerical Officer, Government Information Services
Secretary to Chief Education Officer, Education Department
Education and Outreach Officer

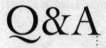

Where are the best cities in which to live to have your job?

Jobs in educational outreach for arts organizations are available in many major cities.

What is your typical day like?

My typical day is spent moving between the office and in the field teaching.

What are your job responsibilities?

I am responsible for the execution, programming and instruction of nine outreach programs; these programs serve a variety of people including children who've been abused or who are juvenile delinquents, battered women and prisoners. The art outreach programs are designed for individuals who would not normally have the chance to be exposed to the visual arts. These programs are an outlet for their self-expression. Many are not able to talk about their problems or issues that they might have. Through art they are able to communicate freely, without any inhibitions about being judged or categorized. I have seen firsthand the way that these programs have worked wonders in the lives of the participants. I am also responsible for all the outreach instructors and I am a liaison to local schools regarding art education and gallery visits.

What is your favorite part of your job?

I love seeing participants gain a sense of pride and achievement when they finally grasp a technique that I have taught them. It makes them feel really good about themselves and that makes me feel good.

What do you dislike about your job?

The most difficult part of my job is to deal with some of the support staff at certain institutions. I sometimes feel that they might have become desensitized to certain things because of their jobs.

Have you had any turning point or "light bulb" moments in your career that have helped you get to where you are today?

This moment came for me when I realized that I was not satisfied to stay in a job where I was not happy and true to myself. I knew that the

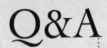

Profile: Education and Outreach Officer

Q&A

only way for me to find the career that would make me happy was to pursue my degree in the art field and get a job doing what I love.

How did you know you wanted to pursue this career?

When I found that an "office" type job was not for me, this job sort of fell in my lap. However I would like to continue my education and obtain my teacher's certificate/diploma or a Master's of Arts in Teaching (MAT) degree in the near future.

How did you get into this industry?

The Director of the National Gallery of the Cayman Islands called my college to recruit me before I graduated.

What do you consider your greatest professional accomplishment?

My first exhibition of works done by outreach program participants that I curated opened with rave reviews and also received a positive response from the community.

If you weren't doing this job, what similar careers might you consider?

I would probably be in a classroom teaching art, or working as a graphic designer for a company, or in some type of art or historic preservation.

To what professional associations do you belong and what professional publications do you read?

I am a member of the International Society of Education through Art (InSEA). I keep up with *Artforum* magazine.

What advice do you have for others who would like to pursue this career?

I would advise one to make as many connections as possible. Visit galleries and see if your work would be a good fit in that gallery. Speak with gallery owners and museum staff. Get involved with the local arts community and be active in the arts community wherever it is you might live. Also research and read about your chosen field. Do as much research as possible to find out what suits you best.

Profile: Program Manager

Name: Ray
Age: 29
Title: Program Manager

Employer: Hyde Park Art Center
Education: BA Studio Art and Biology, MA Art Education
Years in Industry: 5

CAREER LADDER:

Program manager, teen council coordinator, gallery manager, curator assistant, teaching assistant, freelance graphic designer

Did you have an internship in this field prior to starting your job?

Yes, I had an internship at the Chicago Historical Society, working with the Teen Chicago project. The internship was a co-op internship through the School of the Art Institute of Chicago (SAIC). I assisted the Teen Council Coordinator and Project Directors on a variety of tasks, including assisting with the teen group, working with the exhibition planning team, and planning and implementing teen programs.

Do you know of which companies have the best internships in this field that are known to help launch a successful career?

There are many organizations that provide valuable work experience for people interested in the Art Education field. Museums are an excellent place to start, and working with the education departments can give a real sense of what is entailed in planning and implementing programs. If someone is more interested in grassroots organizing, smaller non-profits are a great place to look. Essentially, getting out there, meeting and working with people and tapping into the network are the best ways to start a career in art education.

Where are the best cities to live to find jobs like yours?

Although many people see New York City as the best place to get started because there are so many art museums and artists there, I think any big city is a great place to get started. Typically larger cities have more museums and arts non-profits. Therefore, they have more jobs. New York, Chicago, Los Angeles and San Francisco are all good places to look for jobs, but smaller cities, such as Boston, Minneapolis, Seattle and Atlanta also have thriving arts and art education scenes.

What is your typical day like?

There usually is no typical day, and I don't even work a typical work week. I could have a program running on a Saturday, an artist talk on a Tuesday night, or a film screening on a Thursday, and things are constantly changing. I am often off-site meeting with people, looking at other organizations or participating in programs throughout the city. It all depends on what's coming up. There are usually lulls, where I may be working on a grant proposal or planning for programs, but then the

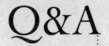

Q&A

days leading up to it are often really hectic as I try to get last minute logistics in, etc. I'm always juggling lots of duties and tasks, and there never really seems to be a dull minute.

What are your job responsibilities?

I manage the Art Resource Center at the Hyde Park Art Center. It's a community space geared towards creativity and the arts. I work with teachers, students, artists, families, and just about anyone else you can imagine. I maintain the space and also plan and implement programming, which can include teacher professional development, artist talks, family days, and various additional community meetings and events.

What is your favorite part of your job?

Working with a ton of fascinating and interesting people. I never feel bored with my job, and there's always so much happening. I get to meet and work on projects with amazingly creative and fun individuals.

What do you dislike about your job?

There isn't much I don't like about my job. The organization is great and I really like what I'm doing. If there's anything that I dislike, I guess it's trying to find money for all the projects that we have. The pot of money for art education programming isn't that big, and there are so many great programs and organizations out there that it's almost impossible for everything to get funded. But they all should be!

Have you had any turning-point or "light bulb" moments in your career that have helped you get to where you are today?

Going to the School of Art Institute Chicago and being part of the art education program really changed my perspective on the field. I went in thinking that I wanted to go into a classroom and teach art, but I discovered that working in community arts organizations and being a part of smaller organizations was exciting and much more productive. I don't feel like I have to fight the system or bureaucracy as much with what I'm doing now.

How did you know you wanted to pursue this career?

I always enjoyed and loved the arts. In fact, I am an artist, but I was never quite convinced that I could make it solely as an artist. I've also always really liked working with students—whether kids or adults—and teaching. It just seemed to be a natural combination of my interests and strengths. Once I got into the field, I loved it!

How did you get into this industry?

I had tried the corporate world and didn't really like having a straight 9:00 to 5:00 job, so I was looking for something else that appealed to me as a career. And as I said, art education seemed like a natural combination of my interests. I had been watching the Hyde Park Art Center and

Q&A

its activities for a while and was really excited about their new building. So when a job opened up, I applied right away. I had participated in a focus group for them during the planning process of the new building, and I think that familiarity with the organization really helped my application.

What do you consider your greatest professional accomplishment?

Thus far, I think my greatest accomplishments have been these: working on the Teen Chicago project at the Chicago Historical Society and *Usingopening*, a major exhibition, and working with the staff at my current organization to open our new building in April 2006.

If you weren't doing this job, what similar careers might you consider?

If I were not in this field, I think I might be a public school teacher in the arts, or maybe even a full-time artist.

To what professional associations do you belong and what do you read?

I am part of the National Art Education Association. I read *Art in America*, *Art Education*, and *Artforum*.

What advice do you have for others who would like to pursue this career?

Get involved and try out different organizations and sites to find the right fit for you. There's so much work to be done, and so many people who need help. Volunteering and interning are great opportunities for people interested in art education, and you'll not only be helping yourself but a lot of valuable causes and organizations!

General Administration

Job Description: Arts administrators manage arts organizations such as symphony orchestras, ballet companies or opera companies. A small company may simply have a company manager who deals with the administrative details of running an arts organization. However, a larger company will employ some or all of the following: executive director, general manager, director of finance, human resources manager and assistants to the executive director.

Training and Educational Qualifications: Almost all arts administrators have completed four years of college, and the majority possess a master's or a doctoral degree. Experience in marketing and business is helpful because promoting events is a large part of the job. Many higher education institutions offer master's degrees in arts administration or master's of business (MBA) degrees with a concentration in arts administration.

Job Outlook: Wage and salary jobs in arts, entertainment, and recreation, in general, are projected to grow about 25 percent over the 2004-14 period, compared with 14 percent for all industries combined. However, the exact job outlook for arts administrators in particular is not provided.

Salary: Salaries vary greatly depending on the size of the hiring organization. Average earnings for chief executives in the performing arts are $171,330. Average earnings for general and operations managers are $106,250, and average earnings for administrative services managers are $73,360.

INDUSTRY RESOURCES:

Association of Arts Administration Educators
975 University Avenue
Madison, WI 53706
Phone: (608) 263-4161
Internet: www.artsadministration.org

Profile: Artistic Administrator– Theater Company

Name: Lynn
Title: Artistic Administrator
Employer: Northlight Theater

Education: BFA Drama
Years in Industry: 25

CAREER LADDER:

Actor, improviser, commercial talent, retail sales/management, bookkeeper, teacher, theater producer, theater designer, theater carpenter, theater grant-writer, theater management, artistic director, NFP non-equity, Director, Theater Arts division of the National High School Institute at Northwestern University (previously, Associate Director, Dorm Director, faculty, faculty associate)

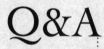

Did you have an internship in this field prior to starting your job?
Being a faculty associate at NHSI was essentially an internship in teaching, acting and directing.

Do you know of which companies have the best internships in this field that are known to help launch a successful career?
I currently am in charge of internships here at Northlight Theater just north of Chicago. The theater internships with the best reputation in the Chicago area are Goodman, Steppenwolf, Lookingglass, North-light—not necessarily in that order.

Where are the best cities to live to find jobs like yours?
Chicago is the best city to actually get to do work in the theater. I have worked in some area of theater since I got to Chicago 25 years ago. I believe in it. But you can really be on the artistic team of a theater company anywhere, I suppose. There's just more people making that scenario work in Chicago than in other places.

What is your typical day like?
It varies a lot. I do some work at my computer and phone. I meet with the Artistic Director and Artistic Associate often. I am in and out of the theater and classrooms regularly, but not daily.

What are your job responsibilities?
I am in charge of casting, internships, the Teacher Training program and I am assistant to the Artistic Director, and part of the artistic team—so I read plays, discuss upcoming projects, seasons, marketing, the future of the theater, etc.

What is your favorite part of your job?
The diversity of tasks and the people. I have learned, sort of the hard way, that *who* you work with is as important as *what* you do.

What do you dislike about your job?

I have more desk work than you'd think I would. The most difficult thing I do is to hire understudies. And that task is not balanced by being greatly rewarding either.

Have you had any turning-point or "light bulb" moments in your career that have helped you get to where you are today?

I've had many of these. I got into teaching by being called to it. I really believe that.

I am more of a leader than an actor. Having been only trained as an actor, anything that I've learned to do along the way that is *not* acting has been a light bulb moment for me.

If you don't pursue acting relentlessly and *get work* all the time, you should figure out what else you do. You get rusty.

How did you know you wanted to pursue this career?

My dad was in theater—a Renaissance man.

How did you get into this industry?

I got both of my most recent jobs in theater by talking my way in. I heard that the woman who preceded me at this job at Northlight was going to take a job at Chicago Shakespeare Theater. I called her and told her that I wanted her old job. She put the person hiring in touch with me—and then I "sold" myself to him.

If you weren't doing this job, what similar careers might you consider?

I'd make a good party planner. I am good at retail. I think I could pass myself off as a costumer. I could be a talent agent. There are lots of options.

To what professional associations do you belong and what do you read?

I'm a member of Actors Equity, Screen Actors Guild (SAG), American Federation of Radio and Television Artists (AFTRA). I read Playbill online and I read Chicago theater reviews all the time.

What advice do you have for others who would like to pursue this career?

Be good at *a lot* of things. Do all the jobs in the theater, including sweep the floor. Be a team player. Be nice. Be the nicest person in the room.

There are many great careers in theater that aren't necessarily acting. That's a hard thing to tell someone who wants to be an actor. Rather than being so focused on one aspect of theater, I think many young actors should consider re-directing their dreams.

Profile: Executive Director

Name: Verdery Roosevelt
Age: 54
Title: Executive Director

Employer: Ballet Hispanico
Education: BA English, MA Business/Arts Administration
Years in Industry: 33

CAREER LADDER:

Executive Director, Ballet Hispanico of New York 1980–present
Assistant Director, Ballet Hispanico of New York 1978–1979
Development Assistant, Lincoln Center for the Performing Arts 1978
Publicity Coordinator, University Theater, Madison, Wisconsin 1977–1978
Development Intern, Exxon Internship Program, Circle in the Square 1977
Editor, Arts Quarterly, Wisconsin Arts Board, Madison, Wisconsin 1977
Costume Shop Manager, Theater Department, University of Illinois 1975–1977
Secretary, Theater Department, University of Alabama 1973–1975

Did you have an internship in this field prior to starting your job?
Internships were a part of my arts management program in graduate school. During my first year in the program, I interned with the local theater. In the summer, I came to New York and interned at Circle in the Square.

Do you know of which companies have the best internships in this field that are known to help launch a successful career?
Every large performing arts organization has internships.

Where are the best cities to live to find jobs like yours?
The city that you love. There are jobs anywhere that you go. If you really want to live in a certain area, find a cultural institution in that area that could use help.

What is your typical day like?
It is certain to include meetings with staff, board and volunteers. This field requires extraordinary flexibility because many events happen in the evenings. A workday could be 9:00 a.m. to 5:00 p.m. or it may 8:00 a.m. to midnight depending on the day.

What are your job responsibilities?
As an executive director, I am responsible for the strategic direction of the institution. I coordinate programs internally and work extensively with the board of directors and donors. It's all about moving the institution forward.

What is your favorite part of your job?
The people I work with—the staff, volunteer leadership and the artistic director. It is an extraordinary joy to work with all of them.

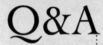

Profile: Executive Director

Q&A

What do you dislike about your job?

There are aspects of every job that get to you after awhile.

Have you had any turning-point or "light bulb" moments in your career that have helped you get to where you are today?

For me, a major decision was coming to Ballet Hispanico when I did. There was a very small staff and they took a gamble on me. That was back in 1978. It worked out because I'm still here.

How did you know you wanted to pursue this career?

I love the arts and enjoy being around the dance, music, opera and visual arts.

How did you get into this industry?

I was fortunate that my graduate program brought experts from the field to speak to students in seminar settings. One of the people who came to an event to speak was Jane Gullong, who is now the executive director of the New York City Opera. At the time I heard her speak, she was president of the board of Ballet Hispanico and working as an associate development director at Lincoln Center. I took a job as a temp working with Ms. Gullong at Lincoln Center. Being around her was invaluable. When a position opened up at Ballet Hispanico, I applied for it and got it.

What do you consider your greatest professional accomplishment?

Allowing Tina Ramirez's vision as the artistic director of Ballet Hispanico to be realized at increasing levels of sophistication.

If you weren't doing this job, what similar careers might you consider?

There are certain aspects of my job I enjoy very much, so it's hard to think of something else but I might try. Perhaps I would enjoy financial management at another cultural institution if I weren't doing this.

To what professional associations do you belong and what do you read?

I belong to Dance/USA, Association of Performing Arts Presenters (APAP), American Arts Alliance, Dance/NYC, Arts and Business Council. I read all of those organizations' publications.

What advice do you have for others who would like to pursue this career?

You need a variety of experience to work at the top level in arts administration, so consider taking any job in an arts organization to learn skills you'll need later as an executive. I recommend that people inter-

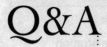

Profile: Executive Director

Q&A

ested in arts administration volunteer a lot, see a lot, create a network of people you know in the field and keep your eyes open to opportunities.

About Ballet Hispanico: With Verdery Roosevelt's leadership, Ballet Hispanico has transitioned from a community-based organization into an internationally recognized dance institution. She has produced over 50 repertory works commissioned by Ms. Ramirez for the Ballet Hispanico Company, which has performed in leading concert halls throughout South America, Europe and the United States. Scholarship support for the Ballet Hispanico School has increased to over $100,000 annually for students who train in the school's singular curriculum of classical ballet, Spanish dance and modern. Ballet Hispanico's groundbreaking education program, Primeros Pasos, now reaches over 25,000 children across the nation each year. Ms. Roosevelt also oversaw the purchase and renovation of Ballet Hispanico's permanent headquarters on Manhattan's Upper West Side and is now directing a $12 million campaign to more than double the size of the facility and create the nation's first Center for Dance and Latin Culture.

Marketing and Sales

Job Description: Marketing and sales staff publicize performances and sell tickets. In a smaller organization, the marketing and sales department may double as the box office and public relations department. However, larger companies may divide employees into teams that specialize in marketing, media relations, publications, group sales and public relations.

Training and Educational Qualifications: Almost all arts administrators have completed four years of college, and the majority possess a master's or a doctoral degree. Experience in marketing and business is helpful because promoting events is a large part of the job. Many higher education institutions offer master's degrees in arts administration or master's of business (MBA) degrees with a concentration in arts administration.

Job Outlook: Wage and salary jobs in arts, entertainment, and recreation, in general, are projected to grow about 25 percent over the 2004–14 period, compared with 14 percent for all industries combined. However, the exact job outlook for arts administrators in particular is not provided.

Salary: Salaries vary greatly depending on the size of the hiring organization. Average earnings for marketing managers in the performing arts are $85,340, and average earnings for sales managers are $93,940.

INDUSTRY RESOURCES:

Association of Arts Administration Educators
975 University Avenue
Madison, WI 53706
Phone: (608) 263-4161
Internet: www.artsadministration.org

Profile: Director of Business Affairs

Name: Tom

Age: 51

Title: Director of Business Affairs, DeBartolo Performing Arts Center

Employer: University of Notre Dame

Education: BA Biology, MA Theater Management, MBA Finance

Years in Industry: 29

CAREER LADDER:

Director of business affairs, director of audience development, marketing director, facility manager, professional dancer

Where are the best cities to live to find jobs like yours?

Every city larger than 50,000 and most campuses have positions for arts managers.

What is your typical day like?

My job entails a lot of correspondence—email and phone calls are a part of the day since they are vital to moving projects along. I'm involved in a couple of strategy sessions per week and I do updates in budget as well as meet with the two staff members who report to me.

What are your job responsibilities?

I manage artist contracts, help with visa issues for foreign performers, watch the budgets of the facility and manage funds flow.

What is your favorite part of your job?

Heading to performances as a spectator knowing that I had a small part in making it happen.

What do you dislike about your job?

My current position required that I give up teaching ballet class, and I miss the student contact.

Have you had any turning-point or "light bulb" moments in your career that have helped you get to where you are today?

Not really, but ending my dance career certainly forced me to focus on what's next.

How did you know you wanted to pursue this career?

I got involved in dance in college and I also attended the Joffrey Ballet School. I knew then that I wanted to be a part of the arts in some way always.

How did you get into this industry?

I retired from dance at the ripe old age of 27, wanted to move into management, but made the decision to go to school to get a degree first. My most recent job came from the university making a $64 million

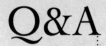

Q&A   investment in a new facility and I moved over from the old facility to the new one.

What do you consider your greatest professional accomplishment?

I am very proud of a short but enjoyable dance career. I have also been proud of developing an audience for theater at Notre Dame. In 1998, we ran over 90 percent capacity for the season.

If you weren't doing this job, what similar careers might you consider?

I would very much enjoy working with a dance company.

What professional publications do you read?

Association of Performing Arts Presenters (APAP), International Ticketing Association (INTIX), *Venues Today*.

What advice do you have for others who would like to pursue this career?

Find an MBA in the arts program.

ADDITIONAL RESOURCES

CAREER RESOURCES FOR ACTORS

Books

The Actor's Other Career Book: Using Your Chops to Survive and Thrive by Lisa Mulcahy
How to Be a Working Actor: The Insider's Guide to Finding Jobs in Theater, Film, and Television by Mari Lyn Henry and Lynne Rogers
Careers for the Stagestruck and Other Dramatic Types by Lucia Mauro

Magazines

American Theatre	www.tcg.org
Backstage	www.backstage.com
Entertainment Weekly	www.ew.com
Hollywood Reporter	www.hollywoodreporter.com
Premiere	www.premiere.com
Variety	www.variety.com

CAREER RESOURCES FOR ARTISTS

Books

New Media Careers for Artists and Designers by Brenda Smith, PhD Faison
Taking the Leap: Building a Career As a Visual Artist by Cay Lang
The Fine Artist's Career Guide: Making Money in the Arts and Beyond by Daniel Grant

Magazines

Art Journal	www.collegeart.org/artjournal/
Artforum	www.artforum.com
NY Arts	www.nyartsmagazine.com

CAREER RESOURCES FOR DANCERS

Books

Ballet Dancers in Career Transition: Sixteen Success Stories by Nancy Upper
How to Make It in Musicals: The Insider's Guide to a Career As a Singer-Dancer
by Michael Allen

Magazines

Dance Magazine	www.dancemagazine.com
Dance Spirit	www.dancespirit.com
Pointe	www.pointemagazine.com

Web site

Career Transitions for Dancers   www.careertransition.org

CAREER RESOURCES FOR MUSICIANS

Books

Beyond Talent: Creating a Successful Career in Music by Angela Myles Beeching
Career Opportunities in the Music Industry by Shelly Field
Careers for Music Lovers and Other Tuneful Types by Jeff Johnson
Great Jobs for Music Majors by Jan Goldberg
How to Make It in Musicals: The Insider's Guide to a Career As a Singer-Dancer
by Michael Allen
Making It in the Music Business: The Business and Legal Guide for Songwriters and Performers by Lee Wilson
Music Business Handbook and Career Guide by David Baskerville

Magazines

Billboard	www.billboard.com
Blender	www.blender.com
Paste	www.pastemagazine.com
SPIN	www.spin.com
Symphony	www.symphony.org

Web sites

www.mbsolutions.com
www.menc.org

CAREERS RESOURCES FOR WRITERS

Books

Career Opportunities for Writers by Rosemary Guiley
Careers for Writers and Others Who Have a Way with Words by Robert W. Bly
Opportunities in Writing Careers by Elizabeth Foote-Smith

Magazines

Writer's Digest   www.writersdigest.com
Poets and Writers   www.pw.org/magazine

Web Sites

www.journalismjobs.com
www.mediabistro.com
www.poynter.org
www.publisherslunch.com
www.publishersweekly.com
www.writersmarket.com

GENERAL RESOURCES

ArtsEdge   http://artsedge.kennedy-center.org
Arts Journal   www.artsjournal.com
Artslynx   www.artslynx.org
Chronicle of Philanthropy   www.philanthropy.org
Idealist   www.idealist.org
New York Foundation for the Arts www.nyfa.org

ADDITIONAL ARTS ORGANIZATIONS

American Arts Alliance
1112 16th Street, NW
Suite 400
Washington, DC 20036
Phone: (202) 207-3850
Internet: www.americanartsalliance.org

Americans for the Arts
1000 Vermont Avenue NW, 12th Floor
Washington, DC 20005
Phone: (202) 371-2830
Internet: www.americansforthearts.org

Association of Performing Arts Presenters
1112 16th Street NW, Suite 400
Washington, DC 20036
Phone: (202) 833-2787
Internet: www.artspresenters.org

Chamber Music America
305 7th Avenue, 5th Floor
New York, NY 10001
Phone: (212) 244-2022
Internet: www.chamber-music.org

Chorus America
1156 15th Street NW, Suite 310
Washington, DC 20005
Phone: (202) 331-7757
Internet: www.chorusamerica.org

Council of Literary Magazines and Presses
154 Christopher Street, Suite 3C
New York, NY 10014
Phone: (212) 741-9110
Internet: www.clmp.org

Dance/USA
1111 16th Street NW, Suite 300
Washington, DC 20036
Phone: (202) 833-1717
Internet: www.danceusa.org

The Foundation Center
1627 K Street NW
Washington, DC 20006
Phone: (202) 331-1400
Internet: www.foundationcenter.org

National Assembly of State Arts Agencies
1029 Vermont Avenue, Second Floor
Washington, DC 20005
Phone: (202) 347-6352
Internet: www.nasaa-arts.org

National Association of Artists Organizations
1718 M Street NW
PMB #239
Washington, DC 20036
Phone: (202) 347-6350
Internet: www.naao.net

National Endowment for the Arts
1100 Pennsylvania Ave. NW
Washington, DC 20506
Phone: (202) 682-5400
Internet: www.nea.gov

OPERA America
1156 15th Street NW, Suite 810
Washington, DC 20005
Phone: (202) 293-4466
Internet: www.operaamerica.org

Theatre Communications Group
520 8th Avenue, 24th Floor
New York, NY 10018-4156
Phone: (212) 609-5900
Internet: www.tcg.org

CAREER INDEX

Find the Perfect Creative College

- Choose the right college to fit your unique needs as a student actor, artist, dancer, musician or writer

- Learn from in-depth profiles of more than 200 programs

- Understand the important differences between BA and BFA programs and an education at a college, university or conservatory

- Get insider tips for the creative component of the admissions process including the audition and/or portfolio

Creative Colleges:
A Guide for Student Actors, Artists, Dancers, Musicians and Writers
ISBN: 978-1-932662-23-8   •   Price: $19.95
Get your copy at bookstores nationwide or visit www.supercollege.com

Get the Money You Need
to Pay for College

- Insider tips from top scholarship winners and judges
- Secrets to writing applications and essays
- Where to find the best scholarships
- Techniques to maximize your financial aid package

Get Free Cash for College
ISBN: 978-1-932662-35-1   •   Price: $19.95
Get your copy at bookstores nationwide or visit www.supercollege.com

Get More Resources and Tools at SuperCollege.com

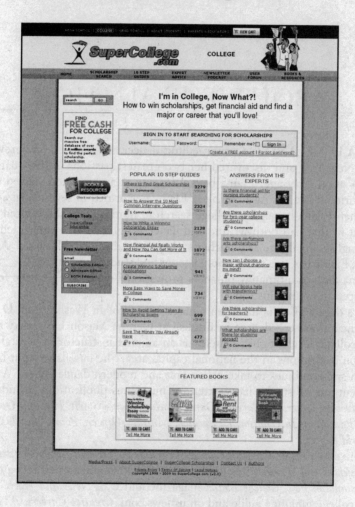

Visit www.supercollege.com for more free resources on scholarships, financial aid and college admission.

ABOUT THE AUTHOR

ELAINA LOVELAND is a writer, editor, dancer and teacher. She grew up in upstate New York and discovered her two greatest passions in life—dance and writing—at an early age. Elaina began dancing at age five and started writing short stories at age 11. As a teenager, Elaina performed in several classical ballets. When Elaina began her college search in ninth grade, she wanted to find a perfect fit that had both writing and dance programs. Her search led her to study English and dance at Goucher College in Baltimore, Maryland. An artist at heart, Elaina has also taken opera lessons and studied sculpture.

Elaina did not ultimately pursue a professional dance career—she followed her interest in writing instead.

For a decade, Elaina has been a magazine editor in Washington, D.C. She also earned a master's degree in English at George Mason University and has taught college-level English courses as an adjunct instructor at several higher education institutions in the national capital area. She has also taught ballet to children and continues to take ballet, jazz and modern dance classes. As an independent journalist, she has written for numerous publications including *Adjunct Advocate, American Careers, Dance Teacher, Dance Spirit, Hispanic Outlook on Higher Education, International Educator, Military Officer, Pointe* and *U.S. News and World Report*.

Elaina's first book, *Creative Colleges: A Guide for Student Actors, Artists, Dancers, Musicians and Writers*, was published in fall 2005 and earned recognition in the *Washington Post, College Bound* magazine and *U.S. News and World Report's* annual college rankings guide and on usnews.com. *Creative Careers: A Guide for Aspiring Actors, Artists, Dancers, Musicians and Writers* is her second book. Visit www.elainaloveland.com to learn more about pursuing a creative life.